How to Make Money in Wall Street

by
Louis Rukeyser

Doubleday & Company, Inc.
Garden City, New York

Library of Congress Catalog Card Number: 73–14055
ISBN: 0-385-07505-7

Printed in the United States of America

For ALEX
My Best Investment

APPENDIX E

Listing Requirements

A key power of the nation's leading stock exchanges is the right to set minimum standards that a company must meet before its stock can be traded there. These listing requirements are raised periodically; the July 1971 increase at the New York Stock Exchange was the sixth in thirteen years. Before a stock can be "listed"—that is, made eligible for trading—on the New York Stock Exchange, the issuing company must have demonstrated annual earning power before federal income taxes of $2,500,000 for the latest fiscal year and $2,000,000 for each of the two preceding years, must have 1,000,000 publicly held shares outstanding, must have 2,000 shareholders each of whom owns at least 100 shares and must have net tangible assets and total market value of publicly held shares both exceeding $16,000,000. The board of the exchange—which also has the authority to suspend or "de-list" a stock whose company falls too far below the requirements—says it decides each case on its merits, but the foregoing standards for initial acceptance are generally required as a minimum.

The American Stock Exchange has lower standards. It normally asks that a company have earned only $750,000 in the last fiscal year, of which $400,000 must be net after taxes. The applicant need have only 400,000 publicly held shares, of which 150,000 must be in 100- to 500-share lots. Where the New York Stock Exchange requires 2,000 shareholders each owning at least 100 shares, the Amex demands only 1,200 shareholders in all, including 800 owners of at least 100 shares each. Of these 800, 500 must be holders of 100- to 500-share lots. Finally, the company's net tangible assets need be only $4,000,000, and the market value of its publicly held shares qualifies if it tops $3,000,000.

APPENDIX F

The "Wall Street Week" Technical Market Index

As explained at the end of Chapter XIII, this index was developed in 1972 by Robert J. Nurock, a technically minded broker and a "Wall Street Week" panelist, in an attempt to summarize the technical strength or weakness of the stock market on a weekly basis.

No pretense is made to long-range forecasting; the idea is to foreshadow changes in the three- to six-month trend of prices (the so-called intermediate trend).

These are the ten indicators, each of which is reported each week as being "positive," "neutral" or "negative":

(1) An advance-decline index. Practically every technician uses some variant of this, which tots up how many stocks went up versus how many stocks went down. The result is a measure of the market's "breadth"—and bad breadth stinks. If the averages are rising but breadth is declining, technicians will assume that the market is already beginning to deteriorate. They were right in 1961, 1966 and 1969–70, but wrong in 1963–64. Nobody's perfect.

(2) A Dow Jones momentum ratio. This compares today's Dow Jones Industrial Average with its longer-range trend to see if the index is getting ahead of or behind where it ought to be—and thereby indicating a possible turning point. (These trends are plotted in the form of "moving averages," such as the "200-day moving average" that is often shown for a stock. Standard & Poor's "Trendline" compiles such figures weekly by averaging the 30 most recent Thursday closing prices for each stock on its list. By comparing a stock's actual performance with its 200-day moving average, the statistics are supposed to help you decide where the stock is going next. Sometimes they even do.)

(3) A New York Stock Exchange high-low index. This measures the number of new highs and new lows reported each day on the New York Stock Exchange, on the theory that any extreme one-sidedness will signal a turning point. For example, five or fewer new

Contents

How to Make Money
in Wall Street

CHAPTER I

To Market?

This is a book about how to live better, feel better and get more fun out of life. Its major themes are lust, power, status and greed —the proper concerns of all great literature—and it will treat them in such modest and undemanding contexts as man against his environment, man against man and man against himself. It is, in short, a book about how to make money in Wall Street.

The underlying assumption, I confess, is that you will find this a desirable personal goal, and that while poverty may no longer be a social disgrace in this country, you do not regard it as an enviable distinction either. Your efforts to escape it, and to construct financial security for yourself and your family, will find encouragement in these pages. The news of your un-chic materialism will go no farther. My own observations, incidentally, which have ranged from villages in India to penthouses in Paris, lead inexorably to the conclusion that the best way to keep money in perspective is to have some. A corollary assumption is that you will require neither moral tutelage nor practical advice on how to dispense the wealth you are about to acquire, and that while remaining cognizant that money cannot buy happiness, you will nonetheless find other uses in your life to which it can be put.

Three reasonable questions ought to be recognized at the outset: Should you be in the stock market? Is it really a good deal for the average person? Why should you believe what's in this book? The first question is asked legitimately and sincerely by most people—but not, I fear, by all. I occasionally am approached by individuals, wearing their smugness like a money belt, who inquire innocently, "I am quintupling my assets each year in Vermont real estate (or Impressionist paintings, or rare speckled goldfish); should I be in the stock market instead?" Plainly, their need is for admiration, not elucidation, but for the record the answer is no. For most of the rest of us, though, who have no such presumably guaranteed highways to fortune, the answer is that if you can afford to have some of your money working in Wall Street, you probably cannot afford not to. There are many ways to put that money to work, as we shall see. But the alternative of leaving all your money "safely" in the bank can be the greatest delusion of all, for there it lies exposed to that most certain of marauders: inflation. Those who believe that our politicians are indeed about to arrest the great dollar robber, that a marvelous new era of fiscal stability is dawning and that a dollar saved today will be worth 100 cents at the supermarket a generation hence, can confidently squirrel their entire holdings under federal guarantee against the more obvious forms of theft. But for those who fear correctly that such a course also guarantees the erosion of their hard-won buying power, the authentic question about Wall Street is not "whether" but "how."

Obeisance should be made to the traditional cautions: The securities markets ordinarily are not the places for your first (or last) dollars. Before investing, you should provide for emergencies. You should have adequate savings and life insurance—though the definition of "adequate" will vary with each individual's circumstances and temperament, not to mention whether the advice is coming from a banker, a broker or an insurance salesman. For those with family responsibilities, simple prudence dictates erring slightly on the side of conservatism; no sensible person will count on the market being exactly right for a sale on the day you need to pay your doctor bills. By one of those distasteful laws of life, forced sales are likely to be bad sales. Wall Street is for your tomorrow; the exigencies of today should be provided for first.

But once there is a sum in the bank that would meet six months' living expenses, or some other sum that meets your personal definition of adequacy, and once the insurance salesman has left your house with an expression about midway between a frown and a guffaw, the time has come to think of investing. If you then have a surplus of anywhere between $500 and $500,-000,000, your actual investment program should begin right now —or better still, the day after you finish reading this book.

For the primary purpose of this tome is to provide a reasoned affirmative answer to that second question: Is it really a good deal for the average person? The notion here is that two aspects of Wall Street most frequently frighten off people who ought to be investing there but are not: the baffling jargon in which it, like most professions, is encased, and the conviction that the market is nothing but a dangerous form of gambling. The unease about the jargon is more easily quelled. Just as surgeons like to murmur imposingly about a cholecystectomy, instead of saying simply that they plan to lop off your gall bladder, so stockbrokers tend to employ an arcane vocabulary that will either impress the devil out of you or make you run for your life. Neither result is necessarily desirable. The processes of investing are a good deal more basic than the daunting jargon would suggest; the working language of our exploration will be ordinary English, with translations from the Wall Street version of Malayalam provided as required.

The fear of the stock market as a perilous gamble, impure and unsimple, is understandably enhanced during those periods when prices are dropping faster than a disappointed investor diving from the twenty-ninth floor. Those who play on this fear during those unsettling times are especially irksome to the poohbahs who are professionally responsible for Wall Street's image. Consider the case of Howard Samuels, president of New York's Off-Track Betting Corporation and an ambitious executive known as "Howie the Horse." In an effort to attract customers to his legal betting parlors, Samuels approved a newspaper advertisement whose headline read, "If you're in the stock market you might find this a better bet."

Among those who were ostentatiously not amused was the chairman of the New York Stock Exchange's Board of Governors, Bernard Lasker, known not as "Bernie the Horse" but as "Bunny." Lightness of touch was not Lasker's forte. He sent Samuels a telegram demanding that the ad be withdrawn and protesting "on behalf of more than 31,000,000 shareholders" the comparison between betting on horses and buying a share in America. "I cannot see any basis," Lasker declared solemnly, "for telling the public your facilities are an alternative to investment." (Samuels, incidentally, had the last horse laugh. "On behalf of the 48,972 horses that raced in this country in 1970," he replied, "I am sure that some feel they have been a better investment . . . than some of the investments on the New York Stock Exchange.")

Even more recently there was undoubtedly a spate of ulcers in the financial district at the occasional habit of New York's afternoon newspaper, the *Post*, to put side by side in the headlines of its final edition "Closing Stock Prices" and "Lottery Winners." Possibly this juxtaposition was accepted with equanimity at the exchange, but I wouldn't want to bet.

The relationship between gambling and investing deserves to be treated both with more sense of humor and with more perspective. Obviously, any sane person who puts his money in the market hopes that in addition to being intelligent, shrewd and industrious, he will also be lucky. The fellow who bought $10,000 worth of Xerox stock in May 1962 made a commendably sound investment, but could he really have anticipated confidently that that stock would be worth about $200,000 ten years later? There are two categories of Xerox investors: those who were pleasantly surprised and the liars. There is nothing shameful about yearning for a little bit of luck, and indeed I wish it to us all, but the trick in Wall Street is to create the circumstances in your own personal portfolio that make that good luck more probable. Contrary to much of the folklore of the field, there is no one certain road to riches—not stop-loss orders, or convertible bonds, or drinking a newt's-eye cocktail before sunrise—but there are proven signposts that can enable the beginner to approach investing with far more confidence in his ultimate success than would be reasonable as he sauntered into a legal bookie joint for a fling at the daily double. Those signposts are in this book.

Veteran market observers recall that the traditional distinction between investing and speculation has become blurred. There was a time, not too many decades ago, when investing was concerned primarily with the preservation of capital—an art that became self-defeating when inflation took on its perennial terror. Speculation was aimed directly at the growth of capital—which is what most people think of today as the point of investing. Investing still implies a greater degree of prudence and long-range foresight, but Wall Street cynics will tell you that an investor is a disappointed speculator, whose hopes for rapid gains were unfulfilled. They are also fond of quoting Lord Keynes, who said,

"In the long run, we're all dead." A nasty lot, those Wall Street cynics. Stay away from them.

Whatever the true distinction between investing and speculation, and it is one we shall explore further as we examine different routes to financial success, there has always been agreement among the cognoscenti that gambling represents a separate, third category, distinguished primarily by the absence of any social utility to the activity. Whereas Wall Street investors and speculators provide the capital that companies need to begin and to expand, and thereby contribute to the growth of the economy and the future of the nation, betting the solid horse to show is of questionable value even for the improvement of the breed. In Wall Street, unlike the track or the casino, it's patriotic to get lucky and deductible if you fail.

But however noble the contribution of the securities industry may be to the national economy, what you are probably wondering is what contribution it is likely to make to your personal economy. And here the evidence is more reassuring than one might suspect from a casual inspection of the financial bloodshed occasioned by the market's brutal zigzagging of the last decade. For one thing, the market is now a better-regulated and safer place for the small investor. For another, it has still been a place where, in any reasonable long-range perspective, the average investor could count on seeing the money he had saved make money for him. There have been various statistical studies that tried to put a number on this; perhaps the most famous was conducted by the Graduate School of Business at the University of Chicago under the sponsorship of the nation's largest brokerage firm, Merrill Lynch, Pierce, Fenner & Smith. The school's Center for Research in Security Prices began with January 1926 —before the Great Crash of 1929—and concluded that an investor over the next forty years, picking stocks at random without guidance or research, would have averaged a return on his investment equal to 9.3 per cent a year compounded annually. A later extension of the study over the next five years, which included the 1969–70 slump, reduced that figure only a fraction, to 9 per cent, and found that, taking the decade of the 1960s as a separate entity, an investor who was around from start to finish would have averaged an 11 per cent return, including dividends and growth of capital. In short, by whatever long-term test we apply, the stock market has been a place where even average results have been impressive. Professional investors, such as mutual funds, naturally aim to beat those averages, and so—with patience, intelligence and the information in this book—should you.

For those who believe in safety in numbers, there is further confirmation of Wall Street's attractions for ordinary citizens. In the last generation there has been a fantastic increase in the ranks of shareowners. The 1970 census conducted by the New York Stock Exchange reported that more than 30,000,000 Americans owned stock, up by more than half from the total reported just five years earlier. By 1972 the exchange estimated that the number of individual stockholders had grown to a record 32,-500,000, and it projected further increases to nearly 40,000,000 in 1975 and close to 50,000,000 by 1980. Can 50,000,000 Americans be wrong? Sure, but not this time. (The steady uptrend suffered a mild but hopefully chastening setback in 1973, when the exchange estimated that the number of individual stockholders had dipped by 800,000 to 31,700,000—the first reported decline in more than two decades and a useful warning to the industry that the typical small investor was less than delirious about his current treatment and success in the market. But the total remained impressive—and by the standards of any other nation, almost beyond belief.)

As recently as 1952, only one in sixteen American adults owned stock. By 1970 the figure was one in four. Stock ownership still appears to be a function of maturity; the average age of the stockholders in 1970 was a ripe forty-eight, though this was down from the riper fifty-one average reported in 1952. Stockholders are either getting younger or lying about their ages. Other findings of the study were that the median household income for those who owned stocks in 1970 was $13,500 (a year later the United States median household income went above $10,000 for the first time) and that, for the first time since the censuses began in 1952, there were more male stockholders than female—though the edge was a statistically skinny 50,000. Nonetheless, I pass the figure on to the Women's Liberation Movement for whatever it may be worth.

Unhappily, no money-back guarantee attaches to Wall Street investing; on this planet the search for rewards must always entail risks. But increasing millions of ordinary Americans have found securities investing an essential and beneficial part of their planning for a lovelier tomorrow. This book is designed to help you match or better their results, which leads us not so coincidentally to the third and last of our up-front questions: Why should you believe what's in this book?

The primary response is that, while the author makes no foolish claim to individual genius, he has had a rare and indeed unprecedented opportunity to distill the collective wisdom of many of the smartest moneymen in America. These men (and a few brilliant women, too) were my guests on the public television program "Wall Street Week," and both on and off the air they displayed a commendable generosity in passing on the essence of their own experiences. These are people who in many instances are capable of replying to that ancient challenge "If you're so smart, why aren't you rich?" with a confident "But I am, I am." More to the point, they have helped many others get rich, too. Other guests on the program, which began in November 1970, have included some of the nation's most formidable critics of the market and its practitioners, and where their shafts seemed accurate, they have made an impression in the pages that follow. Neither the professional investors nor the professional critics are responsible for any of this book's conclusions, which are necessarily my own, but my debt to them is real.

Through all these programs, attempting to represent the ordinary investor and to defend his interests, I was able to sift a fund of expertise whose purchase would have been beyond the means of any of us. Three conclusions are at hand:

(1) Nobody knows it all. Often the most confident in their forecasts were the widest from the mark. I met no one who had never picked a wrong stock nor misjudged the short-term course of the market. The smartest were the first to admit this.

(2) Some people know more than others. One thing that they know is that there is no necessity to be flawless, that a decent batting average can bring very much better than average results in Wall Street.

(3) Much of what they know is in this book. The techniques, the strategies, the attitudes that have brought others success and fortune in Wall Street are here presented in the hope that you will soon be following in their affluent footsteps.

Among the looniest notions in captivity is the idea that Wall Street is a dull place for vested bankers and staid widows. It is a personal testing arena without parallel, an exciting adventure in self-discovery. Here is one sport where everybody can be a pro, and that includes you—so come along now as we endeavor together to make money, not tears.

CHAPTER II

Blessings on Thee, Little Man

The first thing that you will discover about yourself as an investor may come as something of a surprise. It is that you are, like it or not, a Little Man. This applies even if you happen to measure 6-5—or, for that matter, 37-23-36. The Little Man is a permanent fixture in Wall Street mythology, right alongside the Gnome of Zurich—who is, paradoxically, not a Little Man at all. The mythology holds two beliefs about the Little Man: one, that his business isn't worth having, and two, that he is automatically a lot stupider than the big institutional investors. As with much of Wall Street's cherished mythology, it is wrong on both counts.

What is little about the Little Man is anything but unimportant to him: it is the amount he has to invest. This has been variously defined as anything up to $10,000, anything up to $25,000, anything up to $100,000 and anything up to $200,000, which is the minimum amount that many leading investment management companies will deign to handle. One successful financial adviser told me he was no longer able to take on accounts of a mere $1,000,000, thereby creating an improbable new category: the Little Man millionaire. So you're in good company.

Many leaders of the Wall Street Establishment get a bit nervous when the problems and complaints of the Little Man are discussed, and well they should—for their behavior toward him over the last few years has been nothing short of shameful. After courting him for a generation with glittering advertisements urging him to buy a share in America, the industry showed itself to be both incompetent and impolite when he started to come into the parlor.

The incompetence was evident in Wall Street's staggering failure to prepare itself for the increase in trading volume that took place in the late 1960s. Clerical lapses on the most routine transactions occurred on a scale so massive as to create an unruly ocean of unassimilated paper work, an ocean that threatened to drown the normal operations of the marketplace. At times the mighty New York Stock Exchange was forced to shut down during ordinary trading hours, a humiliating confession that it was unable fully to meet its promises to provide a reliable central market for the world. The back rooms of many prestigious brokerage firms were exposed as antiquated enterprises that might have been left intact by Ebenezer Scrooge—a shocking nineteenth-century contrast to the sleek plate glass and glossy leather that beckoned out front to ever more customers. Meanwhile, the executive offices themselves too often turned out to have been peopled by men who operated at or beyond the limits of prudence and solvency. The alibis came nearly as rapidly as the invitations had come earlier: Who could have anticipated such an enormous increase in volume, so much more than the "experts" had projected? Who could have anticipated such a horribly swift moment of truth, with the closely watched Dow Jones Industrial Average skidding from 985 in December 1968 to 631 in May 1970? And so it went, until the air was blue and the ink was red. Yet two facts remained that could not be alibied: The proud names of more than a hundred brokerage firms had disappeared, either through mergers and consolidations or, in at least fifteen major cases, through outright collapse. And whatever might be claimed about faulty projections, it was clear that any other American industry that had failed so conspicuously to prepare for the future would have been punished without mercy by these very same people—on the floors of these very same exchanges.

And who was rudely asked to carry the can for this brokerage incompetence? You get no prizes for guessing that it was our friend, the Little Man. Increasingly, he found his business, and himself, regarded as unwelcome intruders among the more profitable big transactions. This was particularly true in the busy, booming days of 1967 and 1968, and there may be some ironic satisfaction in noting that many a hotshot broker who was snubbing small accounts when the living was easy found himself selling shoes a couple of years later, when prices and volume declined. And selling the shoes, I presume, one pair at a time.

It would be attractive to be able to report that the Wall Street worm has fully turned, and that the Little Man has been restored to his proper position of glory and respect. But history suggests that such an assessment would be dazzlingly premature. What is clear is that the situation for the small investor is greatly improved, not because the Wall Street nabobs have graciously acknowledged the errors of their ways (they being as minimally inclined toward such nobility as most of the rest of us) but because they have sniffed a missing profit. This was evident on the smallest scale; for example, as "Brutus," the author of *Confessions of a Stockbroker*, once expressed it to me, "I know brokers in the industry who in '67, '68 said to their customers, 'Gee, I only accept accounts $25,000 and higher.' And then these same brokers in 1970—someone would come in with an odd lot of Telephone to sell [a very small order], and they'd beat, you know, a path to his door saying, 'I need the lunch money.'" And it was evident on a larger scale as chastened brokerage executives noted the ongoing profitability of the nation's largest firm, Merrill Lynch, which continued to woo the smallest of investors on the excellent theory that they might someday control larger sums and remember where their friends were.

By 1972 the New York Stock Exchange was able to report that 92 per cent of its member firms handling retail customers had neither a minimum requirement for cash accounts nor any restrictions on the size of orders they would accept. In addition, 81 per cent, or 316 of the 392 retail firms surveyed by the exchange, said they would buy or sell for an investor stock at any price—with no minimum price-per-share limitation. The abashed exchange, sensitive to the charge that it had become indifferent to the concerns of the average fellow, established an Investors Service Bureau, one of whose functions is to supply would-be investors with the names of firms in their areas that handle accounts of all sizes.

Another benefit from those Dark Ages that climaxed in 1970 was the passage by Congress and the signing by President Nixon of a Securities Investor Protection Corporation bill, which is designed to prevent you from having a heart attack if your brokerage firm goes bust. Under its provisions each investor has federal protection up to $50,000 per account. That insurance covers a combination of cash and securities, including a maximum of

$20,000 in cash. Anyone worried about the possible failure of an individual firm can spread his holdings around, $50,000 here and $50,000 there and so on into the night, which I'm sure will come as an immense relief to everyone who has been wondering where his second $50,000 will come from. Incidentally, it is perhaps worth emphasizing that the bill protects you against losses only if your firm collapses, not if you pick the wrong stocks.

The value of the Little Man to the market as a whole is controversial; what is less arguable is that his role has, in a relative sense, been diminishing and that the brokerage houses that served the institutional customers became spoiled with the fatter commissions they were generating there. As recently as 1960, 68.6 per cent of all shares were traded by individuals. Institutions such as mutual funds, pension funds and bank trust funds accounted for less than a third of the trading. Six years later the portion of shares traded by individuals had shrunk to 57 per cent, and the trend was continuing rapidly. In 1969 individuals accounted for only about 44 per cent of all the shares traded—and had become entrenched in what appeared to be a permanent minority position. Institutions had come, by any measurement, to dominate the market—for the comparative value of the shares traded by individuals, as opposed to institutions, shrank even faster than the comparative number of such shares. Yet these superficial statistics, so widely heralded within the industry, bypassed the more significant reality that the total volume of individual trading was not receding but increasing dramatically. From, say, 60 per cent of an average 3,000,000-share day in the early 1960s, ordinary investors were accounting for, say, 40 per cent of an average 14,000,000-share day in the early 1970s. The even more explosive growth of institutional business had masked the dramatic accompanying increase in trading by the great mass of Little Men.

The Little Man stood to benefit, too, from an event that may have seemed remote from any of his practical concerns—the decision to negotiate, and thus lower, the commissions on large institutional business. As such big business became somewhat less profitable for brokers, the wise ones began to eye anew the small customers they had publicly lured and privately scorned. Even before the latest cuts in institutional commissions took effect, it was noted that, while institutional trading accounted for

60 per cent of the dollar volume on the New York Stock Exchange (and was expected to approximate 75 per cent by 1975), member firms were deriving only 40 per cent of their commissions from institutions—and the rest from the very individuals whose commissions were about to be raised. In the words of Robert Haack, outgoing president of the New York Stock Exchange, "The brokerage business of the future that has the most to offer is the retail business."

So there is no reason for any present or prospective Little Man in Wall Street to feel any diffidence about the size of his transactions or the service he is entitled to receive. If you run into an uppity stockbroker, thumb your nose at him in return and write to the Investors Service Bureau at the New York Stock Exchange for the names of firms in your area that will give you the welcome you deserve. The exchange has recognized that the industry not only wants the individual investor, but actually needs him. It needs him to carry his share of a trading volume that is expected to reach 27,000,000 shares a day by 1980. It needs him to supply many of the dollars required to buy up an estimated $10,000,-000,000 to $15,000,000,000 a year in net new equity issues for the rest of this decade—dollars that will launch and feed a vast number of American businesses. And it needs him because, despite specious disclaimers, the market simply cannot function without him; more often than not, it is his buying and selling that make the real auction market and accurately fix the prices of stocks. In one recent month on the New York Stock Exchange, where institutional activity is most evident, there were no large block transactions whatever in more than half the listed stocks. Without the individuals, there would have been far less of the market's vaunted "liquidity"—the ability to turn your assets into cash at a reasonable price at any given time. Exchange officials are convinced that an exodus of individual investors would make price changes more abrupt and less predictable, and eventually would discourage trading even by institutions.

All praise, then, to the much-abused Little Man, who not only should refuse to be pushed around, but is entitled to feel authentic pride about his role in the system. But however pleasant and soul-comforting it may be to know you are needed, what the Little Man really wants to know is whether he has any reasonable chance to compete effectively against all those husky Big Men

—the institutions with that overpowering scent of cash to attract information and expertise unavailable to the likes of you and me. The answer is by no means the automatic negative that some would supply. As we shall see in greater detail as we progress, the individual investor may sometimes actually have an advantage over a large institution. For one thing, the very act of moving a massive amount of money on an institution's part can distort the price of the security in which it is interested—and make it cost more to buy and realize less to sell. The individual, by being a relative gnat on the horizon, can proceed as he wishes without changing the basic flow of prices. Often, despite his higher commissions, he doesn't need as large an increase in the price of the stock in order to take a profit. (One mutual-fund management organization calculated that for a large portfolio, actively managed, there would have to be a 31 per cent average change in stock prices for the fund managers to get out and get back in without losing money.) The individual investor also may find it easier to make a move after the facts of a situation have become public knowledge and a stock has already started to rise; frequently, he is more conveniently placed to go along for part of the ride. For another thing, the legendary brilliance of the great institutional investors of Wall Street is to a surprising extent a legend of their own creation. The best statistical evidence is that mutual funds in the aggregate get about the average rate of return of the market as a whole. Some outperform the market, some do about the same and some do a lot worse—which is, wonder of wonders, pretty much the same thing we could say about individual investors. So that, while mutual funds may well be the total answer for many investors and the partial answer for many others, there is no guarantee that they will automatically do better than you will on your own. What is more, as the veteran market sage Gerald M. Loeb put it when I asked him about the ability of the individual investor to compete with the alleged professionals, "I think he has to try. . . . He really hasn't much choice, because today, if he's going to go the other way and put his money in a fund or get a counselor, he has to pick the right one, and this isn't easy. There are over 500 funds and we don't know how many investment advisers, so that he really should make an effort to see if he is adapted to it."

So come another step forward, Little Man—boldly, yet alertly —in the company of an author whose sympathy and concern for the plight of the small investor could hardly be more genuine, for he happens to be one himself.

CHAPTER III

The Care and Feeding of Brokers

When the sun finally began to set on the British Empire, and to set embarrassingly early in the day, many officials in postwar London devised a marvelous new role for the nation in its era of diminished glory: to be the world's "honest broker," the go-between that would settle the disputes between countries whose power, though never wisdom, might exceed Britain's own. The concept failed to materialize (the stronger nations found themselves capable, when they wanted to make a deal, of doing so without Oxonian mediation), but the choice of words was interesting; what Britain felt the world most needed was a single honest broker. Many a disappointed investor would agree.

Rest easy, Diogenes; their fear relates not to criminal deceit but to phony expertise and misleading counsel. And quite often that cynicism is in error. The average stockbroker is neither idiot nor genius, a notion that should be easier to grasp when you realize that the number of accredited brokers in America is vastly in excess of the number of accredited millionaires. The broker's role in Wall Street is to be everyman's scapegoat. If only we had a better broker, we can rationalize, the yacht would be in the harbor, the servants in the kitchen and ourselves in Tahiti. And while there is, perhaps sadly, a bit more to it than that, it is patently more comfortable to have someone else to blame. Perhaps a portion of the broker's commissions should be considered as payment for this useful therapeutic function.

Having emphasized that brokers are very nearly as human as the rest of us, it is time to point the ways that the ordinary investor can find the extraordinary broker best suited to help him toward the realization of his own financial dreams. For like it or not, if you're going to be an investor, you're going to have to have a broker. (Oddly enough, this is not literally true. It's perfectly legal for anyone to buy stock from anybody else without using a broker, a stock exchange or a single word of jargon. You can buy Fred's General Motors from him and sell your IBM to Aunt Myrtle, and nobody even has to pay any commissions—though you will, in some states, have to affix transfer tax stamps. The problems are (1) finding somebody to make the other half of the deal and (2) protecting yourself for tax purposes, which may involve a suitable letter of sale, a newspaper clipping or photograph of the official price listing for the stock that day and assorted other nuisances. As a practical matter, you have to grab your lamp and set out in search of that honest broker.)

Strictly speaking, incidentally, though you will probably call him "my broker" when you are not calling him something worse, the brokerage-house employee with whom you will deal is just a representative of the firm's floor broker, who actually executes orders at the stock exchange. Your contact is what used to be known as a "customer's man" but now usually has some more elegant title such as "account executive" or "registered representative." The idea is to downplay the image of salesmanship, lest you suspect correctly that his living depends importantly on the amount of business he generates, and to stress instead that he is "registered" by the Securities and Exchange Commission—licensed as a professional of apparent good character and a man who has demonstrated his awesome command of matters financial by passing one of the world's less taxing examinations. Nowadays, these "registered reps," as they are known within the industry, often are subjected also by their firms to more genuine training programs than were prevalent even just a few years ago, so there is perhaps a greater assurance than in the past that the broker you acquire may actually know something worthwhile. But you obviously want to narrow your search a good deal more than that.

One way to pick a broker is to look in the Yellow Pages under "Stock & Bond Brokers." A recent Manhattan directory listed four pages of them in that borough alone, and these days you probably won't come up empty in any burg bigger than East Lynn. As a method of choosing a broker, however, this is about as useful a method as it is of picking a brain surgeon (and remember, he's not dealing with your money, only your life). The same can be said about being influenced solely by the biggest advertisements or the most appealing television commercials, guides that are at least as questionable in finance as they are in fluoridation. You need to know more than what the firm, and its advertising agency, decide to tell you.

Obviously, the best way to select a broker is by firm personal recommendation from someone you trust and for whom that broker has made money. Ask around, but be sure that the information you are getting is sincere, for it is as true in investing as in most of the world's affairs that misery simply adores company.

If you are not lucky enough to be recommended to such an authentic Midas, or if he doesn't have time for you when you arrive, then you have to work a little harder. One traditional piece of advice is to ask your banker. That can be fine, but remember that his professional contact with brokerage firms is likely to lean more heavily on their desirability as applicants for loan funds than on their ability to choose securities for their clients. And remember, too, that in many ways he is apt to look on all brokers as competitors for funds that, his conservative instincts and his banker's self-interest agree, ought to be sitting in his bank earning interest.

Another traditional source of brokers' names is your family lawyer. He is unlikely to be an investment expert either, and he has his own brand of professional ultraprudence to contend with, but like the banker he ought at a minimum be able to supply you with a short list of reputable firms. From there, you have two choices: You can do what most people do, wander in to the first one on the list, ask to speak to a broker, be assigned what amounts to the officer of the day and be stuck with him. Or you can take a little more time in the hope of getting somewhat better results.

One of the most significant facts about a brokerage firm, and one most often ignored by the new investor, is the quality of its research advice. This, after all, is usually the source of the buy-and-sell recommendations that are going to be passed on to you. But how can a layman judge this?

Well, you can ask where the research recommendations originate, how big a research organization is maintained, even the names of the firm's security analysts and the industries that they cover. You can ask for free samples of their recent recommendations. Firms that really operate solid research organizations for their small clients as well as their giants are usually delighted to publicize this commitment.

Perfection is not to be attained in this mortal sphere, however, not even in a brokerage house, and so you should be aware that the firm undoubtedly has pushed some losers as well as winners. Judging the track record can be easier if the firm also runs some outside money-management operations, such as a mutual fund, for which the results over the years have been a matter of public record. Otherwise, it may be more difficult for you to make any scientific assessment of the quality of the firm's recommendations over an extended period of time, in scary markets as well as those that promote euphoria. John F. Childs, senior vice president of the Irving Trust Company, told me that he thought "the poor small stockholder" would not be receiving adequate protection in this regard until brokers are required by the government to keep a uniform record of their past recommendations and to show it on request. It is a sound proposal, and one that would give many brokers a fit, but meanwhile you are going to have to make your judgment on the basis of the less complete information that is available.

Having at least tentatively chosen a firm, how do you then go on to select an individual broker? One good suggestion, too seldom followed, is to visit several firms and several brokers before making a commitment. You wouldn't, after all, automatically marry the first person you dated, would you? There might be someone far more compatible just around the next bend.

And compatibility is an essential feature of the broker–client relationship, compatibility both in the obvious personal sense—you'll be on the phone with him more often than many men are in touch with their mistresses—and in the more delicate sense of your investment goals. One useful way to start is to ask to speak to the office manager. Level with him—tell him just how small a fry you are, how active an investor you plan to be and what you are trying to accomplish. Ask him which of his registered representatives he thinks would be most suited to your account. Then talk with that representative and see if you agree.

Your own temperament has much to do with this question. Some people like to deal with the busiest man in the office, assuming he will stoop to take them on, on the ground that he is

obviously a perpetual money machine. Others feel comfortable
only with a fellow whose very manner exudes affluence, experience and gray-haired sagacity—as if they were casting directors
rather than prospective investors. Actually, it's often desirable
for a small new investor to hook up with a relatively small new
broker, a younger member of the firm who is anxious to build a
clientele, is compelled to hustle a little harder and is a bit less
apt to get haughty about the tininess of the money bag that you
are so desperately clutching.

You may even be fortunate enough to find the qualities you
want in a woman broker—a commodity that is still nearly as rare
as (not to put too fine a point on it) hen's teeth. Wall Street has
been among the most unalterably chauvinist of male institutions,
despite the vast amount of wealth invested there under at least
nominal female control, so if you discover a woman who has been
tough and smart enough to buck the established order, chances
are you might be on to an exceptional broker.

But whoever you wind up with, and for the sake of literary
convenience but without prejudice I shall designate that person
as "him," there are two aspects of your relationship that ought to
be settled at the outset. First, you should eliminate both ego and
shyness, and report frankly to your new broker the dimensions of
your present financial situation—your income, your prospects and
your responsibilities. Then (and he can help with this) fully define your investment goals. If you are aged and retired, you may
place primary emphasis on the highest possible income. If you
are young, well-off and plucky, you may be ready to accept major
speculative risks in the hope of achieving major speculative
gains. More likely you will find yourself somewhere in the middle,
anxious to see your capital grow but at least equally anxious not
to see it evaporate through some broker's unnecessarily wild
"gunslinging"—a form of speculative excess that saw many customers (and brokers) slung right out of the marketplace in the
1969–70 slump. To a degree that should be unsurprising on sober
contemplation, Wall Street's risks and rewards tend to run in
absolute tandem; the greatest potential rewards usually involve
the greatest potential risks, but smaller and more consistent rewards can be attained by running smaller and more foreseeable
risks. Tell the broker what you want to accomplish, and ask him
whether you have set a realistic and adequately specific goal. If

you want to take a profitable ride on the Wall Street train, it's helpful to announce your destination in advance.

The second understanding that you should have with your broker is what your working relationship is going to be. Even if you have chosen, as I would recommend, a broker who is not so busy that he is already constantly under the gun with his existing accounts, you cannot expect him to be available for a casual chat whenever you feel like calling. If your investment is small, and your account relatively inactive, remember that he does nearly all his business on that telephone line and that he is likely to be particularly harried between 10 A.M. and 3:30 P.M., Eastern time, when the major exchanges are open. If you just want some data about a stock you are considering, or a price quotation for information, you will generally find a friendlier and more considered reception if you postpone your inquiry until after 3:30 P.M. In return, you are entitled to courteous and fast consideration when you do want to move speedily. The customer who keeps his requests reasonable, concise and specific, and who avoids unnecessary hectoring during market hours, has traveled his half of the road and has earned the right to superior treatment from his broker.

What should such treatment entail? Well, he ought to get called by his broker sometimes and not always wait to be the originator of any contact. He ought to get written material, solicited and unsolicited. He is entitled to see his broker from time to time and to review his holdings. Most important, he ought to see his portfolio performing at least as well as the market as a whole in terms of the goals he has enunciated to his registered representative.

And how much excess cash is enough to start such an investment program? The New York Stock Exchange has a monthly investment plan into which can be put as little as $40 a month (or quarter!). My own feeling, shared by some of the biggest brokerage firms in the country, is that anything from $500 up is a realistic sum with which to begin—since anything less will entail more commissions and inconvenience than they are worth. But I have to confess that I began my own career as a stock-market investor with only slightly more than half that recommended minimum. For what it is worth, here is the full account of that historic transaction:

It was in the early summer of 1950, a season marked by the start of the Korean War and my graduation from high school, events that are modestly listed in their presumed order of importance. They were, in this case, not unrelated. For the stock market, contrary to Marxist rumor, really finds war a very unsettling experience (as it was to demonstrate again at the time of Vietnam). The market plummeted, but I, fortuitously, had the cash at hand to enable me to step in and help rescue the nation. This I did by purchasing three shares of General Motors common stock, then selling for about $87 a share, and paying for it with the entire savings of my year and a half as a high school sports reporter for the New Rochelle *Standard-Star*.

Over the years, before the necessity to make a down payment on a house forced me to leave GM to its own devices, those three shares not only paid regular and handsome dividends, but increased prodigiously in price. The stock split two-for-one in October 1950 and again three-for-one in September 1955, meaning that each of my original shares had been transformed into six of the current shares. And the price of those new shares soared as high as $113.75 in 1965 before bottoming out at $59.50 in 1970—at which depressed price my original shares would still have been worth more than four times what I had paid for them, not to mention the dividends they had accumulated over the years. My youthful confidence that the United States would not remain in a permanent state of financial panic, and that there was money to be made by betting against the hysteria, had been rewarded handsomely enough to suit any Horatio Alger. Obviously, I would have made out a lot better if high school sports reporting had been a more lucrative profession and my initial stake had been greater, but who would be churlish enough to deny me the pleasure I got from starting so small?

The key question for most prospective investors is not how much they should have to get started, but when—and the answer, more often than not, is right now. It was the fabulously successful Jacob H. Schiff who confided that one of his investment secrets was that he never tried to buy at the bottom or sell at the top. And neither should an inexperienced investor attempt to outguess the professionals by delaying the start of an investment program with realistic long-term goals. Launching such a small-scale investment program is "the only way to learn," Donald

Regan, the chairman of mighty Merrill Lynch, once remarked on "Wall Street Week," adding that his firm's 5,500 account executives were instructed to welcome new customers with as little as $500 to $1,000 to invest.

At that stage, you and your broker should both be aware that neither of you is going to get rich on this account overnight. You are then essentially an accumulator; Julia Montgomery Walsh, an astute broker who was the first woman member of the American Stock Exchange, told me that she felt the accumulating stage did not turn into genuine investing until you had a five-figure account, which in her case took ten years. "Brokerage houses today can't handle the $2,000 wheeler-dealer," she said. "But they're not upset about handling the $2,000 accumulator."

My own view would be slightly different. A small investor who is willing to apply the techniques of intelligent investing spelled out in this book can be entirely authentic long before he has run his stake to $10,000, and contrariwise there are plenty of people around with six-figure and even bigger accounts who do not merit the title of investor.

You will start slow, with no more than two or three different stocks (there is something to be said for restricting yourself to just one, and then having to sell it before you can buy another), and the decisions you will be making will be of the same kind that a larger investor would be confronting. He would, it's true, be buying more of each stock—but all that takes is money. The central considerations—what to buy and when to sell—are precisely the same.

The wise broker will encourage you, particularly if you are considerate about your demands on his time when the market is open. After all, a smart investor like you plainly has a brilliant financial future, and he doesn't want to lose you. (Most customers are promiscuous, usually because they don't get the type of service I have outlined; according to one estimate, the average broker turns over his entire list of clients every four years.) If you have chosen with care, yours may be one of the beneficent exceptions—a marriage between shrewd investor and helpful stockbroker that lasts at least till debt do you part.

CHAPTER IV

Order in the House

Now that you've got your broker, what should you do with him? (Please, no obscenities; this is a family book.) Well, what you shouldn't do is metamorphose him into your personal Bernard Baruch, the financial guru whose word is never to be challenged and whose advice is to be followed without question or delay. There are at least four good reasons for not adopting such a subservient role: (1) your broker, though a splendid chap, may sometimes be wrong; (2) if you master the approaches described in this book, you will at minimum bring a second knowledgeable head to work on the problem; (3) if you follow him blindly, you won't learn much about yourself as an investor; (4) it's your money.

There is a certain dichotomy in the broker–customer relationship that is always worth bearing in mind. On the one hand, the success and indeed the continuance of that relationship should depend on his keeping your interests at heart and doing well by you. On the other, the immediate prosperity of him and his family depends on how many commissions he can generate in the here and now. Every time you buy or sell, he makes a commission; every time you decide to be patient and hang in there, his income shows a goose egg. Don't misunderstand me; the wise broker knows that such eggs may eventually turn out to have come from a golden goose—if he shows understanding, counsels prudence and wins your confidence. And every reputable broker-age house, at least in theory, opposes the "churning" of small accounts through excessive trading to generate commissions. But remember that your two aims encompass a significant difference: You want your total wealth to increase, whereas he makes his money by bringing an order in the house.

Doctors, it has been said, bury their mistakes. Brokers just take a second commission. Or sometimes even a third (one when you buy the stock at his recommendation, a second when you sell it at a loss and a third when you replace it with another stock that he is then pushing instead). His personal income from your account at that point is approximately three times as high as it would have been if the original selection had been a good one and you were still holding the stock and watching it increase in price. Obviously, if you continue to get bad advice you will be sensible enough to look for another broker. But much as many brokers will protest, citing their own impeccable ethics and behavior, this inherent conflict of interests will continue as long as your broker continues to get his income, directly or indirectly, exclusively from commissions. Is there any solution? Sure, a very simple one: Borrow the "performance fee" concept from bigmoney management and make at least part of each registered representative's compensation a function of how well his accounts have performed. That way he will make more money when you do and not vice versa, as is potentially the case now; it's the difference between empathy and identity, and I suspect it could make a powerful difference indeed. Such a change has the support of such thoughtful industry leaders as William R. Grant, president of Smith, Barney and Company, who expressed to me the hope that computers would make such an incentive system possible before 1976. At this writing, however, there has been no discernible stampede of rank-and-file brokers anxious to have their remuneration geared to their merit to their customers.

Having thus risked the wrath of the world's brokers, let me balance this with some further remarks about commissions that may be equally displeasing to many small investors. I think it is possible to pay too much attention to commissions. They are not particularly high as such fees go, and they should seldom be the determining factor in a securities transaction. To buy 100 shares of a stock selling for $40 a share, a hefty purchase for a small investor, you would pay a commission of $63.80—or little more than 1½ per cent of the $4,000 invested.

That commission is, incidentally, $5.80 higher than what you would have paid before September 1973, when commission rates increased 10 per cent on transactions up to $5,000 and 15 per cent on larger orders. The justification was to bail out the beleaguered brokers, whose aggregate losses for the year (in a low-volume bear market) were said to be approaching $250,000,000. The squeeze between rising costs and dwindling profits had forced at least twenty more firms into mergers, and Wall Street cynics were suggesting that even this was like rearranging the deck chairs on the Titanic. These cynics, of course, had often been wrong before. A more useful comparison might have been to a department store in the doldrums—thus inspiring the interesting, if unwelcome, question of whether the best way to bolster receipts is to raise prices.

In Wall Street's case, the negative psychological impact of doing just that was deepened because the new rates, which are identical at all brokerage firms that belong to the New York Stock Exchange, replaced a schedule that had gone into effect only eighteen months earlier. The March 24, 1972, scale of commission rates had, in turn, taken the place of a surcharge that was imposed a couple of years before, plus a basic set of rates established in 1958. So it was understandable that the ordinary investor felt battered and victimized, even though the 1972 schedule had been expected to yield only about 5 per cent more than the 1958 rates and in some categories actually provided effective reductions (including those commissions paid by the very biggest investors and, perhaps surprisingly, the very smallest: those whose orders totaled less than $800 apiece).

Nobody enjoys higher prices (except, of course, on stocks and bonds), and the business wisdom of again raising commissions, when the investor mood already was relatively dismal, is certainly arguable. The brokerage industry ought to recognize that antagonizing the customer with ever-higher commission rates is by no means an endless road to riches. The firms would do better to run their own businesses more efficiently—for example, by not going hog wild on office expansion every time market activity peaks and by concentrating on training knowledgeable personnel instead of hiring former competitors at fancy salaries. But from your own financial point of view the critical consideration is that even these slightly higher rates should not be regarded as a barrier to an investment that otherwise seems sensible. The complete current schedule will be found in Appendix A; here are some typical small-investor commissions: on 20 shares of a $30 stock (a $600 order), $18.04; on 100 shares of a $20 stock (a

$2,000 order), $41.80; on 50 shares of a $75 stock (a $3,750 order), $59.13; on 100 shares of any stock costing more than $50, a flat $74.75. (A 100-share order is called a "round lot" transaction; anything less is considered an "odd lot"—but don't take it personally.)

The purpose is not to argue that such commissions are painless, but that they are a slim portion of the total funds being invested. They are a part of the cost of investing that you should realistically calculate, but the quality of the advice you get and the performance of the stocks you buy as a result are the truly central considerations. If it turns out that you made a good investment, the commission will soon be dwarfed by your profit; if it turns out that you ought to sell a stock, the time spent worrying about paying a second commission can be costly in terms of rapidly falling prices. Commissions should not be a dominant element in your investment thinking; it's just that you should be aware that they mean something different to you and to your broker.

Whether such commissions should properly be reduced is a subject of angry debate in Wall Street. Some major firms have suggested that, if they were allowed to undercut the monopoly prices, they would do so. The Securities and Exchange Commission, in approving the 1973 increase, said it would give them a chance to try: Starting April 1, 1975, the SEC said, all fixed commission schedules will be abolished and rates can be set competitively on trades of any size. That doesn't mean you'll be able to bargain with your broker every time you feel like doing business, but it does mean that each firm will be allowed to set and post its charges independently.

One proposed route for commission-cutting has been "unbundling," meaning separate payments for separate services—instead of the one set commission that you pay whether or not you use the firm for such peripheral purposes as research, collection of dividends and custody of your securities. Unbundling is being formally encouraged by the SEC starting April 1, 1974. Obviously, if you know exactly what you want and you use the firm only to execute those predetermined transactions, you are paying for more than you are getting. As a result, some cut-rate brokerage houses have sprung up that operate outside the normal exchange system and claim already to be saving the customer 20 per cent or more on the regular commissions. One such is Odd Lots Securities, whose president, Lawrence Weiss, described it to me as Wall Street's first discount house. Weiss established a strictly cash-and-carry operation, without what he termed "the frills." Another such firm, Source Equities, Inc., promised a flat fee of 50 per cent or less of the usual exchange commissions and also, unlike Odd Lots Securities, offered the possibility of "margin" (loan) accounts. Its services, however, were restricted to customers willing to trade at least 2,000 shares a year—which ruled it out for the average investor. Later, as competition for smaller accounts intensified, Source Equities publicized a minimal plan under which a customer could buy and sell up to 1,000 shares without a time limit, for a set fee of $220. (Weiss, on the other hand, told me he had among his customers "a little man who comes in every other week and buys one share of stock, and he pays me for the one share of stock the following week, by money order, and we keep his one share in the vault and every six months he picks up his several shares of stock, and we thank him.")

The existence of these no-research, cut-rate houses spotlighted the lock-step performance of all the other brokerage firms that did belong to the New York Stock Exchange and, in return for its undeniable advantages, went along with its price-fixed commissions. It is an ambiguity worthy of the Orient that, though it is the centerpiece of the competitive capitalist system, the New York Stock Exchange often seems to regard the notion of stock-market competition as if it were some kind of deep-dyed Communist plot. The discount brokerage houses represented a bold challenge to at least one of those monopoly cravings—the one that said every broker had to charge the same commissions, and what's more, wrap them up in one big package deal whether the customer happened to want the package or not. They spurred Wall Street's overdue re-examination of its traditional practices, and meanwhile offered some independent investors an alternative worth considering. For the typical small and inexperienced investor, however, they are probably not the answer. I would recommend that he stick instead to the conventional brokerage houses, whose additional services might turn out to be of more use to him than he first assumes—and whose commissions are, in dollar terms, very little higher.

Before leaving the subject of commissions, there is another consideration affecting your broker of which you should be aware: His income depends not only on how much you buy, but on what you buy. Up till now we have been assuming that you were buying stocks listed on the New York or American stock exchanges. When you decide on such a purchase, your registered representative passes the word to one of the firm's brokers on the floor of the exchange in question, and the floor broker then quickly gets you the best deal going at the time. The cost to you, in addition to the cost of the securities themselves, is the kind of commission we have been talking about. Your own registered representative would typically keep about a quarter to a third of the total commission you pay.

But there are other things you might decide (or be induced) to buy that would yield significantly higher commissions on the same-sized investment. On a mutual fund that carried a "load," or sales charge, this could run 9 per cent or higher. Or if you bought an "over-the-counter" stock—one that is not traded in the open auction markets at the major exchanges—the dealer profit, which is included in the price, could run as high as 5 per cent. When a firm has such an over-the-counter stock in its inventory, waiting to be sold, there is usually an extra sweetener for the account executive who gets you to buy it. An over-the-counter stock is often an excellent investment, especially for the customer with some experience, but you should be alert to a situation that rewards a broker more for moving a different kind of merchandise —whether or not it is the merchandise that most nearly suits your needs.

Now, though, you are ready to begin your investment career. Your broker is a fine fellow who combines financial genius with a kindliness of spirit that would have put Barry Fitzgerald to shame. Your only conceivable complaint in the years ahead will be that his judgment was faulty and he failed to put you into the right stocks. Or will it? A surprising number of the thousands of investor complaints we have received at "Wall Street Week" related not to money lost through bad advice but to what might be regarded as simple housekeeping failures, problems that persisted years after the back-office chaos of the late 1960s had supposedly been alleviated. Perhaps it would be useful to examine some of the most common complaints, so that if any of them ever become yours you will know what to do about them.

Many problems seem to emanate from a lack of clear communication between client and broker. For example, you tell your registered representative to buy a stock, he doesn't do so—and the price rises. Or you tell him to sell, he doesn't do so—and the price falls. What happened, and what is your recourse?

The most likely possibility is that your broker felt your wishes were not clearly defined. Were you just musing aloud, were you "thinking about" doing such and such, or did you give him a plain and direct instruction to buy or sell? Most good brokers guard against this kind of situation by habitually repeating back to the customer exactly what they believe to be an order or not an order. If your broker doesn't do this automatically, ask him to.

If, however, your order was indeed clearly given and properly understood, the brokerage firm has an obligation to make good on the trade. If your registered representative is balky, contact the resident manager of the office. If that doesn't work, write the president of the firm. And if all else fails, go straight to the Securities and Exchange Commission in Washington.

Going to the top is often the best solution. Suppose, for example, that you were in the place of one unfortunate viewer who bought 200 shares of a stock, was credited on his monthly statement from the firm with only 100 shares, and then when he tried to get the matter straightened out was told that his broker was no longer working there. If something like that happens to you, dry your tears, stop screaming and run, don't walk, to the managing partner or the chief executive of the firm. And if that dignitary fails to resolve the problem within a reasonable period of time, take your complaint to the Securities and Exchange Commission or to the Compliance Division of the New York Stock Exchange.

(Government control of the securities industry is centered in the Securities and Exchange Commission; it regulates the various stock markets, makes rules for companies issuing new securities and is in general charged with assuring full disclosure of the nation's investment activity. Its five members oversee an operation established by Congress in 1933 and 1934—a time when Wall Street ranked just above leprosy on the list of national favorites—and assigned to policing the securities industry as an independent, bipartisan, quasi-judicial government agency. The SEC's staff includes lawyers, accountants, engineers, security analysts and examiners, and it is the logical place for the small investor to turn for justice if he thinks he is being bilked by his brokerage firm or stock exchange. If you are convinced that that most emphatically means you, the headquarters office of the Securities and Exchange Commission is at 500 North Capitol Street, Washington, D.C. 20549.)

Sometimes you can get action another way. An occurrence that is more common than you might expect in the slickly computerized world of finance is the failure to pay an investor dividends to which he is entitled. If that happens to you, before you take your complaint higher you might try this: Ask your broker to give you the address of the company or its dividend dispersing agent and write a polite but firm letter setting forth the full facts of your transactions in the stock in question. There is a good chance that it will not be the first such letter they have received, and if they are smart they will move with all deliberate speed to see that you are getting what you are entitled to. If for any reason they do not, proceed in a dignified manner to hit the ceiling as outlined above.

One problem to avoid if at all possible is losing your stocks and bonds. Someday this problem will be eliminated by eliminating the stock certificate itself, which adds notably to the cost and confusion of doing brokerage business. This change is opposed both by traditionalists who like to hold that piece of paper in their hands and by skeptics who are unwilling to trust their proof of ownership to a computer. Until their objections are met, or overruled, guard those certificates carefully when you receive them from your broker. For if you lose one, you have the obligation to replace it—and that, as they say at the Tour d'Argent, is no simple *pique-nique*. You will have to put up, in cash, a so-called surety bond that usually runs from 3 to 6 per cent of the price of the stock at the time you reported the loss. The transfer agent will then put a stop against the old certificate and issue you a new one. You can avoid this expensive inconvenience if you were not responsible for the loss. If your broker sent you a certificate and you never received it, that's his problem. If it was sent directly by the transfer agent and failed to show up in your mailbox, the agent is responsible. In either of those cases, you will probably have to sign an affidavit of nonreceipt, and have it notarized and countersigned. There are better ways to spend a summer afternoon.

One way to head off this kind of agony is to be especially careful about mailing stock to your broker. Registered mail is one route; another is to send the stock certificate unsigned by you in one envelope and a separate sheet known as a "stock power" (which your broker can give you) in another envelope. If the stock power has been signed by you, the broker can put it together with the stock certificate and make it a negotiable instrument. On the other hand, if your certificate is already signed and negotiable, and your brokerage office is far away, you can take the certificate into your bank, ask for a receipt and get them to mail it under their special insurance policies. Obviously, if you can hand-carry your valuable certificate right into your broker's presumably hot little hands, you've got the safest solution of all. Another useful tip is to write down the certificate numbers of your stocks when you receive them; knowing the numbers makes it easier if you ever do have to replace them.

If all that strikes you as a paper-work disaster area, you may want to consider putting your securities in what is known as "street name." This means that as far as the company whose stock you own is concerned, the stock is owned not by you but by your brokerage house. That's where all the dividends, annual reports, etc. will be sent. ("Street name" is actually a misnomer, since the owner of record is not any street, Wall or otherwise, but your firm—Tayktha, Moni & Run, or whatever.) The advantages to you of such an arrangement are that your securities are held in safekeeping by your broker and that you have a great deal of convenience in collecting dividends or buying and selling. You will no longer have to worry about storing and carting your certificates, because you will never even see them. The disadvantage is that you won't get your reports from the company as quickly as you should; brokers tend to be lax in sending them on, and the delay can run into weeks. For most investors who plan to be reasonably active, buying or selling at least several times a year, the convenience of leaving securities in street name probably outweighs the disadvantage, and they should tell their broker that that is how they want to proceed. (If this is your decision, don't worry about possible danger; your securities, though formally in the name of the firm, are still protected up to $50,000 by the Securities Investor Protection Corporation.)

Another frequent investor complaint is that, while brokers make you pay up for your stock within five business days (the so-called settlement date or due date), they can outsleep the sloth themselves when it comes to paying you when you sell the stock. The answer one gets from the brokers goes something like this: The pressure on you when you buy comes not from the noble brokers but from the mean old Federal Reserve Board, which requires some unpleasant paper work if a customer is as much as two days late. (The Federal Reserve Board is the government agency that sets the rules for all stock-market borrowing.) When you sell stock, on the other hand, there can be delays in getting the stock to your broker, getting it processed, getting it sent on to New York if you do business elsewhere and getting it delivered to the buyer. It's not till then that a check is likely to be sent out to you. All well and good, but it's my feeling (shared by many efficient firms) that, if you are consistently delivering your stock on time and getting your check several days late, you should assume that the clerical department in question is located in Nome, Alaska—and get yourself another broker.

A related problem arises regularly when customers ask to have their securities sent to them—and then wait months and months for delivery. This seems particularly prevalent where bonds rather than stocks are concerned; in the case of newly issued securities, the normal delays can be painfully extended because of such mundane hurdles as getting the printing done. Here's another case where, if the delay becomes unreasonable, your best bet is to go first to the resident office manager, and then, if necessary, to the president of the firm. At the same time, write a letter to the secretary of the corporation whose securities are concerned, so that he can put pressure on the transfer agent to get your holdings to you. And by the way, if you want to sell the security before it is physically delivered to you, you can go right ahead and give the instruction to your broker. If you have paid for the security, you will have received a confirmation slip from the broker immediately thereafter, and that's all you need. Let somebody else go crazy waiting for the actual security to be delivered.

As a sample of how quickly it is possible to get action if you can get to the right executive, let me tell you about a nasty trick I pulled on Donald T. Regan, the head man of Merrill Lynch, on network television October 22, 1971. Without prior warning, I told him of a complaint we had had from a Merrill Lynch customer in Rochester, New York, who said she had not yet received certificates either for 100 shares she bought in March or another 100 shares she bought in August—despite repeated letters and telephone calls to her registered representative. What the poor lady wanted to know was, "Why should it be so much easier to get a piano than a stock certificate?"

Regan rallied gamely. The August nondelivery, he thought, was "not too surprising": "The transfer of securities is a long and cumbersome process; not only are brokers involved, but banks are involved, and the like. And while we used to pride ourselves on two- to three-week delivery, during the paper crunch conditions got to be very bad, and now six to eight weeks is normal for delivery." But the earlier half of the problem appeared to have him baffled: "The March nondelivery I cannot understand," he said, "and I wish that person would write to me directly, and I'll straighten that one out but quick."

What happened thereafter is encouraging to those of us who believe that no Little Man is an island. The following Monday morning, according to some of my informants within Merrill Lynch, the Rochester office was turned upside down in an attempt, not only to locate the anonymous customer, but also to excavate any other potential skeletons buried in the deepest clerical closets. And the complaining woman's problems were quickly settled, though not without an element that may add fuel to those with smoldering doubts about the supremacy of the computer age.

The August problem turned out to have been easily explainable; the firm was holding those securities because an opportunity was coming up for the holder to get a special deal on ten additional shares, and her broker wanted to be sure that she did not miss this subscription opportunity. But as Regan later wrote me, "The story of the initial confusion is rather an interesting one. The customer . . . requested that our Merrill Lynch office in Rochester forward to her a certificate for 100 shares of National Lead, which she had purchased earlier. At the time of her request, National Lead changed its name to NL Industries, and therefore when the computer scanned her account it did not find any National Lead therein. The consequence, I am sorry to say, was a good deal of delay."

Just another dumb computer—with months of annoyance the result. To get action you have to get real live human beings involved, and while plainly not everybody's problem can be raised on television, the top executives of the most reputable firms are concerned about customer satisfaction and their firms' resulting images—and they should be your targets if you think their local offices are pushing you around.

So now you know how to pick the right broker, and what to do with him once he's in tow. The chief thing you need to know now is how to pick the right stocks, so let's get on to that simple question next.

CHAPTER V

Socrates Was Right

You might not immediately guess it if confronted with the enormous array of literature on the subject, much of it heavy as an elephant and about as digestible, but there are really only two ways to pick stocks—and this applies whether you are an ordinary little mouse or an imposing fat cat. These two methods are "fundamental analysis," which attempts to find out what a stock is worth, and "technical analysis," which tries to make short-term predictions about what a stock's price is going to be. The fundamentalist assumes that hard work and native shrewdness will enable him to discover a stock that is currently undervalued and that will therefore bring him impressive profits in the years ahead. The technician tends to be rather cynical about the whole concept of "value"; a stock to him is worth only what someone else is willing to pay for it at any given moment, and he believes that he can detect the future price on the basis of the past performance of the market itself—a performance that may or may not bear much relationship to the underlying merit of the stock in question.

The purist in either category is increasingly hard to find; most successful investors borrow freely from both disciplines. Asking which is more important is like asking the relative importance of an arm and a leg. The compleat-investor-to-be (that's you) will logically begin by searching for stocks whose fundamentals give them the potential for long-range greatness. But his investing equipment will be imperfect until he is also knowledgeable about the techniques and timing that will guide him as to when and how to act. You will, in short, want to master both halves of the equation; but never fear, that's what we're here for, and you will, you will.

First, though, it will not have gone unnoticed by you that the names of both these systems for picking stocks have a common word—"analysis"—a word whose association with just about everything concerned with the stock market cannot be dismissed as mere coincidence. Despite the austere and humorless face it tries to present to the public, despite all that jargon and all those computers, Wall Street is about as scientific and logical as the most incurable manic-depressive at your local asylum. In the long run it will respond to forces more powerful than itself, such as a truly expanding economy, but in the short run it is difficult to predict precisely because its behavior is so unscientific and illogical. It goes to extremes of excitement and depression; it's as jittery as your old Aunt Gertrude, and it finds it almost impossible to cope with any change in its environment; for maddening stretches it will seem to ignore the obvious and to overreact to the unessential. What it seems to need, then, is analysis in the psychiatric sense as well as the scholarly.

Once you have understood that Sigmund Freud can be as important to the stock market as Adam Smith, you will find it easier to forget the myth that Wall Street—the storied haven of so much of the nation's supposedly "smart money"—is a brilliant forecaster of the nation's economy. It is a myth that ranges from scary newspaper headlines to the government's list of "leading economic indicators," but much of the time you would be just as well off mucking about in soggy tea leaves. It has been calculated, for example, that the stock market predicted eleven of the last four recessions—a performance that may exceed the combined record of the nation's opposition politicians.

Were it not for the market's eventual awakenings to reality, investing would truly seem a hopeless gamble for the ordinary person. But the market's short-term capriciousness can be a source of hypnotic fascination—and a joy when you analyze it correctly. For what the market truly represents is not a crystal ball or anything else of such mystic magnitude; it is an instant photograph of the ephemeral mood of a significant chunk of Americans. Consider the dramatic example of May 1970. President Nixon had ordered a military incursion into Cambodia, the campuses were in an uproar and many prominent Americans who should have known better were vying with one another in prophecies of doom for the republic. Economically, on the other hand, the only sensible forecast was that things were going to get better slowly—which they did. And which siren do you think the so-called smart money heeded? Why, the market staged its very own Cambodia panic—presumably on the theory that if World War III were about to start and we all were going to be hydrogen-bombed into oblivion, the only prudent course was to hold cash instead of IBM.

The Dow Jones Industrial Average, an index of the prices of 30 big old-line stocks that is the market's most familiar indicator, plunged to a sickening low around 630, after nearly touching 1,000 less than eighteen months before. Did Wall Street know something that the rest of the country didn't? All it knew was the hysteria it captured and magnified from its television screens and newspapers. And here is something that to the inexperienced investor is very much worth knowing: The worst pessimistic excesses, the greatest panic selling, took place on the purportedly supersophisticated East and West coasts—the headquarters of most of the lofty financial wise guys and supercilious institutional investors. Investors in the Middle West, in comparison, were heavy net buyers. The real smart money turned out to belong to the Iowa farmer who, perhaps less inclined to stare at his navel and proclaim the demise of America, telephoned his broker to observe calmly that Xerox had gotten down to a level where it looked like a good buy. For lo and behold, the panic passed (as panics do), and less than a year later that same Dow Jones Industrial Average stood fully 50 per cent above its levels of May 1970.

Now, the lesson of this is not that we should all get back to the earth and grow corn, or wave the flag, but that an investor with independence of intellect and spirit is by no means at a disadvantage in a wildly gyrating market. He need not know exactly when his day is coming in order to make the confident assumption that it will. It was John M. Hancock, a partner in Lehman Brothers, who first observed that there are times when the market throws all bad news into the wastebasket, and times when it does the same with all good news. The bulls and the bears are often nothing more than the herd on the Street, and the wise individual will remember the maxim of the senior J. P. Morgan, who remarked at a moment of pessimistic frenzy that "it always stops raining."

(A "bull" on Wall Street is one who believes that stock prices are going to go up, like a bull's horns; a "bear" believes prices are going to go down, like a bear's stomach. Neither beast is omniscient, though over any extended period the over-all price level has rewarded the bulls. Another of Wall Street's adages is that "a bull can make money, a bear can make money, but a pig never can." There is much truth to this, in terms of setting reasonable goals for yourself, but if it were taken absolutely literally, the market might have to shut down permanently tomorrow.)

Plainly, then, the initial analysis you do in the stock market should be of yourself. Are you capable of resisting the comforting jostle of the crowd? Can you train yourself to develop an intelligent investment program, and then to stick to it when everybody at the cocktail party tells you you're nuts? Do you really want to make money in the stock market, or do you have some other motivation—a jolly social experience, perhaps, or punishment for your sins elsewhere in this vale? Most of the genuinely insightful writing that has been done on human beings and the stock market starts with the famous dictum of Socrates: "Know thyself" (a dictum so famous that it has also been attributed to Plato, Pythagoras, Chilo, Thales, Cleobulus, Bias, Solon and the Delphic oracle, among other famous dictors). Socrates, among others, was right.

Mark Appleman, author of an engaging book called *The Winning Habit*, is convinced that about 75 per cent of an individual's investment success or lack thereof is determined by his emotional equipment. He even made up a quiz designed to reveal, on the basis of your personality, whether you would be a big loser, a small loser, a break-even type, a small winner or a big winner. Appleman told me that he thought the most essential personality factors for doing well in the stock market were objectivity, a desire to win and the ability to learn from mistakes. The characteristics of a loser, he said, were hanging on to a stock that had gone down in price simply to try to break even, attempting to get rich too quickly and failing to recognize and learn from his own mistakes.

I'm not convinced that as much as three quarters of your investment record will be determined by your personality, rather than your information and the course of the economy. (Appleman was writing and speaking during a bad year for the market, when many masochists were ready to be told that they had picked the wrong game.) But it is undeniable that two different investors, given access to identical information, will produce two widely differing investment results—and the task for you is to develop the habits that will produce maximum results. This is not quite the same thing as a Dale Carnegie charm course; as my maternal grandmother used to recite, "Money doesn't care where it goes."

Any broker can testify from his own experiences that his customers' psychological approaches to the market strongly influence their results. (In fact, he is usually eager to so testify, since it helps get him off the hook with the losers.) Many brokers have spoken to me of what are sometimes called "barometric customers," the ones who are always so wrong that the minute they walk into the office the brokers instantly are aware that it is time for the market to turn around. These customers apparently are akin to the fellow in military tradition who is always the last to get the word. They are the ultimate creatures of the crowd. When pessimism is rampant and the market is at its low, they panic and decide to sell; when euphoria is supreme and prices are peaking, they finally drop their vows of "never again" and come roaring back to buy. There is only one thing that has worried me about these tales of barometric customers, so amusing to all but the losers concerned. If a broker is lucky enough to have such a barometric customer, and knows it, why isn't that broker a zillionaire? Can it be that brokers are human beings, too?

The tendency to run with the crowd, even when the crowd is heading for a cliff, can be overwhelming. When I asked Alan Abelson, managing editor and columnist of *Barron's* financial weekly, what he regarded as the sensible course for the small investor, Abelson gave a wry smile and replied, "I think to think for himself. It's not even a bad course for the big investor—not too many do it, so I think it would be a novel approach."

Equally strong is the tendency to seek scapegoats for our own failures. The broker, being closest at hand, is usually the readiest target; this is also the logical reverse of the inclination of some brokers I know to speak of "your stocks" when they are losing money and "our stocks" when they are rising. But however satisfying it may be to castigate your agent, it is far more productive to analyze yourself. None of us never makes a mistake in the stock market, but the most successful, from Bernard Baruch on down, have been those who were willing to subject themselves to painful self-analysis. Where did I go wrong (or right—that can sometimes be a helpful analysis, too)? Was I jumping at a tip I heard on the golf course instead of checking it out first? Did I hold on greedily instead of selling when the prospects changed? Or, alternatively, did I get so upset because the stock lost three points that I sold just before it really started to move?

Most basically, do I really understand what I am doing in the stock market? Do I want growth of capital, or income, or some combination of the two? If growth is my objective, how much growth? (If I want to win a yacht, I have to be prepared to lose my shirt; but if I want to average at least 10 per cent a year compounded over the next five years, I have set a realistic goal that can be met with a different, more conservative kind of behavior.) Do I actually believe that calling something an investment is just to give a fancy rationalization to a speculation that went sour? Or do I have a coherent investment plan that both my broker and I fully understand?

If raising these questions suggests to you, as a prospective entrant into the stock market, that investing is going to require some time and thought, then you are already on the right track. Those who are unwilling to make that kind of effort are probably better off putting their money elsewhere, such as a mutual fund, and letting the fund's directors have the headaches (and the fun) of investing for them. This may also be the route for those who shy at examining their own fragile egos in the light of the unflickering numbers of their stock-market results. If, however, Wall Street represents to you an exciting challenge to your intellect and spirit, here is confirmation of the desirability of taking an active role in your own investing. Analyzing the broker's mistakes may be more pleasant, but it is less likely to be as profound or as profitable as analyzing your own—unless, that is, you have been fortunate enough to locate a "barometric broker." If your attitude is right, then all you need is the facts—and those we are about to get.

CHAPTER VI

What's It All About, Seymour?

Asking what's the best thing to buy in Wall Street is like asking what's the best thing to buy in Macy's. It depends on what you're shopping for. If you're looking for secure income, for a return on your savings a bit higher than the corner bank is offering, then there are several departments designed precisely for your needs—stocks that pay high and consistent dividends, for example, or bonds that pay good interest every six months or perhaps a special category of securities known as "real estate investment trusts." We shall visit them all in time. If, on the other hand, you're an experienced swinger looking for something a little wilder in the line of fun and games, there is plenty of merchandise to suit your tastes, too—esoteric pastimes like buying on margin, selling short, trading in commodities and dealing in puts and calls. Blanch not; all will be explained. For the typical new investor, though, everything he needs is right out there in full view on the ground floor. It's in the "common stocks" department on the counter marked "growth."

Now, despite its decidedly unaristocratic name, "common stock" is the kingpin of investing. The holder of common stock gets paid last; all other claims against the corporation, such as bonds and preferred stock, are settled ahead of his. But his compensation is that he is a residual owner of the company, which means two things primarily: (1) for each share of common stock he owns, he has one full vote in the election of the board of directors that runs the corporation; (2) there is no limit to the profits he can make if the company does well. Common stock, like all securities, is issued originally by the corporation whose name it bears. This is the prime way that corporations obtain the capital they need to get started and to keep going.

Unless the stock you buy is brand-new—what is called a "new issue"—the money you spend for it will not, however, go to the company whose name is on the stock. Nor will it go, as some people quaintly believe, to the stock exchange. It goes, of course, to the last person who owned the stock you buy.

Hence it was popular a couple of generations ago for pompous corporation executives to pretend that they had no interest in the price of their company's stock once the initial lot had been sold. This fiction has been abandoned for several reasons, including (1) the possible need, with the consent of the existing stockholders, to issue new stock from time to time and to get the best possible price for it; (2) the increasing use of common stock as a form of extra compensation for the company's key executives—who, being as avaricious as the rest of us, want the price of that stock to keep rising; (3) the use of stock owned by the corporation itself to buy up another company, which means that the more the stock is worth, the fewer shares will be needed in the takeover. So if it is any consolation to you, you can be sure that the president of the great corporation of which you are about to become a stockholder is as anxious as you are to see your shares make a handsome profit. He is, in fact, your hired hand—since you and all the other stockholders own the firm "in common" (thus the name). By buying common stock, your personal desire for financial security has led you to put up some of the capital that keeps everything from the largest airliner to the smallest piece of tissue paper in production; you have become (come close now while I whisper, for the mob is at the gate) an American capitalist.

And how should you begin? Well, first by realizing that the key to wealth in the stock market for most people is to be found in the purchase of "growth" common stocks—the stocks of companies whose earnings are likely to increase rapidly over the years and whose profits have a motive power greater than the average push behind the United States economy as a whole. Companies that have the capacity to increase their earnings year by year are the darlings of the stock market, and should be the objects of your affection, too. We are going to discuss in detail how you can identify and select these growth stocks, but your initial decision must be to make them your target. This means that, where your greatest fortune-building is concerned, you will be wary of the large industrial giants whose prospects are chained to the rise and fall of the general business cycle. They can be solid investments, and there will be times when you will want to own them, but you should start by telling your broker that your interest is in proven growth stocks.

In investing, as in such comparably challenging activities as skiing and sex, it is patently advisable to walk before you run. This means, for example, that you should always pay cash for those first stocks you buy. Don't buy them "on margin"—a technique for the sophisticated and courageous investor that will be discussed later—and don't borrow part or all of the purchase price from your local banker, the finance company or your Cousin Sam. A falling investment made on borrowed money is doubled agony, and here's where you can save yourself some needless torment right at the start. Buy only what you can afford.

The wise beginner, in my judgment, will also buy only "listed" stocks, and specifically those that are traded every day on either the New York or American stock exchanges. To be "listed" by these exchanges is to meet certain minimum requirements (higher on the New York Exchange, which is known as the "Big Board"), and thus the mere fact that the stock is trading there gives you some assurance that it will not disappear overnight. This is not an absolute: Many fine companies, for reasons of their own, never bother to get listed by an exchange—and being traded on the New York Stock Exchange didn't keep Penn Central from going bankrupt. But your odds are better in sticking to listed stocks at first; more people are watching them, and the available information on them is likely to be more complete. (Don't worry how you're going to know whether or not a stock is listed. Look in your newspaper's financial pages for the prices of stocks traded on the New York and American exchanges. If you find the name of the stock in which you're interested, it's listed.)

This leads us logically to what I would regard as a central rule for inexperienced investors: Don't buy a stock just because it's cheap. I realize that this flies in the face of one of the most attractive temptations for many investors, new and old. With, say, $1,000 to invest in a stock, you could buy 20 shares of a $50 stock or—wow! zowie!—200 shares of a $5.00 stock. Somehow the second purchase seems more impressive when you casually mention it to your friends. Resist the tug. While many a $3.00 stock has eventually soared to greatness, many, many more have vanished entirely. Wise guys will ply you with all kinds of phony statistics designed to convince you that a $5.00 stock is far more likely to rise to $10.00 than a $100 stock is to rise to $200. That's the kind of "statistic" that has accounted for more Wall Street disasters than the 1929 Crash. A $5.00 stock can just as easily go down to $2.00 or $0.00. Playing with low-priced stocks is a dangerous game that requires extra-strong information about the company and its prospects. It's not a safe game for beginners, who are all too apt to buy junk in the mistaken belief that its price makes it a bargain. Don't be afraid to buy "odd lots" (less than 100 shares) of higher-priced, quality stocks; the slight additional cost of odd-lot purchases can be the biggest bargain you ever found if it keeps you from buying "round lots" of a losing cheapie.

I've already indicated that I think you ought to restrict yourself at first to no more than two or three stocks. This would be true even if your initial investment runs into several thousand dollars. You will be much better off trying to learn as much as you can about two or three companies than spraying your money around as if you were a miniature mutual fund. While the other method may spread your risk, it doesn't enable you to gain the early discipline that can result in optimum investment results. By limiting the number of issues in your portfolio, you not only are telling yourself to deepen your knowledge of their prospects, you are confronting yourself with a valuable question about any possible new investment: Is it a better prospect than any stock I now own?

Another discipline that the typical stock-market beginner ought to impose on himself is the realization that he is not equipped for success as an "in-and-out trader." This means that you're not going to be constantly buying and selling stock in an effort to outguess the professionals for a few points here, a few points there. Later, we shall discuss some of the theories and practices of that art, but be forewarned that it is a losing game for most people even after years of experience; even in darkest Wall Street it's true more often than not that "investors drive Cadillacs; traders drive Chevrolets."

Now, here's a tip that you may find distasteful: Don't spend your dividends. Dividends can be marvelous things to those who need them; they are the portion of a company's profits that its management decides to pay out to stockholders instead of plowing back into the business. Never, never spend them unless you really, really have to (really, really now—not tempted, tempted). What should you do with them? Reinvest them at the first suitable opportunity. Since your total return on your investment includes both the rise in the price of your stocks and the dividends they pay out, you are plainly building more for the future if you put those dividends to work in the form of additional shares of stock. (Investment funds often make it possible to do this automatically, and in recent years some major corporations have belatedly joined the parade. When American Telephone and Telegraph, old Ma Bell herself, made a dividend reinvestment plan available to her legions of stockholders—the biggest single army in the field—about 11 per cent of the company's new shareowners promptly subscribed.)

Having thus taken much of the fun out of dividends for the average investor who doesn't immediately need them to live on, let me downgrade them even further—and get back to our theme that what you are looking for is growth. Too often the new investor gets hung up on dividends; if one stock is paying a 7 per cent dividend and another is paying 2 per cent (or less), he's likely to head straight as Supermouse for that big 7 per cent cheese. And he will usually be wrong to do so. Wall Street expresses that figure as "yield"; to find out what a stock is "yielding," divide the annual dividend by the current price of a single share. Almost invariably, the higher the yield the lower the growth. The company that pays out a smaller portion of its earnings in dividends has that much more left over to put to work for the future growth of the company. The companies whose stock prices rise the fastest seldom pay much of a dividend in terms of the current price; investors are willing to pay more for earnings that are likely not to remain level but to become much greater in future years. In the words of Frank A. Cappiello, Jr., the astute financial vice president of the Monumental Life Insurance Company (and a regular "Wall Street Week" panelist), "Investors who say they need income should meet those current income requirements by withdrawals from capital [in other words, selling shares of stock]. If you have a choice between buying a stock that yields 2 per cent or one that yields 7 per cent, and have absolutely no other information at all about the two stocks, you can without hesitation select the stock yield-ing 2 per cent. In nine times out of ten it will turn out to be the better investment of the two."

So now you know one characteristic of the kind of growth stock for which you will be looking: Its management will reason that it can use that dividend money more profitably than you can, and it will implement that reasoning with a policy of low (or no) dividends. Don't be frightened off by this lack of immediate return; in addition to everything else, it gives you a tax advan-tage—since dividends (after the first $100) are taxed at regular income rates, while stocks sold at a profit after being held more than six months get the more favorable treatment allotted to capital gains. You win each way by getting your return primarily from the rise in the price of your stock.

Another helpful precept for the novice investor is to remember that there is no requirement that you put your entire investment bundle into the stock market on your very first day. This is a temptation that seems to be particularly potent when the market is roaring ahead, and euphoric brokers and friends are eager to exploit your anxiety to jump aboard before it's too late. How long has this been going on? you wonder—and by the way, how much longer is it going to last? The answer is that the market will reopen for business every Monday through Friday at 10 A.M. local time, and there is seldom a genuine "last chance" to make a good purchase. Just as you are going to be patient once you have made an investment, so you are going to be thoughtful before you plunge. You may well decide to invest smaller amounts over a longer period rather than all at once, thus picking up valuable experience as you go.

And by the way, don't be frightened by the newspaper financial page. That's where you can find information about your stock each day, so now is as good a time as any to learn how to read a stock listing. Let's dream up a mythical name for the company in which you're investing. "Getridge Quik Inter-national" comes to mind. Now let's look it up in the alphabetical listings headed "New York [or American] Stock Exchange Transactions." Running your finger down past such companies

as GenMot (General Motors), you find your very own stock—
and this is what you see: DIV   P/E

43½ 26¼ GetriQuik .20   22   211   44   42½   43¾   +½

Now what's it all about, Seymour? Well, if it all looks like some
kind of forbidding gibberish, relax and go through it item by
item. The explanation for each figure is at the top of the column.
From it we learn that $43.50 was the highest price per share at
which your stock had previously sold this year, and that $26.25
was the lowest. The .20 tells us that the stock pays an annual
dividend of $.20 a share—nice and low. The next figure, 22, gives
us the "P/E," or price-earnings ratio for the stock—compiled by
dividing the closing price for the day ($43.75 in this case) by
the earnings per share reported by the company for the last
twelve months. In this case, the earnings per share would have
been about $2.00. (As we shall see in detail in Chapter X, the
P/E is a useful fact, but unhappily not the philosophers' stone
that some investors take it to be.) To the 211 figure that follows,
we have to add two zeros—thus finding that 21,100 shares of
Getridge Quik International were traded that day. The next
three figures give us the highest price at which the stock traded
that day ($44.00), the low for the day ($42.50) and the closing,
or last, price for the day ($43.75). The +½ at the end tells us
that this closing price was $.50 higher than the last sale on the
previous day. Your stock has edged forward to a new high for
the year. Tomorrow the first number in the line will be 44 instead
of 43½, and hopefully your glory days have just begun. Isn't it
great to know all that without having to call and confess
ignorance to your broker?

Another possible source of confusion for the inexperienced is
all the current talk about a "third market" and even a "fourth
market"—much of it somehow darkly suggesting that the plain
old "stock market" in which he is participating is just a false front
for the suckers. So you will know what all the squealing is about,
here is a quick rundown on precisely which piggies go to which
markets:

At the top of the totem pole, and intensely conscious of its
lofty status, is the New York Stock Exchange—the nation's first,
and by far its largest, exchange. It traces its origins to 1792, when
twenty-four merchants and auctioneers began to meet daily at

regular hours to buy and sell securities under an old buttonwood tree on Wall Street. (They had the good sense to move indoors, into the Tontine Coffee House, one year later.) *"The* Exchange," as its officers and admen still like to think of it, does not buy, sell or own securities; it is simply a marketplace for those who do. But since the members of the exchange make most of the rules, their powers are considerable. (One power they are about to lose in 1975: Over the years they have fixed minimum commission rates for small investors—subject to review by the Securities and Exchange Commission—and forbidden any member broker to charge less.) Officially, the members of the New York Stock Exchange are all individuals: 1,366 of them, each of whom has purchased a "seat." In the early years, the members really did have seats, but now there's not a chair in sight—and shoe leather is the market's most expendable commodity.

Since only individuals can own seats, concerns become "member firms" by having a general partner or voting stockholder who is himself a member of the exchange. Many firms have more than one member. About half the members are partners or officers in "commission houses"—the brokerage partnerships or corporations that deal with the public. Their job is to get the best possible price available at the exchange when one of their customers wants to buy or sell securities. Their executions of your orders are the primary reason for the commissions you pay. Other kinds of stock-exchange members, in addition to those who directly represent the investing public, include "odd-lot dealers," to whom your firm's broker will go with an order for less than 100 shares; "floor brokers," who assist the commission-house brokers and are known as "$2.00 brokers," because that is what they used to get for their services; "registered traders," of whom there were just sixty-nine left in 1972, who buy and sell for their own accounts; and finally the most controversial category of all, the "specialists," who comprise about a quarter of all the exchange's members.

The specialists get their name because they specialize in "making a market" for one or more stocks; specialist firms are located at fixed points around the exchange floor, and each one has exclusive rights to the stocks assigned there. That does not mean that your firm's broker has to buy from, or sell to, the specialist; often the commission-house brokers clustered at the post will make their own deals. But the specialist is required by the exchange, within limits that the officials deem reasonable, to stand ready to risk his own capital when the ordinary buyers and sellers are too far apart. (Let's say the last transaction in a stock was at $50 a share, that the latest offer to sell is still $50 and that the highest bid to buy is only $45. The specialist would normally be expected to narrow that $5.00 spread by making a bid of his own somewhere in between.) The specialist's job is to lean against the wind, buying when stocks are falling and selling when they are rising—to provide stability and liquidity in moments of hysteria. Since the system relies on human beings, and individual judgments, its workings have seldom approached perfection and have repeatedly been the subject of investigation; some critics believe specialists will eventually be replaced by computers—but until someone invents a computer with courage, character and capital, some variant of the traditional specialist system is likely to survive.

A further power of the New York Stock Exchange, and one that retains for it its blue-chip status among the nation's exchanges, is the right to set minimum standards that a company must meet before its stock can be listed there. (The requirements are given in Appendix E.) These standards are the most stringent on any exchange, but they have made listing on the Big Board that much more desirable. In December 1972 the number of stocks listed there climbed to 2,000 for the first time. The number of companies represented was a record 1,500, some of which listed more than one kind of stock. James J. Needham, chairman of the exchange's twenty-one-member board of directors (ten from member organizations, ten from outside the industry, plus the full-time chairman), gave this explanation: "Corporations come to the New York Stock Exchange because they like the auction market and believe it is in the public interest and, therefore, in their interest. In addition, they also like the publicly disclosed and authoritative daily trading information that is available for N.Y.S.E.-listed issues. And they find that exchange membership makes the raising of new capital easier and less expensive." That might be regarded as a brief statement for the defense of the financial "first market"—the nation's stock exchanges.

The most significant junior partner in the first market is the

American Stock Exchange, which is the Big Board's neighbor in downtown New York and in most respects operates quite similarly. No leading brokerage firm would think of belonging to one and not the other. Not until 1953 did the American Stock Exchange acquire that prestigious name; previously, it was known as the New York Curb Market, in recognition of its outdoor origins in the 1840s, when fearless phone clerks hung from the windows signaling orders and brokers were on the curb doing business in all kinds of weather. That rugged existence continued until 1921, when the Curb Market moved indoors into a six-story building at 86 Trinity Place. (Paradoxically, during the first winter inside, the brokers' sick rate went up; trading fever, I guess.) The American Stock Exchange—or "Amex," as it is commonly nicknamed—honors tradition by retaining the colorful hand signals that were a necessity in the old outdoor days; in other respects, however, it has been notably swifter than the New York Stock Exchange to modernize its equipment and adjust to the changing times. From computerization to topflight public representation, it has shown the way.

The average price per share is notably lower on the Amex, however, and so are listing requirements (see Appendix E), so it is inevitable that it operate to a great extent as a proving ground for companies that will later qualify for listing on the New York Stock Exchange—even though some eminent companies remain on the Amex by choice. On average, the American Stock Exchange caters to smaller companies (and a far greater percentage of its trading is done by noninstitutional investors, ordinary folks like you and me). The commissions are the same on both exchanges. It is periodically suggested that they ought to merge, and the practical trend is in that direction, with the consolidation of many of their technical operations already under way.

Finally, the first market also includes the "regional" stock exchanges—the Midwest Stock Exchange, the Pacific Coast Stock Exchange, the PBW (formerly Philadelphia-Baltimore-Washington) Stock Exchange and those in Boston, Cincinnati, Detroit, Pittsburgh, Salt Lake City and Spokane. These exchanges were born as marketplaces for local companies, but they now do more than three quarters of their business trading stocks that are also listed on the New York Stock Exchange. There is also a National Stock Exchange, which is actually just a little fellow in New York

City, organized in 1962. All these exchanges must have their
rules and regulations approved by the Securities and Exchange
Commission.

If the nation's stock exchanges constitute the first market, the
second market is the over-the-counter market—and there is one
central difference that defines it. The first market is an auction
market; its prices are set by open negotiation between brokers
acting as agents for buyers and sellers, and the forces of supply
and demand predominate. The second market, in contrast, is a
dealer market, which means the prices at which securities may be
bought and sold are set by dealers. These dealers may negotiate
—with other dealers or directly with customers—but there is no
continuous auction in progress. Several different dealers may
habitually make a market in the same stock; there is no one specialist with exclusive rights. You don't pay a commission when
you buy an over-the-counter stock, but the price you pay includes a nice profit for the dealer. The over-the-counter market
is not really a market at all, in the sense that there is a physical
meeting place like an exchange; the over-the-counter market
occurs wherever anyone wants to do business in a particular
stock. Yet since the vast majority of the country's stocks are not
listed on any exchange, and thus must be traded "over the
counter," this market is in another sense the giant of them all.

It is easy to see that, without an open auction to set its prices,
the market in unlisted securities can be vulnerable to great
abuses. Announced prices may be withdrawn without notice, and
various manipulative techniques become alluring. The Securities
and Exchange Commission has been tightening its surveillance
of this area in recent years, notably in giving a large degree of
self-regulatory authority to the National Association of Securities
Dealers, which represents more than 4,000 dealers. But perhaps
the most significant improvement was the inauguration in 1971 of
the National Association of Securities Dealers Automated Quotation System, or NASDAQ, under which any broker can instan-
taneously punch up on his electronic screen the retail price
quotations of all dealers who make markets in the leading over-
the-counter stocks. This cuts down on the red tape and finagling
that were involved in less modern methods, such as the telephone and printed quotation sheets. Not all the problems have
been solved, but at least in making sure that you the customer

can ascertain the best available price at that moment, either to buy or to sell, many of the opportunities for dealer sleight of hand have been curbed.

The over-the-counter market in unlisted securities is essential to the capitalist system; this is where young, untried companies get the money they need, if they are ever to be mature, proven companies. And a good many seasoned companies, which would be more than qualified for listing on the major exchanges, choose to remain where they started. The "counter" is automated now, and that is all to the good.

The third market is a hybrid; it is a market where listed securities are traded over the counter. For the average individual investor, it does not have much direct significance. But for major institutional purchasers, it is a daily fact of life. Third-market dealers are not members of the exchanges and therefore not bound by their rules; they do not charge set commissions and they often undercut the prices quoted by the New York Stock Exchange's specialists. They can shave the asking price and still make good profits in handling the buy-and-sell transactions of such institutional investors as mutual funds, banks and insurance companies. The New York Stock Exchange regards them as parasites and has tried to put them out of business two ways—first, by allowing exchange members to negotiate lower commissions of their own on large transactions (the minimum was set at $500,-000, then lowered to $300,000), and second, by calling for congressional legislation to make the third market illegal.

These mavericks who trade in exchange-listed stocks away from the trading floor have been having an accelerating impact on the lucrative institutional-investment business. In terms of dollar value of stocks, the third market accounted in 1972 for trades equal to 9 per cent of the New York Stock Exchange's own volume—and that figure had more than tripled since 1966. The Securities and Exchange Commission was unwilling to accept the argument that the third market should be abolished, but it did want to place its dealers under closer supervision—requiring, for example, that they stick by their stock quotes and that they stay with stocks in which they were making markets even when prices were tumbling.

The SEC also talked of giving us small investors some stake in all this by requiring eventually that third-market firms and other dealers in large blocks of stock allow the specialists to link small orders from the public with larger institutional orders. The intent would be to assure that small investors were getting the best prices possible. (This commendable aim also would be helped along by plans for a composite stock ticker providing investors with price and volume figures on all transactions in listed securities—whether on the first or third markets. The idea is that, if a fellow is aware that he is not getting the best deal going, he is less likely to tolerate that situation placidly.)

And last, there is that fourth market—and this one, I'm afraid, will be of no use to you at all. The fourth market is the title given to transactions directly between big institutions. If the Tayka-chantz Fund wants to buy 50,000 shares of a stock, and the Weegot-burnt Fund wants to sell, they can negotiate their own deal—and save zillions in commissions. (As noted earlier, you and your Uncle Charlie can play this same game on a rather smaller scale—so if it does your heart good to consider that the "fifth market," it's okay by me.)

In the battles of the markets, vast sums of money routinely are involved. For example, the onset of negotiated commissions on large transactions and the growth of outside trading in listed securities both served to diminish the monopoly advantages of a seat on the New York Stock Exchange; seats sold for a record $515,000 in 1968 and 1969, but in June 1973 the price fell to a fifteen-year low of $72,000. I'm sure this creates boundless sympathy in you for the poor members of the New York Stock Exchange, but you need not take up a collection for them just yet. For that matter, the individual who is pursuing a sound personal investment program ought not to be unduly diverted by the passing, and brain-bogglingly technical, controversies over market regulation and the competition for institutional investment funds. You will make out fine if you keep your eye fixed firmly on your own ballgame—intelligent personal investment—and that is the game whose rules you will truly want to master.

Since you are presumably a taxpayer, and about to become a more significant one, you are also entitled to be aware of some rules for investors prepared by your government servants—in the form of a Securities and Exchange Commission booklet entitled "Investigate Before You Invest." Its ten unexceptionable suggestions follow: "(1) Before buying . . . think! (2) Don't deal with strange securities firms. (Consult your broker, banker or other experienced person you know and trust.) (3) Beware of securities offered over the telephone by strangers. (4) Don't listen to high-pressure sales talk. (5) Beware of promises of spectacular profits. (6) Be sure you understand the risks of loss. (7) Don't buy on tips and rumors. . . . Get all the facts! (8) Tell the salesman to: Put all the information and advice in writing and mail it to you. . . . Save it! (9) If you don't understand all the written information . . . consult a person who does. (10) Give at least as much consideration to buying securities as you would to buying other valuable property." I would commend all the foregoing to you, and the only thing I can add is that you should be a bit wary if a stranger wearing snappy yellow suspenders offers you a sensational deal on the Brooklyn Bridge.

At this point, however, you should have some sense of what you're about. You're about to become an investor. You're not going to jump in wildly, you're going to pay cash for your stocks, you're going to buy only stocks listed on the New York or American stock exchanges at first, you're going to buy no more than two or three of them, you're going to avoid the temptation to prefer cheap stocks, you're going to eschew in-and-out trading, you're going to reinvest your dividends (and you're going to look for stocks that don't pay much in the way of dividends anyhow) and the one magic word on which you are going to set your sights is "growth." Now, it's time to narrow your search for the stocks that will fill the bill.

CHAPTER VII

Does the Toothpaste Play "Dixie"?

You can get a lively, if somewhat academic, argument going on Wall Street over the question of whether it is now easier or harder than it used to be for the average investor to pick the right stocks. You will not, I suspect, get overly exercised about this one way or another, since however glorious yesteryear may have been, you (and your creditors) have to live in the here and now. For what it may be worth, though, the most cogent argument goes something like this: The average man has many advantages that were not available in times past. The flow of investment information to him has never been greater. And new laws and regulations protect him against some of the more blatant forms of manipulation that pocked the market's past. On the other hand, the search for truly exceptional results may have become more difficult. The same at least theoretically simultaneous availability of information to the entire investing public makes it more difficult for any one investor to capitalize strikingly on that information. And the very rules and regulations that were designed to protect the ordinary investor may act to thwart the extraordinary player. Perhaps most important, there is simply very much more competition at every level of investing, as the stock market has changed from the private battleground of a comparative few to an authentic marketplace of the millions.

In my judgment, two less debatable conclusions emerge from this little history lesson: (1) Even the statistically average investor has done impressively well, particularly if he has avoided the foolish tendency to enter the market only when it was surging to new records and to sell his holdings at a loss the first time a major market slump came along. (2) Those who have produced the most dazzling results in recent years have been identifiable not by the initial size of their investment but by their ability to concentrate on the accurate selection of growth stocks.

A generation ago, all you really needed was faith in the future of American industry. You could invest in the major corporations that everybody knew—the so-called blue chips—and, more often than not, your results would be excellent. (The "blue-chip" reference was taken directly from the poker table, where the blue chips usually represent the largest amount of all, the reds an intermediate denomination and the whites the smallest unit in the game. But since the New York Stock Exchange keeps telling us that investing must never even be mentioned in the same breath as gambling, I guess this is just another one of those crazy coincidences.) Take the years between 1940 and 1970—years when the cost of living more than doubled, as measured by the Bureau of Labor Statistics Consumer Price Index. In the same period, one of the standard indexes of stock prices, Standard & Poor's "500," finished at a level more than eight times where it started. (Additionally, the dividends on these stocks advanced about twice as fast as prices did.) So all it took for most people was the decision to go into the stock market, to buy the safe and secure names that every household knew, and then to sock those stocks away and forget them—confident that wealth would be the reward.

By the 1960s, however, such "buy-the-blue-chips-and-forget-'em" techniques no longer supplied the magic answer for the average investor. In 1960 what chip could have been bluer than U.S. Steel? Yet the investor who bought its stock that year at the high of $103.50 would have found his stock selling for less than a quarter that amount by 1971. What may have seemed conservative had actually proved disastrous. Contrast that with the performance of investors who were shrewd (or fortunate) enough in 1960 to invest $1,000 each in Avon Products, International Business Machines and Xerox—three stocks whose greatness lay not in their past eminence but in their future potential. By 1971 the Avon $1,000 investment would have been worth $8,360, the IBM $3,760 and the Xerox $24,500. What is more, each of these companies had increased its earnings and its dividends in every year since 1960—and had been relatively impervious to minor swings in the business cycle. Avon stock reached new market highs in ten of those eleven years, IBM in eight and

Xerox in ten. Here were truly the chips that a smart investor would want to have been holding, the modern version of what one fund manager calls "a one-decision stock"—the kind you can buy and hold for years.

All very well and good, you may be thinking, but does it really accomplish anything but make you drool to read about brilliant investments that you didn't happen to make? The answer may actually be yes—if we can isolate the ingredients that made these stocks great and apply the same analysis to the issues you will be considering now. (This is not to say that you will automatically exclude those that have performed well in the past. As William G. Campbell, president of two Hartwell and Campbell no-load mutual funds, put it to me, "Today's Xeroxes may be tomorrow's Xeroxes." He argued that the biggest moves in "tomorrow's Xeroxes" could be realized after you knew they were "real, not phony companies.") What was it that stocks like Avon, IBM and Xerox had that triggered such strong and consistent price rises? And how much of their remarkable stories really can be adapted to your future investing?

Well, first let's see what these stocks had in common, aside from their undeniably inspiring price rises. I have already indicated one characteristic, their consistency of earnings increases. The inexperienced investor seeking a profitable growth situation should shy away from unproven companies, however highly they come recommended by the butcher, the broker or the candlestick-maker. Maybe they have come up with the most sensational idea since the Wright Brothers, but your odds of success are better if you let them prove it for a while first. (On an adjusted basis, present IBM stock once sold for $1.13 and Xerox for $.04. You could have given them plenty of time to establish themselves and still hopped aboard for an extremely profitable ride.)

Another characteristic of these winning growth companies is that they were leaders in fast-growing industries. Their sales and earnings grew not only consistently but faster than that of the economy at large. Thomas C. Pryor, chairman of the investment policy committee of White, Weld and Company, observed on "Wall Street Week": "I think it's fair to say in the case of IBM [in computers] and in the case of Xerox [in office copying equipment] that they were not only in a good industry but they in fact created it and today dominate it." As for Avon in cosmetics,

Pryor noted that it offered "unique marketing competence with
its door-to-door sales organization." There was no need in any of
these cases to consult a ouija board about the quality of the
products or of the company's management; these were being
demonstrated objectively year after year in arenas other than the
stock market.

And this suggests that the alert individual investor may not be
at as great a disadvantage as is sometimes assumed in locating
these supergrowth situations. Some aspects, such as the company's financial position, may not be immediately apparent.
(Solid growth companies tend to be aggressive in sales but conservative in finance, without excessive long-term debt.) The
initial interest in a potentially great stock, however, often comes
simply from keeping your eyes open in everyday life. Brilliant
investing stories have been written by ordinary people who just
liked the early Polaroid cameras and decided that a lot of other
people might like them, too. Mom may have enjoyed the convenience of shopping with the Avon lady—and reasoned that
many others would feel the same way. Watching all the new
construction around town may have led Dad to look into home-
building stocks. Practically any kind of business or profession offers opportunities for insights into potentially growing fields. A
merchant seeing what was moving locally—the Instamatic
camera, say—might have been in on the rebirth of Eastman
Kodak's stock. Housewives attuned to thinking in terms of possible stock purchases can be market-testing for their own account
every time they buy a tube of toothpaste or contemplate the
new fashions for spring.

There is a limit to this, of course, but the point is that not all
the big profits have been made in computers, electronics or
similarly exotic fields. Obviously, just liking a new brand of toothpaste isn't reason enough to sink your savings into the stock of
the pharmaceutical company that makes it; nor should you
automatically avoid the stock of a company if one of its products
once displeased you. (There can be aesthetic considerations
here; I have always refused to buy the stock of a certain soft-
drink company, for example, because I didn't want to be reminded of its taste when I looked at the financial page every
morning.) But these initial impressions can be valuable clues for
an investor who is turning his natural curiosity and common sense

to practical financial use. If you become intrigued with a new product that seems to offer an important technological or marketing innovation, that's reason enough to start asking questions. Ask the druggist if other customers are also going for that new kind of toothpaste whose tube plays "Dixie" when you squeeze it. And ask your broker to dig up the facts and figures on the companies involved, so that you can judge them against the standards of the great growth stocks we have been discussing.

As we shall see in the next chapter, much of your search for growth stocks that will genuinely live up to their name will involve reasoning from the outside in. In other words, you will begin with an understanding of the economic problems that confront America and the over-all prospects for the economy in the foreseeable future. You will move from there to a search for industries likely to prosper in that environment. Third and last, you will get around to picking an individual company. But what we have been talking about up to now have been those so-called special situations in which the bright individual investor can profitably reason from the inside out—by finding a company with one striking aspect that is apt to bring success beyond that of the national economy or even of the industry. Institutional investor William Campbell told me that he had prospered by making timely purchases of stocks like Levitz Furniture—before the price ran away with itself and became vulnerable to severe correction —that enabled him to use his "broad-brush concept," in which "all you have to focus on is one little point" (for example, "that people want furniture now when they go into the store; they don't want to wait three months"). That "one little point" sparked the investigations that in several cases led to spectacular growth jackpots. I asked Campbell how many of the techniques he used as a large institutional investor could be adopted for use by the ordinary investor. "I think the ordinary investor can adopt everything I'm saying," he replied. "When I started to make money in this business is when I started to think the way I think an ordinary investor should think."

CHAPTER VIII

Look, Ma, I'm a Groupie

The truly great one-decision stock is beautiful to behold, an El Greco in a sea of Warhols. If you can turn up one or more of these wonderful masters of technological and/or marketing surprise, and if your subsequent investigation confirms its consistency of earnings growth, conservative financing and potential for further expansion, you have found a stock to cherish, a certificate worth hanging on the living-room wall. But these stocks are rare, even the accredited great ones sometimes stumble, and once they have established themselves they seldom come cheap in terms of their current earnings. What do you do the rest of the time, when you are unable to locate a stock with such singular brilliance that it practically seems to beg you to buy it? Why, you do exactly the same thing as all those high-priced (and often fallible) institutional investors are doing: You use your noodle and try to figure out what the country is going to need next. You think in terms of the areas of the economy that are most likely to prosper in the years immediately ahead. You thus narrow your thinking down to groups of stocks, and then embark on the task of selecting the most promising prospects within those groups. If your thinking is sound about the nation's future requirements (and we're going to try to help that thinking along), you may well arrive at the happy conclusion that what this country needs most is a stock that will make you rich.

The best way to find that stock is to begin by taking your mind as far as possible from the quotidian hysteria at Broad Street and Wall. Think big about this country, where it is going in the world and at home, what changes are affecting its people and the kind of lives they want to live. What will life be like in America five or ten years from now, what trails will the pursuit of happiness have taken? Superficial observers are forever being surprised at the extent to which a philosophical and historical turn of mind can be a highly practical starting place for investment success. Anybody can get you a report on the last quarter's earnings, but the larger rewards await those who can envision the next quarter century's potential.

Let's see how this kind of thinking might eventually affect your approach to individual stocks. First, let's look at some examples of how that approach might become negative. In the 1960s overwhelming profits were taken in the areas of electronics and military technology. Will the seventies truly become a more peaceful period, in which America is enabled to beat at least some of its swords into plowshares? If that is your conclusion, it will undoubtedly be a joyous one for us all; but it may make you think twice about investing in sword-makers.

Similarly, can anyone believe that in the decade ahead any administration of either party is really going to crack down effectively and permanently on the soaring wage rates of the American workman? Not only does this suggest a pressure toward continued price inflation, it also suggests that there are certain industries that the growth-minded investor will tend to avoid. He will favor companies whose enlightened labor policies promote internal harmony and stability, but he will try to find them in areas where labor is a relatively small portion of the company's total costs. Some of the older industries, such as steel and railroads, have as much as a 50 per cent labor factor in their annual expenditures, and the squeeze on such companies' profits is unlikely to be released.

Companies whose labor costs cannot easily be offset or passed on in the form of higher prices often overlap into another questionable category for the years ahead: mature industries with a high degree of government regulation. Particularly in an era of aroused consumerism, companies in these industries are unlikely to be permitted to grow with exceptional rapidity. Electric utilities, for example, may be excellent investments for those whose programs give a heavy priority to dividends—but as a group they are unlikely to entrance the seeker after growth. If their profits started to rise impressively, the howls before the state public service commissions would be audible from one nuclear generating plant to the next.

The search for outstanding growth is also unlikely to take you into industries that are especially vulnerable to foreign competition. There has been a significant change in the 1970s in the American attitude toward foreign trade, a change that climaxed in the devaluations of the dollar and the simultaneous decision to stop acting like a benign big brother toward countries whose own trade policies were highly nationalistic. In the philosophical sense, this might be seen as part of the broader process of America's turning inward, away from internationalism both in foreign policy and in foreign trade, and toward a heightened concern for what were perceived to be the country's internal interests. Whatever judgment you make, however, you are unlikely to conclude that the United States will quickly regain its postwar supremacy in international trade—or that the threat of foreign competition in certain key industries is about to disappear. American auto-makers, for example, have many hurdles to overcome before they can again be considered among the most promising groups for growth.

A similarly jaundiced eye ought to be cast on any industries whose profits rely heavily on their own activities abroad, especially when these take place in areas of probable political volatility. As one who lived in India for more than two years, and has traveled widely in the underdeveloped world, I can attest to the propensity of most of these emerging nations to subordinate economic logic to emotional nationalism. The confiscation of mining and other properties, the heightening barriers to imports, the discouragement of cruelly needed investment all represent a trend that is more likely to accelerate than reverse. Investment in international oils and other companies vulnerable to foreign expropriation is risky economically because it is risky politically; it should be done only by those willing to appraise these risks and to watch developments carefully, and it is less likely to attract those looking for a "buy-it-and-forget-it" growth situation.

None of this is to suggest that the occasion will never arise for investment in any or all of the above-mentioned areas. For one thing, the market may from time to time overdiscount the risks involved, thus creating temporary bargains. And the nation's need for oil, for energy, for electricity is going to be immense in the next decade. It is, however, to suggest that your own ex-

ploration for groups likely to qualify for long-range supergrowth
can more profitably begin elsewhere.

But enough of this surly negativism; what are the trends that
are more likely to lead us to more positive investment conclusions? Surely one such trend in the 1970s is that toward increased
leisure. The average man will have both more time and more
money to spend, and companies geared to capture their share
are favorable candidates for growth. Assessing the probable
tastes of the average American in his expanding leisure time—
what he will buy, where and how he will travel—can be a pursuit
profitable enough to earn you some more affluent leisure of your
own. (As an example of the phenomenal potential of this
market, and of the constant need to re-evaluate specific entries,
consider the spectacular performance of Winnebago Industries,
the leading maker of self-contained motor homes. It was listed
on the New York Stock Exchange in September 1970 after an
ascent so steep that $1,250 invested in the stock in 1964 would
have been worth more than $200,000 by mid-1969. And there
was an amazing ride still to come; in 1971, Winnebago stock increased in price by no less than 466 per cent—the best single
performance on the exchange that year. Such enthusiasm is, however, always prone to excesses—especially when, as in Winnebago's case, red ink suddenly begins to appear among the gold;
in 1972 and 1973, when its price seemed to have motored far
ahead of its earnings progress, Winnebago became a notable
market casualty. In order to qualify as a premier growth stock,
a company must keep on performing—showing continuous increases in earnings—and those that falter are quickly consigned
to a less glamorous market category. And a sharply lower price.)

Just as the steels and rails seemed unappealing because of
their high labor content, government intervention and fierce
competition, so you will look for companies with what Howard
P. Colhoun, president of the T. Rowe Price New Era Fund, has
described as "more control over their destiny"—both in the narrow sense of a patent or market position that gives them greater
freedom to set prices and in the more enlightened sense of a
history of innovation that can attract top people and become
self-perpetuating. One characteristic of such industries will be
high, and demonstrably effective, expenditures on research. This

is what generates the technological eminence that keeps such companies ahead of the field.

As with individual stocks, no industry group is automatically worth buying today simply because it has performed well in the recent past. As a jog to your own thought processes, though, it might be useful to relate exactly which groups have been outstanding. (Skeptics point out that there is often wide divergence among individual stocks within a group, but there are undeniably strong and changing fashions among the groups as groups. Roger Williams, former chief economist for Standard & Poor's Corporation, has calculated that the eleven best groups [out of 100 to 120] rose in every year from 1953 to 1971, with an average annual gain of 38 per cent, while the eleven worst groups had an average decline of 18.2 per cent.) In 1971, for example, the eleven best industry groups and their percentage advances, as reported by Williams in the New York *Times,* were: restaurants, 100.3 per cent; truckers, 81.8 per cent; mobile homes, 76.4 per cent; radio-TV broadcasters, 67.7 per cent; air transport, 66.9 per cent; leisure time, 55.8 per cent; machinery and services—oil well, 55.5 per cent; offshore drilling, 55.1 per cent; air freight, 48.5 per cent; retail—variety stores, 45.6 per cent, and beverages—soft drinks, 44.7 per cent. And lest you believe that everything was for the best in the best of all possible worlds, here is the accompanying list of the eleven worst industry groups, in each case with their percentage of decline from January 1 to December 31: sugar composite, 11.4 per cent; lead and zinc, 11.5 per cent; containers—metal and glass, 15.6 per cent; sugar beet refiners, 17.3 per cent; gold mining, 19.1 per cent; textile products, 19.1 per cent; copper, 20.2 per cent; forest products, 21.4 per cent; metals miscellaneous, 24.8 per cent; aluminum, 28.1 per cent, and building materials—heating and plumbing, 31.5 per cent. (Incidentally, collectors of macabre statistics might be interested to know that the single worst-performing stock on the New York Exchange that year was Boise Cascade, off 59 per cent.) Plainly, picking the right groups is not the end of the job, but it can be a heck of an important first step.

There is an inevitable rotation among such groups. For a while the pace may be set by housing, mobile homes, retailing, airlines or cable television. Then investors may conclude that the prices of these stocks have fully caught up with their prospects;

attention will be diverted elsewhere, perhaps to financial services (such as banks, insurance companies and finance companies) or to the quality technology stocks. But such shifts need not be the dominant concern of the investor seeking growth over a period of years rather than weeks, and as noted it can be a mug's game to try to make it your concern. What is more important, and indeed more possible, for the average investor is to cast his mind ahead as to the probable shape of the country's future and, on that basis, decide which are the most fertile fields for investment. The decision is political and social, human and psychological, as much as it is economic.

The records can tell us which fields are already growing faster than the over-all economy, but what further projections can you make based on your vision of what America is to become in the next ten years? What is the significance of the fact that the twenty-five- to thirty-five-year age group will be increasing more than four times as fast as the general population? Will the purchasing power of these young adults go less for the glamorous automobiles of the past and more for the intangible satisfactions such as travel? Which industries are poised to benefit from the heightened concern about pollution and ecology—and, at least equally important, which ones will be hurt most severely in their profit-and-loss statements? What is the significance of the rising sales of such do-it-yourself equipment as power hand tools and easy-to-apply, one-coat latex paints? Will changing life-styles put even more emphasis on such labor-saving devices? Is the liberated woman going to have a smaller clothing bill? Will she buy as many cosmetics? Which industries are best geared to meeting her evolving needs? Is the vacation home going to become a permanent part of the American dream? What kind of recreation will these growing numbers of young Americans be seeking? And at the other end of the adult age scale, which industries seem most alert to the needs and desires of the increasingly numerous "senior citizens"? We know the popularity of convenience foods, but if, as some predict, the leisured American is going to want to eat better than he has in the past, will there be a broader market for those who cater to the aspiring gourmet? Health seems certain to be a more pervasive concern; which industries are best poised to exploit it?

Simply to pose these kinds of questions is to suggest how your own mind will begin to work as you transform yourself into a successful investment groupie. Don't be paralyzed by the notion that such broad-gauge assessments can be made only by trained professionals, or that the competition is too intense for an amateur like yourself. There is room in the market for all sorts of images of America's future, and there is no guarantee that those that come with the most imposing imprints will necessarily be more accurate than your own. The questions themselves are less diffuse than they may at first seem. Arthur Zeikel, the incisive board chairman of Standard & Poor's Inter-Capital, once told me that he instructed his researchers to keep three questions in front of them at all times: "What's new? What does it mean? And what should we do about it?" These are the questions that you should now be considering, too, as you plan your investment career—although, as we are about to see, you will have a lot of help in answering them.

CHAPTER IX

Is Your Analyst
Fundamentally Sound?

Just as a psychiatrist must begin with a basic medical education
(your problem might be not your mother, but your pancreas),
so the wise investor will master the facts before he considers the
emotions. His kind of analysis, too, is most likely to be successful
if it begins with the fundamentals. Those who were burned worst
in the 1969–70 market conflagration, and who are most apt to
assure you now that investing in stocks is an occupation only
for crooks and fools, are usually those who never learned this
simple lesson. For the fellow who really believes that the average
person can pick stocks effectively from casual tips, or following
the crowd, or throwing darts at the financial page, might as well
pack his family into the old sedan, drive to Florida and spend
his time at the track. His chances of financial success are every
bit as good there as they are in the stock market, and he will at
least get a suntan while he is going broke.

Wall Street has its chart players, too, and just like at Hialeah,
their systems sometimes work. Both kinds of systems tend to be
infallible in telling you what happened yesterday, but something
less than that in telling you what's going to happen tomorrow.
Technical market analysis has its fervent advocates, as we shall
see, but the ordinary investor is far more likely to prosper if he
makes his first and central concern fundamental analysis of the
corporation whose stock he is considering or actually holds. My
own view is that the price of an individual stock can most usefully be defined as "a bet on future earnings," and if you have no
sound basis for estimating what those earnings are likely to be,
you have no sound basis for investing.

Fortunately, you are not alone. You have access, to start with,
to a great mass of significant corporate information. You can take

a free look at the basic financial manuals—Standard & Poor's, Moody's and Fitch—at your broker's office or in most banks and large libraries. You will give more than a cursory glance to the financial section of a big-city newspaper each day (believe it or not, some of them have even begun to be written in English), and you probably will want to see *The Wall Street Journal* as well. Such periodicals as *Barron's, Business Week, Financial World, Forbes, Fortune* and *The Wall Street Transcript* give the professionals many of their insights into the passing investment scene, and are equally available to you. (The one remiss medium has been television, which has persisted in telling people everything about the moon and almost nothing about their money. They tell me there is, however, one splendid program called "Wall Street Week.") The flow of usable financial information is a veritable Mississippi these days, so the problem is not access so much as analysis.

I have held for last your most obvious source of investment information because I think you will make more effective use of it if it is not your only source: your broker. The major brokerage firms provide him, and you, with extensive analyses of the economic outlook for the country, rundowns on the prospects for specific industrial groups and fact sheets with recommendations on individual stocks. It would seem obvious that the quality of the securities analysts who provide these recommendations is as important in the selection of a brokerage firm as any other single factor, but it appears easier for the industry to recognize this in good times than in bad. When the averages are soaring, and everybody is looking for a stock that will triple before Christmas, research is the golden pursuit. When the indexes are declining and the customers are deserting, research departments are among the first to feel the ax. This means that investors get the least good information when they need it most, which reconfirms my earlier hint that the industry is not populated exclusively by geniuses.

Your ability to judge the quality and scope of the research effort of your own brokerage house will be helped if you have some understanding of how the analysts operate. In particular this may aid you in deciding whether a recommendation is based primarily on the transmittal of undigested statistics or has indeed involved some independent brainpower. When I asked Frederick

Frank, the brilliant young director of research for Lehman Brothers, why he thought there had been so much recent criticism of investment research, he replied candidly, "A great deal of what's purported to be analysis is in fact reporting. And I think this is the reason there's been a considerable amount of criticism, very much of it in my opinion valid—because the function is an analytical one, not a reportorial one." Arthur Zeikel, whose three prime questions for investment research were quoted in Chapter VIII, expressed a similar view when he declared, "The research process should not continue beyond the point when the time spent learning new facts becomes uneconomic." In other words, in a world in which facts are endless but sense is in short supply, the analyst's job is not to impress his firm with how many wheels he has spun but to get you to your money-making destination.

So how does a typical securities analyst work—and how many of his methods can you appropriate for yourself? Well, basically he should follow the same train of thought as is recommended for the ordinary investor. He should begin with a consideration of the broad economic factors in the country; some firms separate the economic research function from specific securities research, but the latter can proceed sensibly only in the context of the former. The analyst will typically be responsible for more than one industry, so his next task is to decide how the national economic factors will affect the outlook for these industries. Which areas are likely to grow faster in good times and to decline less in bad? Which will be damaged by underlying economic trends or by new government policies? Next, the analyst will bear down on the individual companies within each of his assigned industries—to see which is likely to beat the industry average, which is likely to match it and which is likely to do worse. And, finally, the analyst's job is not done until he has examined the current selling price of each company's stock in terms of his other findings—so he can tell you, in his written recommendation, whether that stock seems overvalued or undervalued, and for what kind of investor it seems suited.

An excellent analyst will operate much like an excellent journalist, and is approximately as rare. He will be expert at unearthing information but will be skeptical about those who give it to him. He will talk not just to a company's authorized

officers but to other employees, to suppliers, to customers and
to competitors. He will visit industry associations and government agencies. He will read trade journals and anything else he
can find. And when he puts it all together, the analysis will be
his own.

One of the starting points for the analyst will be the annual
reports of the companies in his industries. If you're like most
people, the thought of having to read those reports yourself is
probably about as appealing as holding your hand in the pot
while the water boils. Your mother never wanted you to be a
certified public accountant, did she? Actually, though, these
reports are not as intimidating as they appear. Their official
function is just to summarize the history of the company for the
past year, and to put that year in perspective with the company's
previous record. Their unofficial function, of course, is to convince you that the company's management miraculously combines the wisdom of Solomon, the salesmanship of the Music Man
and the touch of Midas. Toward that end, the report is likely to
divert you with smashing photographs, glossy paper and dazzling typography, all of it designed to take your attention away
from the less impressive statistics. This technique tends to be
successful only when the stock is.

Outright lies are frowned on in annual reports. They are not
only considered in corporate bad taste, but can land a fellow in
jail. The numbers have to be approved by independent auditors,
acting in accordance with accepted accounting principles, so
they are liable to be accurate as far as they go. That qualification
is important, for the shrewd analyst or investor will look beyond
the figures for outside assessments of the company's management,
its record and its place in the industry. Within the report itself
he will be especially wary of any indication that the accounting
methods have been changed from those used in previous years.
Was the change really necessary, or was it intended to mask some
negative developments?

Reading a financial report, and its "income" and "balance
sheet" statements, is a skill you can master more quickly than
you may suspect. Merrill Lynch has a useful free pamphlet, in-
geniously titled "How to Read a Financial Report," but for those
who want some further immediate hints, I thought it might be
edifying to let you in on some of the things Lewis Gilbert told

me he had learned in forty years of studying corporate reports as part of his role as an annual-meeting gadfly. For example, Gilbert said, when the annual report starts off, "Last year was a year of transition for the company," you can be sure you know what that means: It means the company lost money. When the "transition" is upward, the directors find they no longer need the Serbo-Croatian baffle-gab; they can say it in English. Another kind of double-talk cited by Gilbert related more to length than to linguistics: If the auditors' report runs more than two paragraphs, he said, it's time to start asking a lot of questions about the accounting methods the company has decided to use. And finally, said Gilbert, speaking as a man who had endured more than 2,000 annual meetings, if the annual report's footnotes are in especially small print, you can bet there is something going on that the directors would rather not have the stockholders read about. So read them and weep.

The balance sheet is a good place for the analyst to begin, but only that—for remember that the single most important determinant of the price of a stock will be not the earnings record but the earnings future, the "bet on future earnings." Mary A. Wrenn, a topnotch analyst who became the first female vice president of Merrill Lynch, put it this way: "We believe that the market is always discounting the future, so we place a lot of importance on the analyst's estimates of future earnings." Past earnings are obviously an important guide to this estimate, but the company statement may not give full details on the quality of those earnings, their source and the trend. Putting such information in the context of the performance and prospects of the company's competitors and of the over-all economy is part of the analyst's job—and you should look for evidence that it has been done in any research report given you by your broker.

Another point to remember about earnings is that investors will pay a higher price for a stock whose earnings are rising rapidly than for a stock with comparable but more stable earnings. That is why the trend is so critical; investors are buying the future. It is also why the surest route to prosperity in Wall Street lies in the accurate selection of growth stocks. A problem, however, is that many analysts tend—especially in a rising market—to be overexuberant in their estimates. You might think that this is because they are easily swayed by optimistic executives, yet a surprising number of good companies claim they spend much of their time discouraging analysts from estimating too high. O. Glenn Saxon, Jr., former vice president for corporate communications of the Singer Company, told me, "I've been in this investor relations business for perhaps twenty years, and I think I can honestly say that I've knocked down ninety high estimates for two low estimates. By and large our target is to try and keep people from getting too far off base." It is interesting to speculate on why so many analysts apparently are inclined to estimate higher than the company itself would. Is their information really that much better, or do they believe that a striking prediction is more likely to get attention? In any event, when you are confronted with glowingly specific long-range earnings forecasts, a dash of salt often improves the digestion.

Finally, every financial analyst I've ever talked with has told me that a crucial element in his evaluation of a company is the quality of its management. Frankly, I don't believe it. It's not that the management of a company can never be a key, or even *the* key, to the stock's future performance. It's that I don't believe most analysts really are capable of evaluating it, even when they think they are doing precisely that. There have just been too many companies over the years that the investment community regarded as having whiz-bang managements all the time their stocks were rising, and that somehow suddenly developed terrible managements the instant their stocks started to fall. Some of the giant conglomerates—darlings of the sixties, despised in the seventies—provided dramatic examples of this Wall Street tendency to equate the management with the results; the names have been deleted to protect the guilty.

I think it's simply impossible for most trained analysts (to say nothing of an ordinary investor) to make an informed judgment about an isolated commodity called "management," and I don't think you even ought to try. Let the management stand on its record, and subject that record to your closest scrutiny; your judgment of the management will then necessarily be the same as your judgment of the company, and you will not be attempting to segregate the inseparable.

What you really want to know about management is what it has done and is doing for the company and its profits. You will

want to compare the company's performance with that of others
in its field to make sure that the firm is in a successful and leading
position. You will want to check its profit margins—in other
words, how many cents does it keep on each dollar of sales?—
and those margins should be higher than average. You will want
information on its return on investment, on its ability to finance
growth without going disastrously into debt and on its ability to
withstand economic slumps and other adverse developments.
These are all the results of management, and can be considered
objectively by themselves.

The best analysts acknowledge the difficulty in evaluating
"management" as such, as opposed to what management has
produced, but they continue the effort. In Mary Wrenn's words,
"Companies have failed even in very strong growth industries
because of poor management. On the other hand, if you have a
company that has developed a unique method of merchandising,
it certainly helps if you're in the right industry. The company
that comes to mind is Avon Products, which benefited by the
fact that it was selling cosmetics in a fast-growth industry. [Yet]
I think that Sears Roebuck's success in its field was tied to the
fact that it had a progressive approach toward its employees,
and it made them profit-conscious—and this is important as a
motivation for increasing productivity."

What it really comes down to is that good managements
maximize their possibilities, and that what you want from your
broker and his analyst is not just a glib evaluation of the company's management but the factual information on which that
evaluation is based. Sometimes a poorly run company may suddenly get interesting—because of a new product, for example—
but you will want to know what was objectively lacking in the
company's previous record. So don't worry if you find it difficult
to assess management except on its results; that's the only
authentic method that anyone can use.

If you insist on making a separate "management" rating, however, I commend to you a test employed by Charles W. Shaeffer,
the perspicacious president and board chairman of T. Rowe
Price and Associates. "I like to find companies where the management has some stake in the business themselves," he told me.
"If they make a mistake, it's going to be an honest one."

CHAPTER X

What Price Earnings?

No matter how you pick stocks—whether you're a fundamentalist, a technician or a tea-leaf reader—in the long run how well those stocks do or don't do comes down to only one thing: earnings. If a stock goes up, it means that investors think the company's earnings are going to increase. And if those expectations change, or those earnings fail to materialize, the stock will go down faster than a Polaris submarine on red alert.

But if the price of a stock is, essentially, a bet on future earnings, how can you and I at least get the odds working in our favor? In other words, how can we best interpret what we are told about a company's present earnings and future prospects in order to make money on Wall Street? The answer to that lies in an examination of one of the stock market's favorite concepts, the "price-earnings ratio."

The price-earnings ratio, which aficionados customarily abbreviate chummily to "the P/E," purports to give you both sides of the investment equation: what you are getting and what you are going to have to pay for it. The first task in successful investing, as we have seen, is to find a sound, promising company; you will have looked for growing revenues, attractive new products, a position of leadership in an expanding industry and management that (while as difficult to rate in isolation as is the director of a Broadway play) has the company both financially and commercially on the right track. You may not have done all or much of the investigating yourself, but your awareness of the process enables you to do some intelligent questioning when your broker presents a recommendation from one of his company's analysts. But now comes your second major task: to decide whether the stock, however appealing on its fundamental merits, is worth buying at the price for which it is selling today. And that's where the P/E can provide a useful clue.

It's not hard to figure a price-earnings ratio, or price-earnings "multiple," as it is sometimes called. You simply divide the net earnings per share into the selling price. Let's see how that works. If XYZ Company earns $10,000,000 a year net profit and has 5,000,000 shares outstanding, its earnings per share are $2.00—a total pie of $10,000,000 divided into 5,000,000 equal slices. Let's say that the current market price of XYZ stock is $36 a share. If you divide the earnings per share, $2.00, into the price of the stock, $36, you find that the stock is selling for eighteen times earnings; its P/E is 18.

Now, you already know where to find half the information you need to determine a P/E; the market price is listed daily in any good newspaper or you can get it from your broker. But how about the earnings figure? That you will not find in the newspaper each day, so don't make the mistake of confusing the dividends (which appear alongside the stock's name in the daily listings) with the earnings. Dividends are only the part of earnings that is paid out quarterly to the stockholders, and the other part of earnings—that which is retained by the company and invested toward future growth—may be much the more important. In the example given above, XYZ Company might be paying $.50 a share as the annual dividend, and retaining the other $1.50 of earnings to plow back into the company. The market price would be 72 times dividends, but only eighteen times earnings; and the latter is the P/E.

Where can you find the earnings per share? Well, for a particular stock, you could always ask your broker, but there are other sources and they will be helpful if you want to do some broader research. Earnings per share are reported quarterly in the financial section of any self-respecting urban newspaper; if this kind of information isn't carried by your local daily, it's time you thought about supplementing it. For less immediate reports, *Barron's* weekly carries the latest figures, and so do the basic financial manuals such as Standard & Poor's stock-buying guide. A number of services and year-end publications give the range of price-earnings ratios, industry by industry—which will help tell you not only how that particular field ranks but how an individual company ranks as compared with its competitors. Major brokerage houses often publish this material on a biweekly or monthly basis. The Standard & Poor's report on a company, which your broker can get for you, will give you information both on the current earnings per share and on the range of price-earnings ratios the stock has commanded in each of the last ten years. As we shall see, this historical data can provide a second useful clue.

Finding a stock's P/E, past and present, is the easy part (even easier since October 2, 1972, when the Associated Press started giving each stock's current P/E as part of its daily market tabulations); knowing how to interpret it is what separates the investors from the schlemiels. Inexperienced investors often leap at a low price-earnings ratio, assuming that, since you thereby are paying less for the same amount of earnings, you are automatically getting a bargain. The shaft of mature insight that should pierce that gassy balloon is the knowledge that the stock market is not in business to provide you or anyone else with automatic bargains.

It is, in fact, characteristic of the growth stocks we have been discussing that their P/E's will be higher than average. If two stocks have identical earnings, the higher P/E—and thus the higher price—will go to the one whose earnings are accelerating rapidly rather than to the one whose earnings are relatively static. For example, in late 1973 you could have bought American Tel & Tel for about 10 times earnings, while you would have had to pay an awesome 40 times earnings for a proven growth stock like Avon Products. Did this mean that A.T.&T. had to be a better buy? Not necessarily. The telephone company, whose stock was selling well below its 1964 peak of $75 a share, was a heavily regulated industry whose growth record was grossly inferior to that of Avon. It was being recommended primarily for conservative investors who appreciated its liberal dividends. The higher P/E for Avon meant that the market was betting that its future earnings would continue to increase at an above-average rate.

Only the future could tell if either of these bets was correct, but it's easy to see that a higher P/E for a growth stock is merited if the earnings do meet expectations. If today's P/E for XYZ Company is 18, and the earnings increase from $2.00 a share now to $6.00 a share five years from now, the P/E for the stock bought at $36 would be reduced in effect to 6. Not only would XYZ have turned out to be an authentic bargain, but the earnings growth would in reality be reflected in the place it counts most—in a much higher market price for the stock. As Julius Westheimer, a knowledgeable partner in Baker, Watts and Company, put it, "More money is probably to be made in the high price-earnings ratio stocks than in the low price-earnings ratio stocks; just because a stock is cheap doesn't mean it's good."

The possible pitfall here is obvious. If high P/E's are based on great expectations, stocks with high P/E's are vulnerable to dramatic tumbles if those expectations are not realized. Where the ratios have been especially high, there have been cases where stocks have taken sickening plunges simply because one single quarter's earnings did not come up to snuff. The growth stocks with the highest P/E's are expected to live up to their names without faltering, and without the usual peaks and valleys; when they don't come through, the market can be merciless.

How, then, can you protect yourself? Well, there are certain guidelines the professionals use to decide whether a stock is overpriced or underpriced. A stock whose earnings are growing 12 to 15 per cent annually, for example, might ordinarily command a P/E of 25 to 30; if the P/E went above 35, a shrewd investor would begin to consider a sale. There might be some good reason for the accelerating P/E—a new product about to be launched, say, or some other highly favorable corporate development—but if investigation failed to uncover such a possible justification, the P/E could be a highly useful danger signal.

And here's where you will want to look closely at the ten-year P/E record in the stock report you can get from your broker. Generally, you will be safest when the current P/E is around the average of recent years and is roughly comparable to those of companies with similar earnings records. If the stock is selling at a premium, and you can't find any good reason for the increase, those who buy it are in peril of succumbing to the Greater Fool Theory—the notion that no matter how much you pay now for a popular stock there will always be a Greater Fool around willing to pay a higher price when you decide to sell. Experience indicates that in such cases the supply of fools tends to dwindle just when you desire it to expand.

Most sophisticated investors are aware of price-earnings ratios, but not ensnared by them. Their arithmetical exactness is in a sense misleading; while the multiple is based on a stock's current annual earnings, its real meaning is as an assumption about the future—which is necessarily inexact. High multiples have been characterized as based on a "price-to-future-earnings" ratio. Investors don't buy current earnings, they buy the future—and the future has a way of being awfully difficult to quantify.

As experienced an analyst as Arthur Zeikel says bluntly that "price-earnings ratios are a game people play," adding that in his view stock price movements respond more to changes in the forces that make earnings than to the actual realization of the earnings. "The focus," he told me, "should be [on] watching what's happening and not what's being reported by the company, or what's being estimated—because the earnings estimate changes after the fact, not before it. . . . You have to move abreast of the stock and abreast of what's changing." In other words, the market is likely to respond to changes in a company's potential long before that change has been translated into numbers, real or estimated. In support of that view, market cynics often have noted that analysts tend to raise their estimates when a stock's price is rising and lower their estimates when the stock is falling. It's as if the earnings estimate was following the price of the stock rather than vice versa. In kindness to analysts, though, let's remember that it is possible that the estimates are simply catching up to the news that provoked the change in market price.

So it's plain that the P/E is an indication of the market's current opinion about the growth potential of a stock or group of stocks, and is no more chipped in stone than any other market indicator. Anticipation counts more than realization. In the early seventies, for example, the same earnings would be rated lower if reported by an automobile stock than if reported by an antipollution stock. The latter was in one of the favored groups, one of the fields that Wall Street expected to grow fastest in the years ahead. Sometimes this confidence has been justified, and it is then that the so-called glamour stocks (which is a fancy name for those with high P/E's) truly earn the appellation. Sometimes it is not, and a group—such as the nursing-home industry—can fall from favor even quicker than it arrived. The careful investor will be suspicious of price-earnings ratios that seem overly high, but equally so of those that seem overly low (analysts may have detected further trouble ahead, such as a dividend cut or a decline in earn-

ings). But most of all he will devote himself to discerning the
conditions likely to produce exceptional increases in earnings in
future years, because if profits grow faster than expected, so
will the stock's price—and indeed its P/E. Similarly, only the
supremely incautious investor will "buy 'em and forget 'em" if the
P/E is already high; if conditions change, he is likely to wind up
with "glamour" all over his face.

Experience suggests caution when the analysts project especially rapid and persistent growth in earnings for a stock. Most
analysts tend to be bullish, and those who make optimistic forecasts are likely to get the friendliest receptions from their industry contacts. It is the equivalent of the pressures on a resident
foreign correspondent—if he wants to be lionized at the local
cocktail parties, he is apt to suffuse his dispatches in the rosiest
feasible glow. Thus the correspondent, and the analyst, may be
most worth reading when they deliver unexpectedly bad news.
These reports are likely to be based on the best information and
require the most independence and courage.

Some kinds of companies are easier to estimate than others.
As indicated earlier, such regulated industries as utilities and
railroads must provide a tremendous amount of public information; by custom, so do such other major concerns as the auto-
makers. But even in these areas, earnings estimates can go awry
because of unexpected developments within the company, its
competitors or the general economy. Clem Morgello, the *Newsweek* columnist, calculated that Wall Street missed even a 10
per cent margin of error in its estimates for about half the closely
watched 30 stocks in the Dow Jones Industrial Average for 1970
and 1971. A fair number of these estimates, interestingly enough,
were on the low side—a situation that often prevails when Wall
Street is emerging from a badly depressed bear market. It's when
the averages have been roaring upward, as in 1967 and 1968,
that the analysts' normal optimism is likely to go to greatest
excess—and you get what Robert W. Doran, executive vice president for investments of the Wellington Management Company,
has called "underanalysis and overpricing."

A final consideration in weighing the price-earnings ratio of
an individual stock is to investigate the quality of the earnings
being reported. It's commonly assumed that we poor individual
investors have no way of doing this, but as usual with this variety

of Wall Street hauteur, it ain't necessarily so. Some of the tricks are pretty obvious, once you know what you are looking for. For example, companies like to play with their depreciation expenses; if they stretch out the theoretical life of their equipment (that is, write it off over a longer-than-normal period), this can substantially increase their net earnings in the intervening years—without really improving the company's prospects. Another questionable procedure to watch for: In the late sixties, when the conglomerate balloon was still being inflated (as many chastened investors can attest, it burst with stomach-curdling rapidity), a company with a high price-earnings ratio would buy one with a low P/E. The takeover instantly bolstered the first company's earnings per share. The idea of the game was that its stock would then sell even higher, and it would then take over another low P/E company, thereby again increasing its over-all earnings, and so on into the jazzy night. The trouble was that the earnings increases were not based on sound growth of sales and profits but on acquisitions and manipulations. And as it must to all pyramid clubs, the game finally ended. This is not to say that it will never start again, but if it does you can protect yourself by questioning whether an acquisition will pay its way over the years or whether it was taken over solely to provide a temporary—and misleading—increase in earnings per share.

Here's a sneaky one: A number of major corporations in recent years have announced programs for buying their own stocks, especially at times when the prices of those stocks were depressed. (There are restrictions on how much of this they can do; normally, for listed securities, company purchases are limited to no more than 20 per cent of the shares traded that day and no more than 15 per cent of the average daily trading during the previous four weeks.) Now, on the surface, an investor might think that this is a splendid confirmation of his own fine judgment; after all, if the corporation itself is buying its stock, it must augur great things to come, right? Well, maybe, but don't count on it. It could be a device to increase earnings per share. When those shares come into the company's treasury, there are that many fewer shares outstanding—so the same amount of earnings will produce higher earnings per share. Companies may do this legitimately when they temporarily find themselves with excess capital and decide to utilize it to "buy in" their shares, as it is called, and thereby reduce the number outstanding, improve the per-share earnings on those still outstanding and perhaps wind up with a better return on their capital than some other investment would have provided. The corporation might have other motives, too, such as buying shares with a view toward using them in a future acquisition of another company or employing them internally for executive stock options. But in the view of a skilled securities analyst like Frank Cappiello, "If a company does this continuously, year in and year out, buying in its own shares to bootstrap its earnings, you have to ask yourself: 'If management can't find a better use for the money, what are we paying management for?'"

A pitfall that inexperienced investors often encounter in attempting to assess earnings per share is failing to distinguish between "fully diluted" and "undiluted" earnings. Undiluted earnings can be as powerful as 100-proof bourbon, and equally apt to lead you astray. You buy stock in a company in the expectation that its earnings will increase, the earnings duly increase—but the earnings per share do not, because there are suddenly, say, 50 per cent more shares outstanding. So what happened, Seymour? The answer could be that there were numerous "convertible" securities lurking in the background all the time. There are various kinds of issues that may have the right eventually to be converted into the company's common stock at a given price: convertible bonds, for example, which pay interest at a set rate until they are converted; convertible preferred stock, which before conversion is entitled to a set dividend that is paid before the common-stock dividends, and such other types of securities as warrants, which entitle their purchasers to buy common stock at a given price and usually during a specified time period. Whenever there are any kinds of convertible securities outstanding, there is potential "dilution" of the common stock—and any financial analyst or ordinary investor who fails to consider the impact on earnings per share in the event these securities are indeed converted into additional common stock is merely deluding himself. In the 1970s the accounting profession has taken note of this danger by tightening some of its corporate reporting procedures. Companies often report their earnings per share both undiluted—that is, in terms of the number of shares of common stock currently outstanding—and fully diluted, or in terms of what the earnings would be if all potential conversions into common stock took place. Such information can in any event be gleaned from a careful reading of the annual report (watch those footnotes), and any decent written or oral report you get from your broker should alert you on this one. Otherwise what is most likely to be diluted, I fear, is your very own investment capital.

Another method that some companies have used unwisely to expand current earnings at the expense of their firms' fundamental growth has been excessive debt. (This is not to say that high-P/E companies always should have little or no debt; some observers, such as Joel M. Stern, vice president of the Chase Manhattan Bank, believe these are precisely the kinds of companies that benefit the most from debt financing. The issue here is why, not how, the capital was raised.) John F. Childs, senior vice president of the Irving Trust Company, cited to me the example of a company that borrowed $10,000,000 at 8 per cent to invest in a plant whose products would earn a net return of 6 per cent. The company is not absolutely crazy, incidentally, since after taxes that 8 per cent interest costs only 4 per cent—so there is a 2 per cent profit on the deal. Earnings per share are kicked up, and superficially everything is marvelous. But since the return on the new investment would be too low to sustain adequate growth in earnings later on, investors eventually would sour on the stock—and both the P/E and the price would fall. Whether it is taking over another company or borrowing to build a plant, Childs observed, a soundly managed company "should look at the return on investment at the price it's paying for that investment over the long run, and not look at the current increase." Investors who buy sharp immediate increases in earnings without investigating whether those increases are soundly based and sustainable are apt to see their stocks behaving like paper versions of the famous Duke of York—except that after marching smartly up the hill the stocks are likely to beat their retreats in unseemly haste.

So price-earnings ratios, in conclusion, are simply one additional fact about stocks—and an item that should be handled with care. They are creatures of investor emotion, a perennially changeable commodity. In 1961, though earnings generally fell, prices increased—because price-earnings ratios went to what was to be their postwar peak. The following year, with earnings rising, prices—and P/E's—sank. You figure it out. Or better still, realize that the long-range investor should concern himself more with earnings than with price, more with the company's future than Wall Street's tastes—for the former can become an informed estimate, and the latter at best only a hopeful guess. If the company grows, even the highest P/E's can be bargains; if it doesn't, choosing a stock because its P/E is low is like trying to economize on meat purchases by buying tainted pork.

CHAPTER XI

If It's New and Hot, Should You Handle It?

Anyone who still cherishes the notion of Wall Street as a hangout for conservative chaps in stiff white collars ought to take a gander at the average investor on the scent of a hot new issue. No bitch in heat ever had a more undignified pursuer. His eyes will glaze, his heart palpitate, his glands salivate. This, he will eagerly believe, is what the great game is truly all about: a little company nobody ever heard about (except me! except me!), with stock that is to be distributed at first only to a fortunate elite (including me! including me!) and that will then increase in price so rapidly and geometrically as to bring wealth beyond the dreams of Midas to its chosen core of initial investors (that's me! that's me! that's me!). Am I so churlish as to suggest that this vision is never realized? Certainly not. What, then, are that investor's chances of realizing it? About one in a thousand—which happens to be the exact equivalent of the chances that he will win tomorrow's numbers game.

Like many things in Wall Street, the enthusiasm for "new issues" (securities that have not previously been traded) moves in readily discernible cycles. Its peaks are danger signals for market professionals: warnings that the least knowledgeable members of the public are racing to buy anything available, that prices are escalating absurdly, that there is far more froth in the glass than beer. In recent memory this happened in 1961 and again in 1968–69, when just about everything went up and up —and if it happened to have a fashionable name (something ending in "-tronics" was ideal), making money was as easy as being touched with a Fairy Godbroker's wand. The trouble was that midnight struck, with its usual resonant inevitability, and the new-issues market turned into a particularly odoriferous pumpkin. And had the lesson been learned, as tens of thousands of disappointed investors cursed their timing, their luck (anything but their judgment)? For a while, sure; but then, in 1971 and 1972, the number of new issues coming to market again began to increase rapidly, and by 1972 their prices—out of the basement at last—were once more outpacing the rest of the market. The collection of new issues was a long way from the garbage heap of 1968–69, and investors were being more selective in buying or selling them after they appeared. But as the scent of quick profits began to grow, as the average investor again began to salivate, it became apparent that the warming trend could once more make the pursuit of new issues a chase over very thin ice.

The beginning investor, in my view, should regard new issues as he would leprosy. This is a race where even the professionals falter. Listen to what William G. Campbell, president of the Hartwell & Campbell Fund, Inc., told me: "The record since 1946 of companies that have specialized in investing in emerging companies has been rather dismal in terms of the number of companies that have succeeded. I am talking more on the quasi-venture-capital type 'emerging growth' company, and I think that history proves that the companies that were around in 1961 are not here today. And I think that we will find of companies that are very small companies, they will be used as wallpaper in coming years." Campbell was speaking particularly of companies with less than $10,000,000 in annual sales, without established product lines or managements. But his skepticism could be adopted by the average inexperienced investor toward nearly all new issues and small companies. The risks are simply very much higher for him in these areas than in proven securities with a history of trading on the New York or American stock exchanges.

There may come a time, however, when this caution no longer will prevail—when an investor with some experience (which should be the unalterable first requirement) wants to yield to the itch to buy a new issue. Perhaps he will hear tales of friends who have done so with spectacular success. (Somehow there is far less cocktail-party conversation about investments that have lost money.) Perhaps his broker has just called him with the surest thing since Thomas E. Dewey. Or perhaps (let's be charitable) he just wants to take part in the romance of the

American dream—helping a small young company on its way, hoisting the banner of capitalism in an era of despair, offering a hand so that a potential new Xerox or IBM can struggle ahead. And if that should bring mythic prosperity to the benign sponsor who bought the stock the very first time it was offered to the public, why, what could be more just than to satisfy one's greed while advancing the republic? So whatever your motives may eventually be, we ought not to leave the subject of how to pick stocks without a few further words on the subject of shimmering little acorns.

One of the features that adds to the social cachet of owning new issues is that they are often hard to get. Anybody who has the money and the desire can buy stock in General Motors or U.S. Steel, but when a company issues new stock there are only so many shares to be had at that first offering. In 1968–69 it became a mark of one's prestige to be permitted by his broker to buy "hot" new issues, those so widely sought that their prices were thought certain to rise far above that at which they were offered to initial purchasers. To be allowed in on such deals was regarded as a license to make a guaranteed profit, a reward for previous yeoman service to the broker. And sometimes it was even true. From this psychology grew a certain cynicism about those issues that were, indeed, available to the small or average investor. If he could get it, the feeling seemed to be, he shouldn't want it.

How, then, do you go about buying a new issue? Well, the easiest way is if your broker is trying to sell it and gives you a call. But you can show a little initiative, too, and the best way is to be aware of which new issues are about to appear. *The Wall Street Journal* reports on new issues both of companies coming to market for the first time and of companies issuing additional shares. When these companies file prospectuses about the new issues, this is reported in a publication called *The New Issue Digest*. Normally, the offering will not take place for another twenty days. So your next job is to get what Wall Street significantly calls a "red herring," a preliminary prospectus from the underwriter of the new issue. (We'll see precisely how he functions a little later.) All prospectuses are on public file at the offices of the Securities and Exchange Commission in Washington, but I'm going to take the liberty of assuming that you have already seen the Jefferson Memorial and are not anxious to race back to the District of Columbia for another peek every time you want a prospectus. Here's an easier, if less scenic, method: Call your broker and express your interest. No matter how you have heard of the new issue, he can quickly consult such periodicals as *The Commercial and Financial Chronicle* weekly and *The Investment Dealers Digest* monthly to learn who is the lead underwriter, the manager of the offering. From that manager, he can get you a prospectus.

Once you get it, what will you have? Well, you will have a booklet that should eliminate any doubt you may have entertained about the high degree of risk involved in buying new issues. The standard disclaimer on page one is worth keeping in mind: "These securities have not been approved or disapproved by the Securities and Exchange Commission nor has the Commission passed upon the accuracy or adequacy of this prospectus. Any representation to the contrary is a criminal offense." Duly forewarned, let the buyer beware. But if that doesn't scare you, read on. You will encounter a classic of the school of unreadable literature written by lawyers for lawyers. Full disclosure of all possible threats, from technological competition to tapeworms, is the motif—but the morass of figures and cautions is likely to tell you everything but what you really want to know: Is the company going to be a success? Senator Harrison A. Williams, Jr., the New Jersey Democrat who was chairman of the Senate Securities Subcommittee investigation of Wall Street, aptly described the typical prospectus to me as "a forbidding document" that "really requires intense professional knowledge," adding, "Simplification, or a summary form together with all of the detail, would be indicated."

The senator was getting at a central problem in dealing with new issues. For while it is certainly excellent advice to read the prospectus (a step that can instantly put you ahead of the field), there is no guarantee that what you read will be fully informative or even fully comprehensible. When the Securities and Exchange Commission proposed extensive new rules in 1972 to bring more sense and stability to the new-issues market, it concentrated on clarifying prospectuses. Suggested additions included a statement of anticipated cash resources and cash expenditures, by category; more detail on the company's competition, on the company's actual development of new products and on its market studies concerning these products, and some explanation of how the tentative price of the new stock was determined. Stress was placed on the underwriters' responsibility to make sure that the issuing company was telling the full truth, in particular in disclosing the experience and background of its key executives. "The hot-issue hearings have shown that one of the most important items of disclosure to a venture capitalist relates to the character and experience of the management," the SEC said, and its chairman, William J. Casey, declared in a separate statement that the commission's proposed new disclosure requirements were "intended to give public investors information approaching the quality and type generally required and received by venture capitalists and other professional investors."

All well and good, but the SEC did not at that time decide whether companies, old or new, should be required to add carefully documented forecasts of sales and earnings to the regular reports they file with the commission. That suggestion had been opposed by the Securities Industry Association on the ground that reputable companies and underwriters would make conservative estimates while fringe operators would promise the moon. But most analysts and investors would welcome such estimates. Not only have prospectuses not included earnings estimates, but brokers have been forbidden by law to comment on estimated earnings for a stock that was in registration as a new issue. Yet the most critical element in selecting any stock, as we have seen, is the estimate of its future earnings. (Casey indicated later on "Wall Street Week" that he leaned toward permitting—though not yet requiring—such projections.) One would not have to accept blindly the company's own estimates in order to find them a useful tool in analysis.

Assuming, though, that you have actually read the prospectus and still want to buy the new issue, what do you do next? If your local brokerage house is participating in the underwriting, fine; pressure your broker to get some for you. If not, he can tell you which firms are part of the underwriting syndicate, and he may even be able to get what is called "selling-group stock" though his firm is not a syndicate member. If your interest is genuine, it is worth determining how much effort your broker is willing and able to make in getting you this kind of issue. And even if he fails, remember that a stock truly worth buying before it comes on the market should remain an excellent investment a few days later, when it is available to the general public, even if it does become slightly less exhilarating as a topic for conversation.

The business of underwriting new issues of companies that have not previously offered their securities to the public is both speculative and romantic. The underwriter is chosen by the company for any of a number of reasons: a recommendation by accountants or lawyers, a tip from friends, observations of earlier performances for other companies. The executives tell their company's story to the underwriting firm, much as you would tell your story to a banker when seeking a loan. Then an experienced underwriter, if he is interested, will generally visit the company and make an extensive examination of the facilities, the financial statements and the commercial situation. One of the most successful underwriters, A. Robert Towbin, partner in C. E. Unterberg, Towbin Company, told me, "We find, though, with new issues, particularly with smaller companies, that one rarely makes a mistake on numbers—one really only makes mistakes on people." Yet the numbers are important, for they lead to the key number for the new-issue buyer: the price at which the underwriter is going to offer the security to the public. To determine this he will take one part annual earnings, one part comparable price-earnings ratios for stocks in the same field—and one part eye of newt, because pricing a stock properly requires a touch of magic, too. His effort will be to lean toward the conservative side, so the issue will quickly sell and he won't be stuck with it. Even the United States Government, when it has a new bond issue, likes to price it a little below the market—so you will buy that issue instead of whatever else is around. Should Zowie Ultratronics do less?

Towbin is so conscientious about his pricing that he thinks a stock that came out at $10 a share and then quickly rose to $12 a share probably ought to be sold. If that goes too much against the grain, he believes that any stock that so much as triples in a short period of time should definitely be sold—and then, if you still like it, repurchased later when the price falls.

Meanwhile, while you are mooning about those lovely possibilities, you still have to concentrate on how to select a new issue that is going to perform that well. Reading the prospectus and consulting a knowledgeable broker are the first rules. Then, as you would with any stock, concentrate on the earnings potential—the realistically likely growth of the business in terms of its industry position and its product. The risk is going to be immense in any case, so you owe it to yourself to minimize it by doing enough homework to enable you to judge whether the company's hopes have anything going for them besides crossed fingers. Often it is difficult to get regular information after the stock has been issued; always this is a sophisticated market in which extreme hotness may result only in somebody getting burned. So emulate Smokey the Bear.

An especially dangerous part of the new-issues forest is what is called the "after-market"—that is, the trading after the initial distribution—and it is here that the careful investor will be on the lookout for any manipulation or creation of artificial shortages. Among the suggestions that have been made for reducing these dangers are adoption of the European system of new issues by tender (everybody just sends in a price, and the highest bid is the price of issuance) and a possible one- to three-day moratorium on trading after a new issue is brought to market (so that a large number of buys and sells can accumulate, and they can be matched to make a realistic opening price). The latter idea was opposed by the Securities Industry Association, which argued that a trading moratorium would permit demand for a hot issue to build up to explosive proportions. Probably the only final solution to the problem of wild gyrations in the prices of new issues would be to eliminate the speculative urge from mankind—and we wouldn't want to do that, now, would we?

As another indication of the difficulty in spotting precisely which small company is likely to be the next Xerox, consider those professional venture capitalists who try to do that for a living and who invest their money before stock is issued to the public. Don A. Christensen, president of Greater Washington Investors, Inc., which was one of two such venture-capital investment companies listed on the New York Stock Exchange, said his firm had to look at more than 1,000 companies each year in order to find perhaps ten that were worth putting in its portfolio. Of the 1,000-plus, he told me, his executives would meet with the managements of about 200 and then begin "really detailed" investigations of maybe 50. Against that kind of compe-

tition, what are the average investor's chances of hitting a home
run with the first small company that catches his fancy? "The
real characteristic of venture capital," in Christensen's expert
judgment, "is this one-in-a-thousand sort of success. For professional venture capitalists, it's really probably one-in-a-hundred."

Professional underwriters and venture capitalists tend to work
closely with the new companies they are helping; often they go
on the board of directors. It is a much more personal relationship
than is usually possible with an established corporation. (In this
connection, Christensen offers a useful tip for all investors: "One
management is not necessarily good for all parts of a small company's growth. The sort of gentleman who could be an entre-
preneur and form a company [he said earlier that this should be
a "guy who goes for the jugular" and "just is not going to give
up, no matter what happens"] is very often not the same man
who can run it when it's doing $10,000,000 or $20,000,000 in sales.
You require different abilities, a different type of man.") It is
a kind of investment best suited to those with a highly developed
parental instinct, and should never be attempted by those who
like to "buy-'em-and-forget-'em." When you are dealing with the
new issues of small companies, you are dealing with one of the
most fragile and speculative commodities on Wall Street. The
rewards may conceivably be enormous; the risks are certainly
so. The more experienced investor, who is the only one who
ought to consider such issues in the first place, should find part
of his compensation in the knowledge that he is performing the
most classic of investment functions—providing the capital to
start a business or make it grow. I asked Christensen if this was
not as close as a male capitalist could come to being a mother.
"Very much so," he replied. "They say about small companies
that they are like small children; you know, they have all sorts
of very serious illnesses, none of which are fatal. But they keep
you awake at night."

CHAPTER XII

Was It News to You, Too?

There are many who regard the stock market as wholly perverse, the daily product of an evil genie who would have bankrupted Aladdin. It is moved, they feel, by forces mysterious and Satanic, not discernible by those of honest minds and pure hearts (i.e., themselves). How else, they demand, can one explain a situation in which a company announces increased earnings—and sees its stock decline? What is the justification for a day on which all the news is bad—and the market rises? In an arena so devoid of elementary logic, what chance has the proverbial Little Man to emerge with his skin (and savings) intact? These questions, not surprisingly, are the sort that often leap to the lips of those whose own adventures in the stock market should be consigned to the category of great natural disasters. But such sentiments can be needlessly discouraging to those who have not yet dipped their first tentative toes in the muddy waters of Wall Street. The antidote is not some bland assurance that the market always knows what it is doing, because it often does not and, as we have seen, its value as a predictor can lie somewhere south of tarot cards. But the market does tend to behave in some internally consistent patterns, and the investor who wants to understand them ought to begin with a basic comprehension of the interrelationship between news and the market.

I say "interrelationship" because, just as the news can affect the market, so the market can affect the news. Many Americans, whether or not they personally own stocks, watch the changing averages in the persistent belief that Wall Street must know something they don't know. When the stock market is booming, when stocks and spirits are rising on Wall Street, it tends to have an identifiable effect on over-all consumer confidence. So the euphoria can, for an extended period, be self-sustaining. On the other hand, when the averages dive, so do the expectations of many who would no more buy a stock than fly to Mars. During a time of market weakness in 1971, Walter E. Heller, who served Presidents Kennedy and Johnson as chairman of the Council of Economic Advisers, worried aloud that this might have "a negative effect" on the mood of business executives, whose attitudes he reported as ranging from "pessimistic to apoplectic." To at least some veteran observers, this recalled the philosophical speculation early in the century by William James, the Harvard psychologist, as to whether people are happy because they laugh or whether they laugh because they are happy. (Stock-market losers should be advised that James pondered similarly about crying.) As it turned out, most business executives were not pitched so totally into gloom as Heller suggested; trade and manufacturing inventories were rising at the very time he spoke, and the market soon rebounded from its lows. As is often the case, when the selling was bad enough to be reported on page one, it was an excellent time to buy. But there is little question that Main Street watches and is affected by Wall Street, as well as vice versa.

Politicians thus pay closer attention to the stock market than many will publicly admit. It is not just a useful gauge of sentiment among an important sector of the public but also a daily fact whose psychological impact ranges far from the trading floor. When the averages are high, the incumbents are delighted; Lyndon Johnson cited the market's move into then-record territory early in 1966 as an accomplishment of which he was proud. When the market began to slide after President Nixon's inauguration in 1969, one of the new President's top aides confided to me that this was taken as satisfying evidence that the Administration was being convincingly tough in its war on inflation. He suggested that there would be no need for official concern unless the Dow Jones Industrial Average dipped below 850. When it submarined about 220 points lower in May 1970, all traces of Administration satisfaction had been removed. Reports on the Dow index were distributed twice a day to White House staffers and drew worried attention. (Not that there is much the White House can do directly to influence the market, as Richard Nixon learned when he said earlier that spring that if he had any money he would be buying stocks. The market promptly fell even more sharply, apparently reasoning that things must be worse than expected if the President had to be out touting stocks.)

Despite this political interest, however, the link between elections and stocks is not strong. Begin by disabusing yourself of the notion that investors are all true-blue Republicans who panic at the thought of a Democrat in power. Statistics indicate, as a matter of fact, that the market has on average done better in this century during Democratic administrations than during Republican—though Republican analysts explain this by contending that the Republican Presidents had to spend much of their time cleaning up the economic messes left behind by the Democrats. Ignore the partisan rhetoric on both sides; what matters is the course of the economy, which can be affected by many considerations unrelated to election results, and there have been periods of tremendous market booms (such as 1952–56, when the Dow nearly doubled) under Republicans as well as Democrats. When the market gets nervous about a presidential candidate, as it did about George McGovern in 1972, the reason can usually be traced to his specific economic proposals rather than to his party label.

If politics does not truly move the market, then, what does? Well, in the end, as we have seen, the rise or fall in the prices of any and all stocks must eventually depend on the earnings of corporations. Thus the market tends to favor expansionist government programs, even when powered by deficit spending, as long as inflation remains moderate (thus presumably making stocks an attractive hedge) and does not threaten to become unchecked. When inflation gets out of hand, as it did in the wake of excessive spending on the Vietnam War and on domestic welfare programs, without commensurate tax increases, it becomes counterproductive on the stock market—eroding corporate profits by escalating costs faster than businesses can raise their prices. The stock market's basic attitude toward inflation resembles that of the girl who would like to be just a little bit pregnant.

There is, however, one news subject that normally has an immediate and almost inevitable effect on the stock market—and that, with brilliant appropriateness, is money. The market traditionally likes to see the money supply plentiful and interest rates low, and any government or private action affecting this area is likely to have a direct impact on stock prices. Here's why: Money

is not just a nice thing to have personally; it's the very blood of
a growing economy, the fuel of a roaring stock market. When
the money supply is expanding and interest rates (the price of
money) are relatively cheap, retail merchants are more inclined
to build up their inventories. Corporations find it easier to borrow to start new plants. Capital spending is stimulated all along
the lines, followed by more jobs, followed by more consumer
spending. It's even favorable for the stock market when banks
and savings-and-loan associations, awash on this tide of money,
find it necessary to cut the interest rates they pay depositors for
passbook savings—because that very act makes this form of saving
less attractive in comparison with securities, and stimulates small
investors to take a fresh look at Wall Street. Easy money also
reduces the yields on bonds and thus lowers the competitive
lure of bonds as compared with stocks.

Money is nice. But the introduction of too much money into
the economy too quickly, as in the disastrous deficit financing
of the Vietnam escalation, can trigger a punishing inflation—and
punishing measures to keep it in check. The stock market doesn't
like the medicine, but it seldom thinks that far ahead. Its bias is
toward loose money, not tight, and low interest rates, not high.
Hence it may react in what to you might seem excessive fashion
to a minor change in what is known as the "prime rate," which
is the interest banks charge to their best corporate customers.
Traditionally, this lowest of bank interest rates is the key to all
others, but of late some of the drama—and the Wall Street over-
reaction—has been lessened because of an inclination to change
the rate frequently in small doses. Banks are trying to get out
from under the gun of Washington, which tends to act as if any
increase in bank interest rates were a high public crime—even,
or perhaps especially, if Washington itself is responsible for re-
leasing the forces that produced the rise.

Whatever the cause, though, a shrinking money supply and
heightening interest rates predictably foreshadowed the market's
tumble in 1969–70, and the reverse situation led to its resuscita-
tion in the months that followed. So investors pay close attention
not only to interest rates but to any changes in the behavior of
the Federal Reserve Board, the independent government agency
that may or may not be working in tandem with the administration of the day.

The "Fed," as it is genially known, likes to operate in conditions of secrecy approximating those of the CIA, and hints as to its possible shifts of policy regarding the money supply and interest rates often draw conflicting interpretations. The Fed can strongly affect short-term interest rates in three basic ways: (1) In its "open market" operations, buying and selling government securities, it expands the available supply of credit when it buys such securities and contracts the money volume when it sells; when the credit supply shrinks, short-term interest rates rise —and vice versa. (2) The ability of banks to lend money can also be influenced by changes in the Fed's "discount rate," the rate at which it lends to its member banks; a tightening of its loan policies and an increase in this rate will quickly be reflected at the private customer level. (3) What has been described as the most massive and infrequently used gun in the Fed's arsenal (fired every couple of years or so) is a change in the "reserve requirement," the amount of reserves banks must keep in relation to their deposits; higher reserves mean "tighter," more expensive money. An increase in the discount rate or in reserve requirements is a signal to banks and their customers that caution may be in order. The Federal Reserve Board has other weapons as well, such as rules for installment-loan deposits and stock-market purchases on credit (which we will discuss later), and its impact on short-term rates is mighty. It has been less successful as the czar of long-term interest rates, however, partly because buyers of bonds and other long-term debt add in such additional considerations as their expectations about the future rate of inflation.

There is a perennial dispute between those who think the Fed's main concern should be with interest rates and those, such as Professor Milton Friedman, who believe it should ignore interest-rate fluctuations and concentrate on sending out a steady supply of money that increases moderately at a set annual rate. This predictable flow would be designed to assist sound growth by avoiding both the cramping effect of too little money and the inflationary effect of too much. Although this approach has achieved greater influence in recent years, in its pure state it has never been tried. (Professor Friedman once confided to me that if he were in government he might not be such a purist himself.) So investors are going to have to keep on figuring out what the

Fed is up to. And whatever its theoretical posture, the Federal
Reserve Board is likely to remain the single Washington agency
most closely watched by Wall Street professionals. For as Dr.
Albert H. Cox, Jr., chief economist of Lionel D. Edie and Company, put it to me: "Generally speaking, the batting average of
money supply in predicting stock prices has been pretty good."

Now that we have some understanding of the kind of news
that Wall Street finds important, let's get back to those questions
about the market's apparent perverseness—its occasional tendency to react to a piece of news with the opposite of what would
appear to be logic. The root answer lies in the word "anticipation"; investors are concerned with the future (a stock's price,
you will recall, is essentially a bet on its future earnings), and
thus the occurrence of an event that has been foreseen may be a
signal for those who have foreseen it to take their profits. Once
the news is out, they back away, following the maxim that what
everybody knows is no longer worth knowing. This may result
in some good news about a company producing selling, and bad
news producing buying—but to get the real picture you have to
look at the recent history of the stock, to see if it has not indeed
already risen substantially in anticipation of the precise piece of
good news that has just been announced. The news, in Wall
Street's term, has been "discounted" in advance. (Scarcely a jet-
age development. Hark to this incisive bit of market analysis:
"The expectation of an event creates a much deeper impression
upon the exchange than the event itself. When large dividends
or rich imports are expected, shares will rise in price; but if the
expectation becomes a reality, the shares often fall; for the joy
over the favorable development and the jubilation over a lucky
chance have abated in the meantime." Joseph de la Vega wrote
that in 1688.)

Interestingly enough, some experienced analysts tell me this
discounting is often less complete today than it was decades ago
when stock ownership was not so diffuse and the federal government not so active in ferreting out abuses of "inside" information.
These days, good news, even if expected by some investors, may
happily surprise enough others actually to send the stock up—as
logic, though not tradition, would suggest. On the other hand,
a stock may fall on news of increased earnings simply because the
increase was less than anticipated. The solution for the long-term

investor is to see whether the stock is continuing to meet his expectations, whatever the expectations of others might be, and if it is, to persevere in his investment program without bending to every whim of the traders. The market's predictive value is usually at its worst when it is reacting to spot news.

As for the market's over-all trend, I advise you to apply your own most skeptical discount to confident Wall Street assertions that it anticipates changes in the economy six to nine months ahead. Prices do usually foreshadow significant profit trends; the market started to turn down in December 1968 and profits followed in the second quarter of 1969, for example, and the market bottom in May 1970 came ahead of the profit upturn in the third quarter. But there are enough exceptions sprinkled through the years to suggest a grain of salt for each sprinkle. The market can remain stubbornly indifferent to the course of the economy for surprising periods. From 1946 to 1949, for example, it kept foreshadowing a major postwar crash—which somehow never quite arrived. In 1962 it again went off in the face of impressive economic indicators and rising profits. Its claim to infallibility does not deserve a high P/E.

On balance, there is probably more money to be lost than won by reacting immediately to a spot-news flash. Bad news can cause such a rush of panic selling that a stock drops precipitously; those who wait may see the stock regain much or all of its initial loss when the news is digested and the hysteria is corrected. Besides, there remains the excellent chance that the news is either incorrect or exaggerated. There was a famous case on a Monday noon in the twenties when the Supreme Court handed down a decision on the taxability of stock dividends. The ticker erroneously reported that the Court had held stock dividends to be taxable as income, and the Dow Jones Industrial Average instantly nosedived 15 points. A few minutes later, the ticker put on what passes for a blush on a news machine, apologized and said that the Court had actually ruled that stock dividends were not taxable as income. On the basis of this revised report, the Dow index promptly recovered its loss and added another 15 points for good measure. The wise guys who had acted immediately got burned; the more tranquil investors could count it just another good day.

And don't think that this sort of danger belongs only to the distant past. A "Wall Street Week" viewer complained in a letter in 1972 that he had been fooled into acting on an incorrect news report that caused a stock nearly to double in fifteen minutes—and then to collapse half an hour later when an excuse-it-please correction of the earnings report was printed. This brought an uncharacteristically sharp, but absolutely justified, reaction from a program panelist, B. Carter Randall, senior vice president of the Equitable Trust Company, who snapped, "I really don't have much sympathy for people who buy or sell stocks based on news that they don't verify for validity. And I don't think it's the proper way to invest money." Neither do I—and neither should you. I am reminded, in fact, of a test that used to be given to freshman applicants for the Princeton Press Club, the organization of campus "stringer" (part-time) correspondents for newspapers, magazines, wire services and assorted other news media. Part of the quiz consisted of a number of actions to be taken in the event the reporter should happen to notice that Nassau Hall was burning down. He was supposed to demonstrate his professional competence by putting these actions in their proper order. The only correct answer for number one was: "Take a deep breath, and then . . ."

Investors are naturally trying to assess each day's news for the impact it will have on their present and potential holdings. Which companies will be hurt by the latest shift in defense policy? Which airlines will gain most from the latest fare boost granted by the Civil Aeronautics Board? Which corporations are best positioned to exploit the possibilities of the government's new trade program? This kind of questioning soon becomes automatic, and it can be helpful to the investor who takes his time and arrives at an independent appraisal. But the tendency is to move impulsively when the news first comes, especially when it is bad news. This probably accounts for the tendency for stocks to go up more slowly than they come down. This is also true for the market as a whole. It is popular to think of this as some sort of modern phenomenon, related to the supposed agonies of life in the America of the seventies and to the country's loss of its traditional confidence in itself. This sort of deep psychological analysis makes brilliant living-room conversation and appeals to the habitual American urge for self-flagellation. Unfortunately, for those who are trying to make sense of Wall Street, it also happens to be absolute bunk. The phenomenon is by no means modern, and in trying to account for it I commend to you the nineteenth-century admonition of Charles Mackey, who wrote, "Men think in herds; it will be seen that they go mad in herds; while they only recover their senses slowly, and one by one."

Just as the market abhors uncertainty (and never finds anything else), so it is made nervous by any piece of unexpected news. A flare-up in the Middle East can cause a one-day scorching of nearly all stocks, including those whose products never venture farther east than Long Island. A pessimistic prediction from a professionally pessimistic predictor (and there is a handful around Wall Street that makes a lovely living from being perennially, but dramatically, wrong) can scare the market's pants off for a few hours. A negative story in *Barron's,* or the New York *Times,* or *The Wall Street Journal,* can send a stock down sharply for a day or two—and then have its entire impact neutralized just as quickly, as more positive information gets added into the investment equation.

What can the small investor do? Well, in addition to vowing firmly not to get panicked by a scare headline or a scared broker, he can resolve to be a critical reader—and not just a trusting consumer—of the daily stock-market reports. Those who prepare these reports are under pressure to account daily for something that may, on a daily basis, be unaccountable—the movement of more than 1,500 common stocks on the New York Stock Exchange alone. Thus they will tell you that "renewed fears of inflationary pressure" sent the Dow Jones Industrial Average down 2½ points yesterday, or "expectations of improved second-quarter earnings statements" moved it up 3. The trouble is that there is almost never one single reason for the stock market's total behavior on any given day. It can thus be bewildering for the neophyte to try to figure out why yesterday's "renewed fears" apparently have evaporated today, or why yesterday's fully justified optimism has been replaced by today's equally rationalized pessimism. The truth is that, while spot news can affect some or all of the market on a day-to-day basis, the underlying trend is what matters—and that takes a little more perspective than daily deadline pressures can permit. The market never goes straight up or straight down for long, and the day it chooses for a short-term reversal may have scant connection with any hard news that appears on that day. But tradition requires a confident daily explanation for what has happened. (Market analysts are always brilliant in explaining exactly why today's market did what it did; it's only the explanation for what the market is going to do tomorrow that provokes any uncertainty at all.) The jargon is such that if, say, the market goes up a bit on December 1, you can count on reading that stocks are having their "traditional year-end rally." If, however, the market should happen to dip on that day, you can be equally sure that you will read that the reason was "traditional year-end tax-selling." If the market were as simple as most daily stock reports suggest, all financial journalists would be rich.

The market has its moods, like a headstrong child. When it wants to go down, when the trend is bearish, it can ignore the most favorable economic developments imaginable. On the other hand, I recall one day in 1972 when the news included the following events: George Meany, the country's most powerful labor leader as president of the AFL-CIO, had walked out on the Government Pay Board. Grocery prices were reported to have soared at the fastest rate in fourteen years. International monetary problems continued far from solution. The prime rate of most banks was increased to 5 per cent. So what happened to the stock market, which at that point had been bubbling along in a full-fledged bull trend? Why, it rose another 11 points. It wanted to go up, and that was all there was to it; it was in no mood to pay attention to contrary news. A few months later, it was just as persistent on the downside.

All this is just further reason for the successful investor to develop a mind of his own—and a detached attitude toward the day's passions on Wall Street. In keeping ahead of the market, he will try not to outguess its ephemeral moods but to search for more basic considerations—to look, as the government does, for those "leading economic indicators" to which the market must eventually respond. (When used in the government's periodic reports, the phrase "leading economic indicators" refers to a composite index that summarizes eight statistics: the average work week for manufacturing employees, the number of initial claims for unemployment insurance, building permits, stock prices, new factory orders for durable goods, new orders for equipment, the ratio of price to unit labor costs, and industrial material prices. The composite is intended to be a preview of what is going to happen to the economy and to those who work in it.) The investor who buys and holds quality growth stocks is often wisely counseled to be prepared to wait at least two to three years for his payoff, but if his judgment is sound and his forecast of economic trends is correct, he is far better positioned to make money in Wall Street than the fellow who calls his broker four times a day and tries to refigure his portfolio with each edition of the hourly news.

Before abandoning the subject of news and the market, I'd like to leave you with one final thought that might make you feel just a trifle more benign about the stock market. It concerns those formidable figures of Communist mythology, the warmongers of Wall Street. In real life they are as hard to find as an amateur skier at the Olympics. In truth there are few places in this world where peace is more revered than on the littered floor of the New York Stock Exchange. As Vietnam again demonstrated so dramatically, war is extremely bad for nearly all stocks. (Investors won't even pay much for the earnings of munitions-makers, realizing these earnings are going to be temporary.) Rumors of war, or any close relative, invariably unsettle the stock market. Rumors of peace are bullish. Wars upset economic relationships, misdirect national resources and endanger earnings. And when each of the wars in this century has ended, and the initial speculative seesawing has finished, the stock market invariably has gone on to new all-time peaks. Happiness and prosperity have descended on those who bought and stayed with quality growth stocks. It may be surprising to some to learn that wars, which are reported to be bad for children and other living things, are also damaging to securities—and that the news that the smart money on Wall Street wants each day is the same news sought by those whose yearning for peace has a more spiritual base. Yet it may be comforting, in assessing this unsung saga of the peacemongers of Wall Street, to realize that Karl Marx couldn't figure out the stock market, either.

CHAPTER XIII

It's Either a Triple Top
or a Spike Bottom

The basic thrust of the last few chapters has been on helping you to pick winning stocks by recognizing the kind of fundamentals to which Wall Street pays attention and by being aware of the sort of news that, by affecting either the general economic picture or the earnings of specific companies, can make those fundamentals change. All this has been submitted in absolute good faith, in the belief that this is not only the way that most people have made the most money in Wall Street but that it is virtually the only way the average beginner can do so. I would be remiss, however, if I did not point out to you that there is a cult in the financial community that would regard all the foregoing as unmitigated balderdash. To the members of this cult—the technical analysts—the fundamentals of a company are as irrelevant as the number of freckles on the nose of the president's daughter. All that really matters, they will tell you, is the pattern on the chart.

A committed technical analyst is a wondrous beast to behold. Immersed in his arcane graphs, muttering incomprehensibly about "moving averages" and "resistance levels," he clumps around a self-contained forest in which all you need to know about stock prices is . . . stock prices. That the pattern of the past predicts the pattern of the future is the code by which he swears. And if on any particular occasion it doesn't happen to work, why, he just swears some more. And draws a new chart.

I enjoy technical analysts, as I enjoy all religious fanatics. They are stimulating and provocative, but I'm not sure I would want to turn my money over to them. For one thing, like wild-eyed theologians, they have a tendency to be disputatious as to which among them has the precise inspired word. Show five technical analysts the same record of a stock's recent movement, and all too often you are likely to wind up with seven explanations (since at least two will be smart enough to hedge). Their argument will be not just about what lies ahead, where honest men will always differ, but on what pattern the stock has already formed. You see, the trouble is that the beautifully symmetrical charts that appear in books are seldom duplicated in the actual, erratic behavior of stocks on Wall Street. So it all depends on how you draw your own lines over the jagged performance of reality, and when one man's "triple top" is likely to be the next fellow's "spike bottom," the typical small investor is apt to be rendered not only bewildered but inert.

Beyond this internal uncertainty in a cult that pretends to preach certainty, there are authentic grounds for skepticism about the value of all those expensive charts and graphs as predictors in the first place. Recent studies with a computer at Princeton University's Financial Research Center are instructive. A group of professors under the initial leadership of Oskar Morgenstern, a brilliant mathematician who appropriately had previously gained world recognition for his work on the theory of games, set out to determine whether there really was anything much to the game of "technical analysis"—which they defined as the use of patterns of past stock prices to predict future prices. The professors fed their computer stock-price records going back to the start of the century, then embellished the diet by constructing equations to express the various theories of technical analysis. When these equations were duly checked against the actual results that had been put into the computer earlier, the message of the figures was unhedged; in the words of Professor Burton G. Malkiel, "There's nothing in past patterns of stock-price movements to allow predictions of future prices."

The reporting of these findings in the New York *Times* was naturally unsettling to hard-core technical analysts, especially when another professor involved in the study, Richard E. Quandt, was quoted as remarking that "technology is akin to astrology and every bit as scientific." One leading investment survey, terming the Financial Research Center a "menace," bought a one-third page ad in the *Times* to fume at what it called "'The Greater Fool Theory,' Summa Cum Laude, from Princeton." But the professors, whose basic mission has been to single out which fundamental economic factors truly do foreshadow stock prices,

were unrepentant in their rejection of the market technicians'
charts-and-graphs approach. Professor Quandt later told *The
Princeton Alumni Weekly* that he believed the problem was that
"if you look at stock prices, there is no signal of when a particular stock is a top and when it's a bottom; while there may be a lot
of noise in a stock-market price series, there is no signal." And his
colleague, Professor William J. Baumol, concluded, "A growing
literature shows that by every test, stock prices approximate a
'random walk.' If you'd known every stock pattern from 1945 to
1960, you could not have used them in any way to predict stock
price patterns in the 1960s."

If technical analysis turns out, then, to be an imperfect ouija
board, is it a game you will never want to play? Not necessarily;
you ought at least to be aware of some of its basic precepts, if
only because so many investors do believe in them and guide
their market behavior accordingly. Knowing what they are likely
to do can be helpful, especially if you decide to move in the opposite direction. Besides, technical analysis that goes beyond the
bare facts of stock-price performance may provide a shorthand
method of reflecting or foreshadowing underlying economic
trends. In that respect it gets away from the simplistic notion
that a stock's past will tell you its future and closer to the fundamentals that purist practitioners profess to spurn. And, finally,
many successful investors combine the best of both worlds by using fundamental analysis to pick their stocks and technical analysis to decide when to buy them.

First you ought to know some of the lingo, an accomplishment
that will impress the devil out of your spouse, and possibly your
broker. Let's start with some easy ones that every good chartist
takes with his morning coffee: "uptrend," "downtrend," "resistance level" and "breakout." When a stock is in an uptrend, it
will regularly move to new highs—and each time it comes down,
it will stop at a higher level than in its previous decline. A downtrend would be the reverse: Each new low point is lower than
the last, and each rally attempt fails to match the previous surge.
An unalloyed uptrend or downtrend should be obvious enough
—but, alas, few stocks ever perform quite so predictably. They
zig, they zag, they spurt, they falter in a most frustrating fashion;
it's confusing to technical analysts, some of whom are likely to
pronounce an uptrend as broken at exactly the moment that some

others are diagnosing it as intact. As with all chart patterns, these trends are usually best seen in retrospect.

A "resistance level" would be that point on the chart where a stock would normally be expected to stop falling or rising, whichever it had been doing. (Some technicians prefer to use "resistance" only for an upward level, favoring the term "support area" for the point at which a stock is supposed to stop falling. Others use "support" and "resistance" interchangeably for the downside level where a rally is expected to begin.) Let's say a stock had gone from 20 to 23, fallen back to 20, risen to 24, fallen back to 20 and was now selling for 24½. The resistance, or support, level would appear to be 20, and technicians would assume that, the next time the stock fell that low, buyers would step in and prevent it from falling farther.

Unless they didn't, of course—in which case we would have a "breakout." A breakout occurs when the resistance level is pierced, and technicians assume the stock will probably continue in the direction it has broken. A breakout on the downside may lead to further selling by chartists who think the stock has gone sour, and a breakout on the upside—when the stock moves though a resistance level where it has previously been stymied —is likely to attract further buying by chartists who regard this as a sign of strength. Thus in both cases the chartists are taking actions that will, in the short run, help to fulfill their own prophecies. And if the pattern doesn't last for long, if it appears that their guess was wrong—why, then, they will simply say the stock has had a "reversal" and is now, quite naturally, moving in the other direction.

Now, you're ready for the big time: a "head-and-shoulders top." Just as "resistance level" and "breakout" turned out to have nothing to do with sex or prisons, so "head-and-shoulders top" does not refer to the amount of dandruff on the analyst's scalp. His chart will, however, look roughly like a man's head and two shoulders. The first shoulder represents a rally, the head represents a second rally attempt that went even higher and the second shoulder covers the third move of the stock—in which it did not get as high as the head. When it comes down this time, the theorists believe, it will keep on coming. The "top" was made by the head, as was demonstrated by the failure of the next rally to match it, and if the charts are right the stock won't stop falling until it reaches the navel. (There is also, anatomy to the contrary, a "head-and-shoulders bottom." In that case there is a drop to a new low, followed by a drop to an even lower low, followed by a third descent that goes only as far down as the first. Chartists will assume that the second drop reached bottom, and that the stock—by refusing to go that low the next time—is now heading higher. Back to the navel, maybe. Perhaps it will help if you think of the man as standing on his head.) In any event, these formations also tend to be much more clear-cut in a textbook than in the real world, where they become most evident long after they have occurred.

As you will have gathered, "tops" are bad and "bottoms" are good (no, dear, we're talking about stocks), in that each signals a reversal of the stock's previous direction. So let's conclude this little discussion of dirty pictures with a dramatic example of each. A "triple top" resembles a picket fence: three moves up to the same point, and then back again. If a stock (or a stock average; analysts would just as soon think big) fails on a third straight rally attempt to break into new high ground, chartists will assume that it is too puny for the effort and is consequently riding for a sickening fall. A "spike bottom" (I do hope your mother's not listening) offers the opposite prognosis; it is a sharp move downward climaxing a steady fall, an emotional sell-off so massive that it brings in the bargain hunters and starts a successful rally. I could draw all these charts for you, and you would undoubtedly conclude that making money in Wall Street was an automatic cinch—until you started wondering why all the market's technical analysts were not riding about in limousines. Real life does tend, regrettably, to be more complicated.

A dedicated technical analyst will, of course, go far beyond the mere examination of lines on a chart. He will, for example, add in such considerations as volume—the amount of trading that accompanied each move. Volume, as it happens, is closely watched by practically all the market's traders (as opposed to investors) because of the clues it affords to the market's essential sentiments. If the market is rising and volume is heavy, it means that the great bulk of investors is optimistic—while an increase on light volume might be written off as purely technical and unconvincing. The same would be true on the downside; if volume is heavier on the days the market is declining, this would be taken as a strongly negative signal. Similarly with an individual stock, an upward move on rising volume would be viewed as more significant than one that occurred without extraordinary activity. A stock will draw attention simply by appearing on the daily list of most actively traded issues; even if its price should be unchanged, many investors will get interested on the assumption that something must be going on. (Yes, but is the allegedly smart money selling or buying, liquidating or accumulating? Ay, there's the rub.) Traditionally, more heed is paid to a stock that is behaving uncharacteristically; we expect Polaroid to be volatile, but if Bethlehem Steel begins to go up two or three points a day on high volume, traders will be intrigued and begin to wonder what's gotten into the old girl. Still another field for volume analysis is a comparison of the total daily trading on the New York and American stock exchanges. Since the issues listed on the American Stock Exchange tend to be (with many exceptions) lower-priced and more speculative in character, many analysts regard it as a caution signal in a rising market when volume on the Amex gets higher than 40 per cent of that on the New York Exchange. They take this to be an indication that the speculative froth is rising, and that the time may be approaching to take your profits and run.

There is a danger, I think, that inexperienced investors will become mesmerized by these and other trading techniques, some of which will be discussed in the next chapter. In buying any stock, there are two considerations—what's it worth and what will people pay for it—but the conflict may be more apparent than authentic. If there are fundamental reasons for believing that earnings will improve, the stock is unlikely forever to blush unseen—so its technical pattern will improve. And if a stock is running wildly upward, without fundamental underpinnings, a crash is foreordained—no matter how many "upside breakouts" its pattern now reveals. Plainly, one of the nicest things you can know about a stock is that it is going up—but if that is the only reason for its attraction, you had better be nimble when it comes time to bail out.

Amateur traders who haven't learned this lesson get badly burned each year. And the average inexperienced (or experienced!) investor has no business playing with this kind of matches in the first place, unless he is willing to admit that his instinct is purely for the casino. Wall Street's refuse bin is clogged with those who thought they could outsmart the market or pick the bottom or top on an individual stock. As a timing tool, in helping you to know where the market fashions are at this moment, technical analysis can have some marginal utility. But I have listened to, and followed the reports of, many a technical analyst and "systems player," and while they were almost all super-self-confident, the most generous comment I can objectively make about any of them would be this: He was sometimes right.

For the average investor the best advice would still be to detach himself from the hysteria of the daily tape. Without overriding reason, he may not want to "fight the tape" by buying when stocks are tumbling mercilessly and without apparent end. But such trends are less common than situations of indecision and confusion, and when those occur he should steel himself to accept the premise that the best time for him to buy a good stock is probably right now. Recall Jacob Schiff's sly declaration that the secret of his success was that he never tried to buy at the bottom or sell at the top. If you have found a stock that appears good for the long haul, then climb aboard, keep a close watch on the engineer, but don't jump off the first time any other passengers disembark. It's entirely possible that you will be the one who gets to the Emerald City.

Should you want to become better acquainted with the sort of indicators that are watched by professional traders, however, you will find in Appendix F the makeup of the "Wall Street Week" Technical Market Index, which was developed one season by Robert J. Nurock, a perceptive broker for Merrill Lynch, Pierce, Fenner & Smith. The index, which is concerned solely with over-all market direction, lists ten different indicators whose behavior is supposed to offer clues to possible changes in the three- to six-month trend of prices (the so-called intermediate trend). The underlying notion is that all trends are likely to go to extremes, and that, when many short-term traders are smiling and buying, the smart short-term trader will start to frown and sell. Similarly, when the selling itself becomes excessive, the technician will decide that a rally is imminent and it's time to buy. Sometimes, in the short run, this conviction about perennial mass error is accurate; sometimes, alas, it is not.

The idea of having a ten-part index (rather than just one magical litmus test) is that while any component might on occasion be misleading, the combination should prove a reliable gauge of the technical strength of the market. I have no doubt that this is true. As for actually predicting usefully for you what stock prices are going to be next week or next season, however, the only guarantee I can offer is this: It will sometimes be right.

CHAPTER XIV

The Kid's Got Great Technique

When a chart resistance level on, say, the Dow Jones Industrial Average shows, in the crunch, about as much resistance as a nymphomaniac, the disappointed disciple of technical analysis may be tempted to sue for nonsupport. Though his grief be as moving as his averages, he has no case. Santa Claus doesn't live on Wall Street, either, and there is no one technique that is always guaranteed success. Books have been written about such alleged techniques; the authors, all of whom naturally could gain unheard-of riches simply by following their own advice, must surely be listed among the world's true philanthropists. My own impression is that, given the right kind of market and the perfect conditions, their advice sometimes works. You ought, though, to know some of the techniques that serious market students have developed to increase their wealth, in the thought that you might want to adapt one or more of them to your own investment program from time to time. If you keep them in perspective, they can be useful tools.

Let's begin with what is perhaps the most familiar, and most misunderstood, of all market techniques: the "stop-loss order." Some of the confusion can be cleared up simply by understanding what the different kinds of orders really mean. When you call your broker and just tell him to buy or sell so many shares of a certain stock, he transmits what is known as a "market order." One of his firm's representatives at the New York Stock Exchange (if that's where the stock is traded) takes your order and goes to the place on the floor where that stock is bought and sold. (There is only one such place for each stock.) There he will inquire cautiously, "How's XYZ?" The answer might be "42¼ to

42¾," or more likely just "¼ to ¾." This tells your floor broker, who has not yet disclosed whether he has come to buy or to sell on your behalf, that the stock is offered for purchase at $42.75 a share and that buyers, in turn, are willing to pay only $42.25 a share. Let's assume your order was to buy 100 shares of XYZ at the market. He might say "⅝ for 100," disclosing that he is a buyer rather than a seller and that he is trying to get you a slightly lower price per share: $42.625 instead of the $42.75 that sellers are demanding. If no one bites, he will have to meet the best available "asked" price, $42.75, since your market order requires him to execute it immediately at the best price going. More often than not, this is how you will want to buy and sell stock—because it guarantees that, when you choose to act, action will be taken and you will get the most desirable deal currently available.

But there are other kinds of orders as well, so let's stick to the hypothetical situation just described for XYZ stock and see how these alternate methods work. Suppose you want to buy those 100 shares of XYZ only if the price comes down a bit—say, to $40 a share. Your broker will enter for you a "buy-limit order" for 100 shares at $40. This order will be entered in a little book kept by the "specialist" in the stock, so that your own floor representative does not have to stand around waiting for the stock to fall—which could be minutes, weeks or never. Your order will not be executed until somebody offers to sell 100 shares of XYZ at 40. Even then you could lose out—that is, not get the stock—if other orders were entered ahead of yours. There might, in that case, be one or two sales at 40, and then the stock would begin to rise again. If, instead, it kept falling, your order might be executed at a lower price than that to which you were committed; you might, for example, have to pay only $39.50 a share. But you would never, under any circumstances, pay more than your "limit."

A "sell-limit order" works the same way. Suppose you own 100 shares of XYZ and are willing to sell it if it goes to $45 a share. Into the book goes your order, and it will not be executed unless and until some would-be purchaser bids 45—or higher. There are two possible twists on these "limit orders": (1) If you are just haggling a little bit, and want to take action today in any event, you can have your order marked for "execution at the close"—in which case you will get the best available deal at the end of the day, even if your limit has not been reached by then. (2) You can stick to your limit but cause your order to be withdrawn automatically if no one wants to play ball at that price. In placing the order you should tell your broker whether you want it to be good for today only, good this week ("GTW"), good this month ("GTM") or good till canceled ("GTC"). Your broker, in turn, should send you a written confirmation of your order, so that you are not taken by surprise four months later when your long-forgotten GTC order is executed while you are cruising through the Bay of Bengal.

Now that you are an authority on the use of limit orders, you are ready to enter the somewhat-trickier domain of "stop-loss" and "stop" orders. Suppose you bought that XYZ stock at $42.75 a share and, while you naturally hope and expect that it will promptly go to $142.75 a share, you want to protect yourself against a big loss should things turn against you. You could enter a "stop-loss order" at, say, $38.50 a share. This kind of order can be entered at the same time you buy the stock, or any time thereafter. If (bad cess be upon it) XYZ ever trades as low as 38½, your stop-loss order is instantly transformed into a market order—and you get the best deal available at the time. Please note, because so many investors do not, that this does not—repeat not—guarantee that you will be able to sell your stock no lower than $38.50 a share. After that first trade at 38½, which was required to trigger your order, the best bid may be something less—and that's what you will get. This is a critical difference between a stop-loss order and a sell-limit order. In the first case, you will definitely be sold out, though possibly at a lower price than that for which you bargained. In the second, if the stock cannot be sold at the price you set, it will not be sold—even if the price starts falling drastically.

Stop-loss orders should sometimes really be called "profit-protection orders." Here's why: Let's say your fondest dreams were realized, and XYZ instead of falling to $38.50 or below started to rise and show you a profit. You might then use a stop-loss order to prevent that profit from evaporating. As the price of the stock kept rising, so might your stop-loss orders. When the stock sold at 55, you might enter a stop-loss order at 50; when it reached 80, your stop-loss point might have risen to 75, and so on.

Judiciously used, stop-loss orders can be useful in saving you from a major loss or locking in at least part of a profit. But don't assume that they are the magic answer for every investor every time. First, as noted, a selling wave might make it impossible for you to get the price at which you have set your stop-loss. Your stock will be sold anyhow, at whatever is bid at the time. Second, the New York Stock Exchange sometimes bans stop orders for particular stocks (and suspends those already entered). It takes this step when the stock has been especially volatile. The fear is that a price decline could trigger a succession of stop-loss orders, each one lower than the last, and thus send the stock on a sickening plummet. (If, in the above case of XYZ, your stop-loss order at 38½ was in fact executed at 38, it in turn would set off all the stop-loss orders at that level, and so on down the descending line.) The market's name for this unpleasant phenomenon is "snowballing," and you can guess who is most likely to get the snowball in his face. Third, particularly with fast-moving stocks of the glamour variety, you are always in danger of being "whipsawed"—that is, seeing your stop-loss order touched off and then seeing the stock quickly move up again. In such cases a policy of benign neglect would have been more profitable. Fourth, even in the event of the major market disasters against which stop-loss orders are presumably intended to guard, they can be counterproductive. A friend of mine who was out in the Far East in 1963 had stop-loss orders on all his stocks. When President Kennedy was assassinated and the market took a fierce immediate plunge, every one of his stocks was sold automatically. The market then recovered its nerves, turned around almost immediately and went right up past its previous level. But by the time the news reached my unfortunate friend, all he could do was get back in with 80 shares where he had formerly had 100.

So stop-loss orders should generally be marked "handle with care." If you want some protection while you're off on vacation drinking ouzo in Piraeus, then enter your order and hope that you have thereby guarded against a possible substantial loss. But trying to play the game by inches, through cleverly chosen stop-loss orders, is a method that tends to trip up even the most experienced traders. Brokers report that surprisingly few cus-

tomers ever use these orders effectively. The average investor
who is really worried about the price of one of his stocks more
often than not ought to go ahead and sell it—and forget it. Professional traders rely on stop-loss orders far less than you might
suspect, because they recognize their very real limitations. If you
or (lucky you) your broker is paying attention, you won't need
them often, either.

Finally, let's take a look at the "buy stop order," which is a
sort of stop-loss order in reverse. This is a favorite device of our
old friends the chartists. In the case of XYZ, now available for
purchase at $42.75 a share, a devoted follower of technical
analysis might enter an order to buy at 50¼, or $50.25, a share.
Why would anyone be so foolish? It's all in the charts. The charts
might show a resistance level just below 50, meaning that if the
stock managed to "break out" above that level it was certain to
keep on going till at least, say, 58—where it would encounter a
new resistance level. So our chartist enters a buy stop order at
50¼, and if the stock ever does trade that high his order immediately becomes a market order to buy at the lowest price
offered (which might then be higher than 50¼). Sometimes a
stock, after such a breakout, does indeed keep marching upward,
and in those cases the placer of this buy stop order congratulates
himself on his brilliant technical acumen and pockets a nice little
trading profit. Sometimes, however, the stock that has just
"broken out" defiantly turns around and marches downhill again
—in which case the unfrocked shrewdie of an investor may be
inclined to wonder why the devil he didn't buy it at $42.75 in
the first place.

A discussion of the different kinds of orders available to the
market trader leads logically to the one kind of order that seems
to excite the most mystery and controversy: the "short sale."
The principle behind the short sale is that a free market is built
on differences of opinion, that this is what makes the auction
process valid and that hence it should be just as legitimate to
make money betting that a stock will go down in price as to make
money betting that it will go up. The short sale provides a way to
make money when a stock falls.

Here's how it works: You decide that XYZ, currently selling
for $42.75 a share, is heading lower. You don't happen to own

the stock, which is comforting in view of your low appraisal of
its worth, but you decide to make some money as it falls. So you
tell your broker you want to sell 100 shares of XYZ short. It's
then up to your broker to lend you the stock you want to sell. If
he can get hold of 100 shares of XYZ, and he usually can, you then
make a sale at the market—which theoretically brings you $4,275,
minus commissions (all on paper; you can't just pick it up and
fly to Rio). In fact, you have to pay your broker in cash whatever percentage of that sum is required by the current "margin,"
or credit, rules; in the past, this has been anywhere between 40
and 100 per cent of the total price. The rest of the total consti-
tutes a loan from your broker, on which you pay interest. Now
you sit back and, you hope, watch that overpriced stock tumble.
If, as you expected, it goes down, say, 10 points, you may decide
to close out your transaction and take your well-earned profit.
Since you began the short sale by selling the stock instead of
buying it, you naturally wind it up by buying instead of selling.
You "buy back" the stock at $32.75 a share (returning it to the
broker from whom you borrowed), and you have a nice $1,000
profit, minus commissions and interest on the loan.

Now what could be wrong with that? Well, to listen to some
people you would think the entire technique was an invention of
the devil. Some of their distaste is probably attributable to the
unsavory uses to which short selling was put by shady cabals in
the bad old days before market regulation. But even more, I
suspect, can be traced to the emotional gap between short selling
and the optimistic American temperament. To gamble on a decline seems to violate much of our tradition, and even many who
are convinced that a stock is overpriced find themselves unable
to act on that conviction by selling short.

This attitude is reflected in the strange array of rules with
which short selling is circumscribed. Whereas it is considered
perfectly proper to buy a stock while it is rising, it is forbidden
to sell it short while it is falling. When you sell short, your broker
must mark the order as a short sale—and it will not be executed
if the stock is declining. There are only two times a short sale can
be executed—when the price is an "uptick" (that is, one eighth of
a point or more higher than the last previous sale) or when it is
an "even tick" (price unchanged from the last previous sale) in
cases where the last previous change in price was upward. In

other words, buyers can accelerate a move upward, but short sellers are forbidden to accelerate a move downward. The purpose of this Securities and Exchange Commission regulation was to prevent market manipulation by bands of intriguers seeking artificially to drive down the price of a stock. But there can be scant doubt that one of its effects is to make the market just a little less free.

A similar discrimination against those un-American enough to try to make money on a decline is shown by the Internal Revenue Service. The IRS would much rather see you being "long" a stock (that is, buying it and owning it like a properly optimistic investor should) than "short" it, and it enforces this moral judgment in the only way it knows how—through higher taxes. Hence if a stock is held for more than six months and then sold at a profit, this profit is taxed at the much lower rate assigned to long-term capital gains. But a similar profit on a short sale, even if you waited ten years to buy back the stock you had borrowed, is always considered short-term—and thus is taxed at the higher rates that apply to ordinary income.

With morality, patriotism and the tax man all ranged against you, why would anyone have the temerity to sell short? Well, the truth is that few people do, even in periods of intense market declines. Short selling normally accounts for only about 7 per cent of all New York Stock Exchange transactions, and most of that is done by the specialists—who are required to sell stock when no one else wants to—and by professional traders.

Beyond all the other disadvantages, selling a stock short involves one risk that is clearly greater than buying the stock: You can lose more money. Here's why: If you buy 100 shares of a stock at 50, paying $5,000 plus commissions, the absolute most you can lose—even if the company's treasurer absconds to Brazil and the stock drops to 0—is $5,000 plus commissions. Now let's suppose you sold the stock short at 50, and instead of falling it kept on rising—and got to 150. You're now losing (would you believe) $10,000, and there's no set limit on how much further the stock may rise—and thus how much more you may lose. When you buy, the most you can lose is your total investment; but when you sell short, look out.

This is why short sellers are by tradition an exceptionally jittery lot, prone to nervous glances over the shoulder and to panicky executions. Those who do it successfully tend to make firm rules for themselves to minimize the emotional factors. They like to get the odds in their favor by shorting only stocks that look bad from the standpoints of both fundamental and technical analysis. They thus avoid shorting strong stocks, even if they are bearish on the market as a whole. Other no-no's include "thin" stocks (that is, those for which there is only a limited number of shares available) and those that have already attracted a large amount of short selling. And they often try to minimize the risk of outlandish losses by entering a "buy stop-loss order." This differs from a buy stop order only in its purpose; in both cases the effect is to enter a bid to buy XYZ stock immediately after it sells at a certain price higher than its present price. For example, at the same time he sold XYZ short at 42¾, the customer might enter a buy stop-loss order at 47¾, thereby hoping to limit his maximum possible loss to about $500 plus commissions. For unlike the investor who buys a stock, the short seller can never really relax when things are going against him even temporarily. As the old Wall Street adage wisely counsels, "He who sells what isn't his'n/Has to buy back or go to prison."

Even if you have decided by now that you would no more embark on short selling than take up skydiving, there is one other related technique of which you ought to be aware—and that is known as going "short against the box." That is what happens when, instead of selling a stock you don't happen to own, you sell short a stock that is already in your possession.

Now why in the world would anyone want to do that? Two common reasons: (1) An investor might want to defer paying taxes until the following year. In December he sells short against the box a stock on which he has a profit. The following month he closes out the short sale not by buying new stock but by delivering the stock he has owned all along. The gain on the old stock is taxable in the new year, but the investor has locked in the profit he had in December. Note that, while this puts off the paying of taxes on the gain, it does not reduce them. The status of the gain is determined by how long the stock had been held on the day the investor went short against the box; if that period was less than six months and one day, the gain is short-term and fully taxable whenever he decides to take it. (2) An investor with a big profit in a stock may want to trade against this profit. Let's say he owns 100 shares of a stock that has gone from 50 to 75. He's a little worried about the stock, and he wants to assure himself of the gain he already has. So he sells short against the box 100 shares of the stock. Now let's suppose the stock falls from 75 to 60, and he begins to think it's a bargain again. He could close out his short sale by delivering his old stock to his broker and still have that old 25-point profit. (The 15-point loss in the stock he owned, as the price declined from 75 to 60, is exactly made up for by a 15-point profit on the short sale.) Or he could get fancy, and cover the short sale by buying new stock at 60—and holding on to the old stock he bought at 50. Then if, as he suspected, the stock began to rise again, he could have had his cake (protection against the decline from 75 to 60) and eaten it too (making a brand-new profit the second time the stock moved from 60 to 75).

In any event, selling short against the box involves no risk; it freezes the profit-and-loss situation at the moment the transaction occurs, and there is never any concern about a call to put up more "margin" money because any adverse developments on the "short" side will be precisely balanced by an improvement in the "long" position, and vice versa. In this sense going short against the box is Wall Street's version of suspended animation.

The stock market offers all techniques to all men, of course, and hence many investors who would never entertain even a mild flirtation with short selling themselves will pay close attention to the activities of those who simply love the gal. This spectator interest is engendered by the belief that the volume of short sales provides a useful technical barometer of what lies ahead for the market. Each month the New York Stock Exchange publishes a report on the total "short interest"—that is, the number of shares sold short and not yet "bought back," or covered. It counts all sales of securities that the sellers do not own or that are completed by the delivery of borrowed securities. Now, logic might tell you that a report that the short interest has risen dramatically over the previous month would be taken as a negative indication—a sign that the brilliant money men of Wall Street, who clearly must be right, think the market is going lower. Well, logic would be wrong, for this is another case of the stock market's penchant for reverse psychology. When the mass of men thinks one thing, so this reasoning goes, it must surely be time for a change. In the case of the short interest, there is a practical consideration as well. A high total signals a large amount of reserve buying power to cushion any decline. Everyone who sells short must eventually buy back, and as stock prices fall and profits begin to appear on the short side, this reserve buying power flows back into the market—and ironically begins to support the very stocks at which it was aimed. This is why seasoned short sellers avoid those stocks that have already attracted a large number of their brethren. It is also why traders read the small print of the New York Stock Exchange report to watch significant changes in the short interest of individual stocks. A sharply rising short interest in a particular stock will draw the same interpretation that it would have for the market as a whole—that there is now a nice comfy pillow under that stock, and it is more likely to go up than down.

Sophisticated investors also look for other clues in the short interest figures. For example, any time a stock is flying high, soaring upward at a dazzling pace, a step-up in short selling of the stock should be expected. Many people just don't believe that kind of good news; they assume that the price has been recklessly inflated, and that what goes up that fast must inevitably come down. Sometimes they are right, although as we have just seen their activity may have the opposite result: Investors will see that there is substantial buying power stacked up at a slightly lower price, and thus will assume that it's safe to buy the high flier even at its present elevated altitude. But now take another kind of situation, in which heavy short selling suddenly appears in a stock that has not risen in price. Investors will suspect that this is one of those occasions when a technical indicator offers a tip-off to a fundamental development. They will wonder whether some people have not learned some bad news about the company, and they will tend to regard its stock as a newly dangerous holding. So the figures, which newspapers report each month, are worth watching.

Technical analysts, those demon scientists whose ways we charted in Chapter XIII, often give special attention to "odd-lot short sales"—that is, to the total of short sales involving fewer than 100 shares each. This is an extension of the reverse-psychology theory, which holds that the most bullish indicators of sentiment are those that show the most widespread expectation of a decline.

Hence it is felt to be favorable to an upward move when short selling increases dramatically and when margin buyers use substantially less borrowing power than brokers are willing to make available to them. All this indicates that people are getting scared—and since emotional traders are usually wrong, the theory goes, the market will probably head upward. A theory based on contempt for the judgment of most speculators will naturally intensify its scorn for speculators of small means, and hence the interest in the odd-lot short sales figures. Some experienced traders regard an increase in such sales as among the best indicators of what is known as an "oversold" market—one in which selling has proceeded too rapidly and an upward correction is due. In a real bear market, such short selling by small investors may increase from perhaps 2,000 or 3,000 shares a day to as many as 40,000 shares a day, and when that happens the cynical old-timers will take it as a signal that light is about to appear at the end of the tunnel.

Over the years this has been a more reliable indicator of the market outlook than the far more publicized question of whether all odd-lot investors were buying more than they were selling. The wise guys like to assume that the little man is always wrong, so when the ratio of odd-lot buying to selling increases, they take it as a signal to sell. But the odd-lot investor's traditional bullishness has made him a lot of money in the course of the century, certainly a great deal more than perennial bearishness would have made him. In recent years, moreover, his behavior has been a poor guide to market ups and downs. There was some very sound bargain-hunting behind his decision to become a net buyer of stocks in May 1970 at the market low, and to continue accumulating during the next two months. But then odd-lotters as a group went on an exceptionally extended, years-long buyers strike that persisted despite strong market rallies. The odd-lotter's decision to remain a seller, in good markets and bad, reflected the negativism felt by many small investors and was ascribed variously to his jolting experiences in 1969–70, to rising commission costs and to a feeling that the market neither cultivated the Little Man nor was an area where he could operate to his advantage. I happen to think that this attitude was incorrect, and that the intelligent small investor has magnificent money-making opportunities in Wall Street, but there is no question that the contemptuous attitude in much of the industry contributed to this exodus. These extraneous factors, however, diminished the predictive accuracy of over-all odd-lot activity.

The most basic of all speculative techniques, and one about which you will have to make a decision for yourself, is the use of margin—that is, borrowing from your broker part of the cash needed to buy your stocks. Your thrifty ancestors might have been appalled by the idea, but the ethics of Polonius are not necessarily the ethics of a society that already puts everything else from cribs to cremation on the credit card. So you ought at least to know what the margin procedure entails.

The reason you buy on margin is that you can thereby control more stock than if you paid strictly cash. How much more depends on the Federal Reserve Board, which since October 15, 1934, has regulated the percentage that your broker can lend you. The Fed's motives are benign, intended to save you from another Great Crash like that of October 29, 1929, when there was no government regulation of margin and speculators piled on debt so excessive that the first signs of trouble touched off a catastrophe. The word "margin" refers to the amount of cash you have to put up, not to the amount you borrow (many people get it the wrong way around), and since the start of government regulation the required margin has been as low as 40 per cent (1937–45) and as high as 100 per cent (1946–47), which meant effectively that your broker couldn't lend you anything at all. Over the years the average margin requirement has been 60 per cent, but it has changed frequently. When the Fed decides that a booming stock market is threatening to run away with itself, it contracts the supply of credit by raising the margin requirement (the technical device is known as Federal Reserve Regulation T). Equally, when it wants to loosen things up and help the market along, it lowers the margin requirement and thereby automatically hands more buying power to all investors with margin accounts. When prices rise in ensuing months, as they usually do, even the cash customers benefit.

To show you how a margin account works, let's assume that the current margin requirement is 50 per cent (your broker can give you today's figure), and that you have decided to put this technique to work for yourself. Your motive is clear: There's a stock you believe in, it's selling for $100 a share and you have $5,000 to invest. If you pay cash, you can get 50 shares. If you buy on margin, you can get 100 shares. If you paid cash and the stock doubled, you would make $5,000. If you bought on margin and the stock doubled, you would make $10,000. How long, you begin to wonder, has this been going on?

Well, long enough for certain rules to be established. The first rule is that your initial margin payment must be at least $2,000, even if that is more than 50 per cent of your purchase. The second is that your "equity" in the stock—its current market value less the amount you owe your broker—must never go lower than $2,000. The third is that this equity must never fall below 25 per cent of the current market value of the stock, a minimum that most brokers have independently raised to 30 per cent. If either of these last two rules is violated, you will get what is known as a "margin call"—a demand that you immediately deposit more cash or acceptable securities in your account.

Let's see how this might work in the example with which we started: a purchase of 100 shares of a $100 stock on 50 per cent margin. You would have had to put up $5,000 cash and would have simultaneously incurred a debt of $5,000 with your broker. Your account will be billed monthly for interest on this debt, which you may find irritating, but the consolation is that Uncle Sam allows you to deduct the interest on your income tax. The size of that debt—$5,000—does not change. If the stock goes down 10 points, it's all your loss but you still owe your broker only $5,000. If it goes up 10 points, the profit is all yours and you still owe your broker only $5,000.

What margin customers have in mind is that the stock will indeed go up, thereby dwarfing the amount of the loan. If the $100 stock doubles, 100 shares are worth $20,000, and even after paying off his $5,000 loan the margin customer has tripled his $5,000 investment. But trouble can develop if the stock perversely continues to sink. After a 10-point drop, 100 shares of the stock bought at $100 are worth $9,000. Deduct the amount you owe your broker, $5,000, and you have an equity of $4,000—still comfortably above 30 per cent of the current market value, $9,000. But suppose the stock doesn't stop falling until it hits $60 a share (it does happen, you know); now the current market value of 100 shares is only $6,000. Deduct your $5,000 debt and you find an equity of only $1,000, well below the minimum requirements. In fact, before it reached that point the customer would have received a margin call, and if he couldn't come up with the assets to meet it, his account would be summarily sold out.

So now we can understand the scary aspects of margin accounts. As with all attempts to extend your funds by using other people's money, both the potential risks and the potential rewards are magnified. If your stocks go up, you not only have a bigger profit but—without having actually to sell the stock and take your profit—you get the right to buy still more stock. Juicy accounts have been written about how this so-called pyramiding technique has enabled great fortunes to rise from tiny investment acorns. Your broker will always be eager to calculate for you how much new "buying power" you are acquiring each day in a rising market. But if your stocks are going down, your losses will be commensurately greater than they would have been if your purchases had been strictly cash. And if the drop is precipitate, you face the danger of a margin call at the very moment you are least prepared to meet it. Thus you could be turned into a sucker at both ends—tempted to buy high when new buying power is created, and compelled to sell low when the margin call comes.

It's not surprising, then, that about nine out of ten stock-market investors decide that margin accounts are not for them. They sleep better at night knowing that, win or lose, their purchases are fully paid. (Lewis Gilbert, the annual-meeting gadfly who has been a successful personal investor, once told me, "I never buy on margin. Therefore when they run into these summer storms or winter storms or what you will, you don't have to worry about them.") Certainly no beginning investor should even think about buying on margin. This is not a game for the unsophisticated. Most investors should accept their inability, economically or temperamentally, to accept the risks of margin trading—and should think no more about it. But I would hesitate to reject it entirely for an experienced investor who recognizes and can handle the double-edged challenge of a margin account. Brokers adore qualified margin customers, partly because they tend to be active far beyond their numbers or their assets. That's nice for the brokers, but it should not automatically frighten you away; sometimes it is possible for you both to make more money. Most short-term traders and other outright speculators probably do use margin, because their activities demand a certain self-confidence that would lead them to look on the brighter side of the risk–reward ratio. All short sellers must have margin accounts (and their accounts will be billed for any dividends that come due on the stock they borrowed). So must purchasers of "put and call" options, which we will discuss in Chapter XVIII.

It's possible for an investor who wants to dip his toe in this deep ocean to establish a separate margin account in addition to his cash account, and thus to try his luck with credit buying on a small scale. All stocks bought on margin must be left with the broker in "street name"—that is, in the broker's name and custody, not yours. You will have to sign an agreement authorizing the brokerage firm to "hypothecate" these securities, a snazzy word that may stir images of perverse orgies in a Hungarian forest—but actually just means to pledge them as collateral for bank loans. Your broker is now in good shape, you will undoubtedly be elated to know. He can sell your securities expeditiously if you fail to meet a margin call. He will charge you a little more than it costs him to borrow the money he lends you (how much more depending on such variables as the size of your loan and the amount of activity in your account; the bigger these be, the lower your interest rate should be). And he naturally will charge you the full commission on each purchase, including the shares for which he advanced the capital. What's more, the lending agreements signed by margin customers provide the prime source for the securities the broker passes on to other customers who want to sell short. (Usually, if you want to sell short, a broker will get the stock he lends you from one of the firm's margin accounts. If it is unavailable in any of these, he will turn to another firm or to an individual who makes a business of lending stock. Sometimes the stock cannot be easily borrowed, and you will have to pay a premium to get it.) Margin turns brokers into bankers—and that can be a profitable business, too.

Margin buying has been enjoying a fresh surge in popularity lately, with the total stock margin debt reaching record levels in 1972. One stimulant has been the broader use of the technique now being permitted. Formerly, only stocks listed on the New York Stock Exchange and a limited number of those listed on the American Stock Exchange could be purchased on partial credit.

Now, several hundred of the thousands of over-the-counter stocks are also eligible for margin; the list is determined by the Federal Reserve Board, and your broker can tell you whether a particular issue is eligible.

The change is justified since, contrary to myth, many well-established, financially sound and mature companies choose to remain on the over-the-counter market instead of moving on to the major exchanges. Interestingly, W. James Price, a partner and over-the-counter authority at Alex. Brown and Sons, told me that in the Fed's decisions as to which of these stocks should be on the margin list, "liquidity's the key, rather than quality." In other words, assurance is sought that the stock can be easily sold—that there is a sufficient number of brokers making a market in the stock and that the number and velocity of shares traded is adequate to make the quoted market price a realistic one. In this respect the criterion differs from that used when, from time to time, margin trading is banned in a specific issue traded on the New York Stock Exchange. That comes about when the board of governors decides that there has been too much speculative activity in a stock, that its price path has been excessively volatile and that investors need to be protected from themselves. When a stock goes on the "100 per cent margin" list, purchasers must put up the entire price in cash—a frightening experience for an inveterate margin trader. (If you bought the stock earlier, however, your own loan situation is not affected. Similarly, if you bought on margin when the required level was 50 per cent, and it is subsequently raised, the change is not retroactive and your account is unaffected except for future purchases.) The prohibition of further credit purchases of a stock should be taken as a flashing yellow light, not only by margin traders, but by those who have bought the security for cash.

One final tip about margin accounts: While the original example assumed, for simplicity's sake, that you were buying only one stock, in practice most margin customers buy more than one issue. In those cases the entire account is viewed as a whole; in other words, a sharp drop in one of your holdings would not bring a margin call as long as the total account showed sufficient equity. If one or more of your other issues had a profit, the loss might be offset sufficiently for you not to be harried for more collateral. Similarly, the account as a whole is figured in an advancing market to tell you how much new buying power you have acquired for possible new purchases—or, alternatively, how much actual cash money you can now withdraw from the account, should that happen to be your bag.

As practically everybody eventually has occasion to discover, the government's efforts to protect people from themselves are often counterproductive—and margin customers recently were added to the list of unintended victims. Until September 18, 1972, a margin customer could perform a "same-day substitution"—selling one or more stocks and buying others of equal market value —without putting up more cash, even if the equity in his account was below the current minimum. This provided a helpful opportunity to switch out of nasty losers. But then the Federal Reserve Board, apparently in a well-meaning attempt to reduce margin debt, ruled that same-day substitutions could no longer be made by customers whose equity was below 40 per cent. When these customers sold stock, they would receive only 30 per cent credit on their sales toward whatever margin was currently required for new purchases. No more full "dollar-for-dollar" substituting would be allowed them. Instead of strengthening margin accounts, however, as was the intention, what happened when stocks tumbled precipitously in 1973 was that many customers found themselves, in effect, "locked in" to heavily battered, highly speculative stocks—unable to switch to other, safer securities without steeply diminishing their total market position, and thus discouraged from seeking stability in a storm. Here's one case where both the broker and the customer would have benefited from less Big Brotherly help; with full substitutions allowed, the broker would have collected more commissions and the customer whose high fliers appeared mortally wounded would have been more inclined to make a timely bail-out. However benign its intentions, the Fed had provided still another potential booby trap for those who buy on margin.

Like stop-loss orders and selling short, margin trading is a fundamental stock-market technique of which the compleat investor ought to be cognizant. This does not mean that he will then want to utilize any or all of these techniques, but at least he will be aware of their possibilities and limitations. The average prudent investor will no more want to buy stocks on margin than he would want to scribble in the margin of a rare book.

Beginners, and those whose eyes are fixed firmly and properly on the long haul, should pay cash for their purchases and avoid the nightmares of the imprudent debtor. It's another case of knowing yourself, your assets, your abilities and your intentions. Those who can undertake that assessment and still conclude that they are ready for the heightened risks associated with margin trading will find that it amplifies their strengths and exaggerates their weaknesses. Self-discovery is less expensive when you are paying cash. If you and your broker are nonetheless determined to give margin a try, be prepared for an intense and perilous relationship that may well last till debt do you part.

While these are some of the major market techniques and theories, there are nearly as many other approaches to Wall Street as there are roads to Rome. There are some investors who swear by "book value"—what a share of stock is worth if you add up the company's tangible assets, subtract the debts and other liabilities it would have if it liquidated tomorrow, and divide by the number of shares outstanding. (Going by the book, as it were, is a pleasant exercise for your new pocket calculator. And particularly in a declining market, it can be comforting to know that your company has genuine assets behind it, even if its earning power is temporarily hobbled. But while book value can be figured with an accountant's exactness, the result regrettably may be a poor guide to the stock's future price; it's the prospective "market value" you really want to know, and even the finest computer on the planet may not help you there.)

There are those who get out their slide rules for "flow of funds analysis" (which attempts to determine the market's supply-demand situation by assessing whether institutional investors and individual margin traders are using up their potential buying power too quickly to sustain a rally), and there are those who claim to get their technical signals just by standing on the corner watching all the girls go by. The "hemline theory" holds that skirts and stocks tend to get too high at the same times, such as in 1929 and 1969, and that, when an excess amount of thigh decorates the boulevards, the wise investor will tear himself away long enough to telephone his broker and sell. I object to this theory on aesthetic grounds, and would point out that dowdy fashions didn't do much for the market in the Depression or late

forties. High stocks and high skirts each do have their own undeniable fascinations, but trying to build an investment program
on the supposed correlation is as inappropriate as putting hot
pants on the Easter Bunny.

Similarly, other theorists will try to predict the behavior of the
entire market by watching the action of one or more so-called
indicator stocks; the value of these apparent bellwethers may
change through the years, however, as conditions affecting their
companies change—so their utility is far from guaranteed. Nor is
success automatic by looking at any kind of chart of the Dow
Jones Industrial Average, a fact that leads many theorists to look
for a "confirming" trend in, say, the average of transportation
stocks, or the Standard & Poor's 500-stock index, or the New York
Stock Exchange index of all common stocks traded there, or in
the number of needles in your Aunt Tillie's sewing basket. By
the time full confirmation is at hand, a new trend is sure to be
starting somewhere, and the ferris wheel may well have passed
you by.

Lately, Wall Street has indulged in a vogue for the "beta
coefficient," which assigns each stock a rating based on how
rapidly that particular issue tends to move up and down, as compared with the market as a whole. In an up market, the theory
goes, you want highly volatile stocks, while in a down market
you should seek stability. That's fine, except for two things: Most
stocks do not become heroes and villains with equal fervor,
and general market conditions have been calculated as accounting for less than a third of the risk in any individual stock.
Adherence to this theory is particularly perilous for an ordinary
investor with only a small number of issues in his portfolio. For
him there has got to be a beta mousetrap.

We have already touched on the erratic conviction that market
success is assured by those who bet against the Little Man by
going contrary to his over-all performance, as evidenced in the
statistics for odd-lot purchases and sales. A recent addendum to
that theory tries to discount the special circumstances often attached to odd-lot activity (an investor might just be selling off
a stock dividend, for example) and concentrates on "small
round-lot activity"—that is, buying or selling by investors whose
orders are in units of 100 shares. But it turns out that they simply
are not the dumbbells that the theorists assume. It may give you

comfort to know that this indicator, even more than its odd-lot predecessor, tends to refute the smug notion that the small investor is a lost lamb in Wall Street. But telling you that after the fact may not help you individually in deciding what to do today.

Finally, though, let's turn our skepticism on what is supposed to be one of the Little Man's own favorite trading techniques: buying stocks that are about to split. A stock split does not increase your wealth; it simply gives you more shares. In a three-for-one split, for example, a stockholder who had 100 shares worth $120 apiece will now have 300 shares worth $40 apiece. In a rising market, stock splits may indeed signal a better price ahead—if, indeed, they come at a time when the company's earning power is growing rapidly. (Some conservative companies won't split their stock without simultaneously increasing the dividend.) But while splitting a stock is supposed to be a signal of strong expansion, the overriding motive is usually just to make the market price more attractive. Lower-priced stocks are believed to have stronger appeal to individuals, who can thereby boast of owning a larger number of shares. (In contrast, the institutions' long-time favorite, IBM, retains snob appeal by keeping its price relatively high.) Any company that announces a stock split—or individual who buys on that basis—is heading for trouble if the split is based purely on market considerations and not on fundamental growth. Splitting a stock can create two little headaches where one existed before, and will not atone for any basic problems the stock may have: Bausch & Lomb sold as high as 191¼ in 1971 before it split two-for-one; in 1973 the new stock sold as low as 17⅛.

Is there, then, no market technique that is dependable for the small investor? There is, indeed, but few have the strength of character to stick to it. It's called "dollar averaging"—that is, investing precisely the same number of dollars periodically in exactly the same securities that offer promise of survival and growth. Having selected a sound stock, one with persistent and expanding earnings, the investor steels himself to buying it in set dollar amounts at regular intervals, whether the market that day is up or down. This method avoids the propensity of too many investors, large and small, to buy in a frenzy and sell in a panic. When the market is down, on the contrary, it works to the "dollar averager's" benefit, since his set investment buys more shares that day. When prices are rising, his accumulation continues but his average price remains relatively low. This sort of systematic long-term accumulation may be less emotionally stirring than reacting to every dramatic daily change, but it also happens to be a much sounder route to financial security.

As would-be swingers are forever being stunned and depressed to discover, most short-term traders lose money most of the time. They might be assisted in gaining perspective on their folly if they realized that the same is true at Las Vegas. Few have the flair to break the bank with consistency in either environment. The difference is that Wall Street can have remarkably favorable odds for those who approach it with patience and realism, and who recognize that all the techniques in Manhattan can and should be laid end to end if they do not begin with the necessary first step of picking the right stocks. Long-term buying of quality stocks is the primeval technique that all the others should augment, lest you wind up a jack of all trading techniques—and a master of no jack. The investment you save may be your own.

CHAPTER XV
Love for Sale

We humans are a race of optimists, however much we protest the contrary. We distrust relationships, but we fall in love; we are skeptical of institutions, but we get married; we find the world deteriorating, but we bring forth children; we regard ourselves as innately unlucky, but we purchase common stocks. And that sequence is not so far-fetched as it might first appear, for most people approach investing much as they approach the other acute emotional experiences of their lives—with a combination of love, hope, ego and self-deception that is as remote from cold rationality as Wales is from Wall Street. Nowhere is this gap between emotions and economics more apparent than when the average investor has to decide when to sell.

It is the one decision above all others that most investors find of supreme difficulty, and surely one underlying reason is that it so often requires them to admit that they have made a mistake. Few find such admissions easy; there is usually more joy at the marriage than at the divorce. But there is no investor yet discovered on this planet who has never made such mistakes, and those who kid themselves into believing that they are indeed free of financial error are victimizing only themselves and their heirs. The most common advice, and the most commonly ignored, is to avoid identifying yourself and your own merits with the stock and its achievements. Just as you do not acquire more class by buying a classy stock, so your character is not diminished when a stock fails to come through in the clutch. There is no relationship between you and the stock that should concern anyone but an accountant, and as "Adam Smith" pointed out in *The Money Game*, "The stock doesn't know you own it." Similar sentiments have been expressed by every experienced

Wall Streeter with whom I've discussed the art of selling: Don't fall in love with your stocks, never marry a security, don't let its past sentimentally influence your view of its future, regard it always as what it is—an indifferent piece of paper representing changing values in a changing world.

It would be nice if we never had to think about selling, and indeed in the not-so-distant past it was a distinctly secondary consideration. Wealth could be acquired simply by purchasing shares in the most eminent American businesses, salting the stocks away, and then settling comfortably into ever-greater prosperity, with generous dividends along the way. To be sure, not every supposedly leading company kept up with the parade; indeed, some of the most highly touted fell by the wayside; but a balanced portfolio of the top American companies was a guarantee that, if not every day in every way, at least over-all, number one would get richer and richer. An intelligently conservative investor would no more sell his U.S. Steel or his A.T.&T. than he would sell America short. There were always two choices: buy more or sit tight. And for more than half a century, while the United States enjoyed the greatest growth of any nation in the history of the world, American products set the international standard.

That that situation has changed is now painfully clear, perhaps especially to the trusting investor who bought U.S. Steel at $104 a share in 1959 and then watched in unbelieving anguish as it fell to less than a quarter that amount in 1971. No one who has observed the deteriorating balance of American trade, or been shocked by the forced devaluations of the dollar, should believe that the course of all things American is forever upward. Until the 1970s the United States had never in this century failed to sell abroad more goods than it was buying. The lopsided change could be traced to a complex of historical and economic factors, but the most basic was quite simple: While costs, particularly of labor, continued to escalate in the United States, relative efficiency continued to escalate abroad. The result was that many United States goods found it impossible to compete effectively, not only in foreign markets, but within America itself. It is uncomfortable for any American to confront a statistic that tells him that, among eleven leading industrial nations in the 1960s, the United States ranked eleventh in rate of productivity gains—

but it is especially uncomfortable for the investor who failed to sell a stock in one of the industries where the United States surrendered its previous worldwide leadership. And it probably will bring him minimal consolation just to sit around grousing about the Japanese every time the newscaster brings him more bad news on his Sony.

When, then, should the wise investor sell? The emphasis in this book has been on buying and holding quality growth stocks for the long term, simply because that is the most tested and reliable method for the average investor to succeed. He is making the "one decision" to invest in a growth situation, rather than the "two decisions"—when to buy and when to sell—that are required when he buys the so-called cyclical stocks, those that tend to move up and down in harmony with the economy as a whole. But that does not mean that any investor, in any stock, can afford to ignore the problem of when to sell—or to regard it as one that is applicable to all those other investors, but certainly not to him and his Consolidated Everskyward. Remember that the only kind of love you should ever feel for a stock should be love for sale.

Some authorities recommend a rigid mathematical formula for when to sell stocks, arguing that this is the only way that an investor can rid himself of the emotional encumbrances that make selling so difficult for most people. We will get to that approach in a moment. But first, let me express my own reservations as they apply to true growth stocks—for I suspect that many investors will get better results over the years if they put such stocks in a separate category, one which they are notably slower to sell. To qualify for such privileged treatment, a stock must authentically possess the growth characteristics outlined earlier, including a persistent pattern of higher earnings. Such stocks may be buffeted in market declines, their price patterns may indeed be perennially volatile—but as long as the fundamental reasons for regarding them as quality growth stocks remain untarnished, the smart investor will not try to "beat the market" by buying and selling them at precisely the right time. For the ferris wheel may be turning a hundred yards higher next year.

Periodically, one hears that the concept of growth is a burst balloon, and that the market will now be turning its attention elsewhere. ("To nongrowth?" one wonders.) Yet on investigation this generally appears to be based on bad experiences with stocks whose growth was more in investors' minds than in the balance sheets. A growing price does not make a growth stock. The genuine ones rarely come cheap these days, though a quarter century ago they could be bought at what seems in retrospect to have been surprisingly little premium over their stodgy brothers. In retrospect, of course, we could all be zillionaires—so let's stick to the here and now, when stocks with truly glittering credentials for earnings growth are likely to be priced at a relatively high multiple of their most recent annual earnings.

Even in this era, growth stocks over any extended period have tended to outperform the cyclical stocks by an impressive margin. Consider what happened between 1966, when interest in growth stocks was already abundant, and 1972, the first year thereafter in which profits reached and surpassed their 1966 peaks. A compilation by the investment-counsel firm of David L. Babson and Company of seven representative industries in each group indicated that the cyclical stocks had suffered an average earnings loss of 33 per cent and their share prices were 27 per cent below their 1966 highs—while the growth-stock group had lifted its earnings by 85 per cent and seen its market value more than double. Because of their inherently less favorable characteristics, the cyclical companies had not been able to increase their profits on balance in a six-year period during which the gross national product had expanded by 50 per cent. Inflation hit far harder at them than at the growth companies. And investors responded in kind.

This is not to say that there is never any time to sell a growth company, or that any time is a good time to buy one. At times, as in 1960–61, many such stocks got so far ahead of themselves that investors had to wait several years before they saw profits; when such stocks are in the upper range of their traditional price-earnings ratios, cautious investors will rightfully be wary of them. But the critical factor in determining when to sell a growth stock is always to deal with its fundamental underpinnings and rarely to become preoccupied with price. Most investors who waited over the years for IBM or Xerox to become more "reasonably" priced are waiting still—and on the opposite side of the coin, as the Babson analysis pointed out, "It has never proven to be a good across-the-board policy to sell growth stocks making strong earnings progress just because their share prices looked 'too high.'"

If you can master that concept, you will be miles ahead of the jittery "professionals" who set the Wall Street fads—and who are forever trying to guess the exact moment to switch from growth stocks to cyclicals and back again. Don't try to make your jack be that nimble.

And lest you think I exaggerate this peril, let me cite two quick examples involving those eminent growth stocks I have just mentioned: (1) Donald F. Kohler is a senior investment officer at First National Bank Trustees, a Louisville bank holding company whose common stock affiliate, First Kentucky Company, beat the 1966–71 growth rate of the Dow Jones Industrial Average by more than two to one. "One of the humbling things about this business is looking back and seeing the mistakes you've made," Kohler said in a *Barron's* interview. "We put $84,000 into Xerox when it was Haloid-Xerox. We nearly doubled our money in a year, patted ourselves on the back and sold out. That $84,000 would be worth over $3,000,000 today if we had been smart enough to keep it." (2) In July 1971, IBM announced that, instead of rising as usual, its earnings for the second quarter had been virtually flat. Investors panicked, sending the stock down 13 points in a single day; it finished the week at $294.50 a share, down from a 1971 high of just under $366 and an all-time high, set the previous year, of $387. Wall Street wise guys acted as if the giant company had been exposed as a front for a Mafia white-slavery operation; its sin was taken to be irreparable, and analysts fell over one another in their rush to downgrade their appraisals of IBM's prospects. One of the market's most respected commentators said the stock still wasn't low enough to buy, but that if you were already stuck with it you could hold it if you were willing to wait two or three years —during which time it was not likely to exceed the averages. Little more than a year later, IBM's price had zoomed to more than $425 a share, and among those who were laughing were the many small investors who had been "too dumb to sell."

There may come days when IBM or Xerox—or any other stock—should properly be sold, but these tales of over-rapid profit-taking and panic selling might be taken as a cautionary guide.

Now for the market mechanics. The most usual method, followed indeed by some quite successful investors, is to sell any stock that goes down 10 per cent from the price you paid for it. This is usually refined to state that if the stock advances after you buy it, you then should sell any time it drops 10 per cent from its high point. When the stock reacts, you act. Rid yourself of all ego and all emotion; do it by the book. This method is based on the (absolutely correct) theory that most investors will try to talk themselves out of a sale, that they will tend to dither and rationalize as the stock descends. The automatic rule is designed to avert the negative investment results of this variety of inner turmoil by forcing you to cut your losses before they become so large as to be disabling.

It is not my intention to mock this method, which for many inexperienced investors may be a useful discipline. If you can't trust yourself to be dispassionate about investment decisions, try being a 10-per-center for a while—and then complete your education by examining the might-have-beens. But as a rigid rule for all investors at all times, I think this one is better in theory than in practice.

The theory is excellent: Cut your losses and let your profits run. It's one of the most basic rules for investment success, yet it is surprising how many investors balk at following it. They convince themselves that "it never hurts to take a profit," so they gratify their egos by selling a winner—thereby presenting themselves with the dual problem of retaining their losers and having to find a new stock in which to invest the proceeds of the gain. All investors should periodically weed out the worst performers in their portfolios, and they should show the most reluctance to sell those that have performed best. Such stocks should be sold, not because they have increased in price, but only if the company's basic growth situation has changed. But the typical investor goes the other way. He convinces himself that his losers will "come back" if he will just hold on—and he deludes himself into thinking he still has his original investment in such stocks. If you bought 100 shares of a stock at 30, and it's now down to 20, you have $2,000 (not $3,000) worth of the stock, and the only sensible question for you to answer is whether you believe this is the one best place you could have that $2,000 invested today.

The typical pattern of unsuccessful investment combines racing to buy with delaying to sell. Give the average guy a hunk of money, by inheritance or bonus or whatever, and he can't wait to invest it all without hesitation—especially in a rising market. Never mind that the exchanges will open again tomorrow at 10 A.M., never mind that a more deliberate program of dollar averaging might bring far better results; he is like a flush crapshooter crying, "Where's the action? Where's the game?" But let his expectations fail to be realized, let that stock that "couldn't miss" make him (or his broker) a liar, and he will find more alibis than a minister in a porno movie house. He will tend to delay most when he should be heading quickly for the exit.

Why, then, is the 10 per cent rule less admirable in practice than in theory? Simply because too many variables can enter into the equation. A fall of a point and a half in a $15 stock, for example, can be a false signal in a market that is itself taking an unexpectedly sharp plunge. Market cycles tend to occur more rapidly than in the past, and individual stocks are often more volatile. Jumping in and out of stocks because of an inflexible 10 per cent rule can be needlessly costly, both in terms of brokerage commissions and in terms of the price you will have to pay to reacquire the stock if its 10 per cent drop turns out to have been an aberration. Even Gerald M. Loeb, who was first credited with popularizing the 10 per cent rule, told me he did not favor its use as an automatic sell signal. But while Loeb said he was "not much for this automatic business of saying 10 per cent or 3 points or so forth," he did quite properly emphasize the necessity to accept losses and take them quickly, before they become too staggering to contemplate. "Admit when you are licked," he said, adding that the intelligent investor should regard such inevitable small losses as "insurance premiums" that are part of his annual price of market success.

And here, I think, we are on sounder ground. If the stock descends 10 or 15 per cent from its latest high point, or from the price at which you bought it, certainly you should carefully re-evaluate your reasons for buying and holding the stock. Sometimes you can do it even faster, which is all to the good. (Similarly, if the stock is crowding the upper end of its traditional price-earnings range, stop and think again whether its basic values are increasing as quickly as its price. You might check, too, on whether the momentum of investor enthusiasm, as measured by the volume of trading in the stock during its rise, has shown any signs of waning.) But if you are convinced that the company itself is meeting all the expectations you had when you bought the stock, you the long-term investor might well conclude that there was no necessity to dump the stock merely because its price had moved temporarily against you.

As James Reston remarked to Chou En-lai in Peking, we Americans have no memory. Reston suggested that this was a charming characteristic, boding well for future Sino-American relations, but in the stock market it can be a costly attribute. Hence when the market is declining, I find the most enthusiasm for automatic-sell rules; investors mutter that if only they had sold every time any stock went down X amount they would have saved themselves all kinds of red ink. True enough. But as an inflexible practice in an irregularly rising market, the same procedure might have seen them time and again struggling to get back into the same stocks at higher levels. It boils down to this: If you can't or won't make an unemotional re-evaluation of a declining stock, then put yourself on the 10 per cent rule —and stick to it. But if you are willing to work for your money, then regard such formulas with the same detachment and flexibility as do most of those who promulgated them in the first place.

The harder, but more reliable, course is to adhere to more fundamental considerations than price. Your basic guide as to when to sell should be the crucial question: Why did you buy it? If your original expectations for the company have been realized, it may be a superb time to sell; a rising stock will often turn dull after an anticipated earnings pattern has been realized. Here's a time when apparently "selling too soon" may make excellent sense. Obviously, it's a caution signal when a company whose earnings have been expanding without interruption suddenly reports a "down quarter" (a three-month period in which its earnings declined as compared with the same period the previous year). As we have seen with IBM, one disappointment does not necessarily a wrecked stock make, but it should be a yellow light directing you to reappraise the security without delay. Other such signals might come through any changes in the company's situation, such as through acquisitions or new competition. Arthur Zeikel, chairman of Standard & Poor's Inter-Capital Fund, told me he figured each investment situation usually was governed by "two or three very particular and very important variables"—factors that might range from the level of automobile sales, say, to the attitude of a regulatory body—and that it was the investor's job to recognize the variables that applied to his particular stock and to take it as "early warning signals" when they changed.

Where all the advice coincides is on the necessity to be willing to act, to swallow your pride and your losses if that seems advisable, and thus to live to fight another day with most of what you started with. Don't forget, too, that while selling a loser may hurt your pride, it can help your pocketbook under this tax civilization: A realized capital loss can be used to reduce your tax liability for both earned income and realized capital gains.

Sometimes prudence will come simply from observing what kind of market is developing; in a weak market, speculative stocks that have soared to illustrious price-earnings ratios largely on unproved hopes may be especially vulnerable to crippling declines. If you were lucky enough to hop aboard such stocks when the market was stronger, this may be an excellent time to bail out.

Except in retrospect, nobody can ever know precisely when to sell, and that is why "selling too soon" is so often recommended as distinctly preferable to "selling too late." Those who pay greatest obeisance to technical analysis will usually sell after the top is reached, however, because the chart pattern cannot develop until the event has occurred. Clem Morgello, in a *Newsweek* column, summed up the judicious uses of such information: "Technical sell signals in general are more precise and automatic than those based on fundamental analysis, but charts and other technical data often give false signals, and most brokers don't react automatically to the signs. Instead, they use the data for clues on where to look for trouble, then examine the fundamentals before deciding whether to sell." I would go further and recommend this kind of cautious double-checking after all kinds of "sell signals," and not just those associated with that particular sect of voodoo known as technical analysis.

Few authorities would quarrel with Charles W. Shaeffer,

president and chairman of T. Rowe Price and Associates, over his statement to me that "your first sale is generally your best sale in a poor, nongrowth stock"—but Shaeffer balanced this with faith, later vindicated, in several genuine growth stocks whose price declines went well beyond the 10 to 15 per cent range before recovering. That's why I think my question—Why did you buy it?—must be the critical factor in determining when you should sell. If you were just speculating and it didn't work out, take your beating. But if you invested based on expectations that have only begun to be realized, then you ought to stick with the stocks whose performances truly merit the word "growth." The market may not have come around yet, but meanwhile you have a fine opportunity not to sell but to buy more at bargain prices. You might take your cue here from William R. Grant, president of Smith, Barney and Company, who told me he thought an investor should buy a stock with the expectation of holding it for at least three years—and should plan on doing so unless and until he got professional investment advice "that the value of the stock is substantially below where the current price may be." Grant also recalled that early in his career he had asked a distinguished senior analyst how to tell when the top of a bull market had arrived and the analyst had replied, "It's a little bit like walking up a mountain that's in the top of a cloud; you never quite know when you're at the top, but you know when you're in the clouds."

Knowing precisely when you are in the clouds can be difficult for an inexperienced investor, and that is another reason why he is likely to be better off in quality growth stocks—which can be expected to go ever higher with each new market peak—than with the cyclicals, which may just keep on cycling the same route up and down the mountain. It's not just that U.S. Steel and American Telephone and Telegraph have not, at this writing, come anywhere near the highs they reached, respectively, in 1959 and 1964. Take another undeniable blue chip like Standard Oil of New Jersey (now Exxon). It could have been bought at $75 a share in 1963 and at exactly the same price nine years later; meanwhile, its dividend yield averaged 4½ to 5 per cent. While holders of growth stocks were chalking up massive capital gains, these could have been obtained in Jersey Standard only by agile trading. The stock sold just above $45 a share at one point in 1962 and at more than twice that price at one point in 1964. In 1966 it was back below $60 a share; in 1968 it topped $85. By 1970 it was again dipping below $50 a share. Compare the adroit timing of sales and purchases required to make money in this stock with the single investment necessary in the leading growth stocks that showed consistent earnings increases, and you can see which is more likely to pay off for the average investor. The adjective in the expression "blue chip" has too often become a description of the disappointed investor's mood.

There seems to be no question in investing that is so widely troubling as that of when to sell. At "Wall Street Week" we regularly receive letters from viewers who are seeking the philosophers' stone—and who seem to think that the lack of a foolproof system is a peculiar deficiency in their own investment equipment. Not so. No one in the world will always guess right as to when to take a profit or cut a loss, and no rigid formula is going to provide the solution, either. The best achievable answer lies in three kinds of knowledge—a knowledge of what the sound basis was for buying the stock in the first place, a knowledge of what has been going on in the company and the industry since then and a knowledge of yourself and your own investment objectives. If you are a serious investor and not a Las Vegas hustler, then act like one. As long as a growth company is growing as you expected, you shouldn't panic every time its price chart shows an unnerving jiggle. This doesn't mean that you should not try to develop a flair for spotting the danger signals and checking them out, but it does mean that you are going to resolve not to be stampeded every time the thundering herd changes course. There is always time to stop and think. And then to think again. In the end you might want to go at least part of the way with William G. Campbell, president of the Hartwell and Campbell Fund, who described this concern over when to sell growth stocks as "the most unnecessary aspect of investing," adding pointedly, "If you took the ten best companies you could find in every industry—or not even industry, just take ten companies that you thought met your four- or five-point criteria, whatever criteria you had—and you bought them blind twenty years ago or ten years ago or five years ago or today, without any consideration of price, I will bet you my last dollar you will make more money than the man who is trying to decide when to buy and when to sell."

The whole answer will never be found either in sitting tight or trading loosely, but the most critical decision, in my judgment, will still be what and when to buy. Solve that one, don't be afraid to take a loss when you're wrong, and the searing problem of when to sell will cool considerably. Just remember that there are only two kinds of people in Wall Street: those who have made mistakes of their own and the liars.

CHAPTER XVI
My Word, It's My Bond

On the scale of financial thrills, investing in the bond market used to be regarded as approximately as exciting as having tea with your rich Aunt Sadie. It was perfectly proper and undoubtedly prudent, but scarcely where the action was. The study and purchase of bonds was viewed as the exclusive preserve of gray-faced bankers and gray-haired ladies, an area of investing that was sedate and maybe a little dull. Suddenly, however, within the last few years, the bond market has taken on a glamorous new reputation as an arena with more than its share of action, and attraction, for many ordinary investors. At times recently it has been considerably swingier than its more publicized partner, the stock market, and you the intelligent small investor can now legitimately ask yourself: If you have only one life to live, should you live it with a bond?

An increasing number of Americans lately has been warmly embracing that proposition, so let's try to find out whether this affection is justified in your case. The likelihood of a positive answer increases in proportion to the priority your own investment program gives to safety and income, as opposed to the possibility of growth. There have been periods recently, such as 1969–70, when practically every investor would have been better off in bonds than stocks—but over the long haul, an emphasis on bonds is more apt to suit those whose income needs are immediate and whose investment psychology is conservative. There are two reasons why, one positive and one negative.

The positive reason traces to something called "the reverse yield gap," which is probably the single best argument in behalf of bonds. The "yield" on any investment is, of course, the dollar return on the dollars invested; when you put your money in the savings bank at 5 per cent, you have just made an investment yielding 5 per cent. Now, in the supposedly good old days, stocks traditionally yielded more than bonds. Dividends on stock tended to be higher than interest on bonds, the theory being that investors needed an extra incentive to take on what was presumed to be the extra risk involved in buying stocks. This gap obtained over most of American history; as recently as 1950 the stocks that make up the Standard & Poor's composite index were yielding a whopping 7¼ per cent—compared to a lowly 2¾ per cent for AA-rated industrial, rail and utility bonds. By 1955 that average yield on stocks had come down to just over 4 per cent, but that was still nearly a point higher than the average return on bonds. Then the ratio began to reverse. From the standpoint of income alone, bonds moved into a clear lead over stocks—and this reverse yield gap, a turnabout of the historic relationship between stocks and bonds, has now prevailed since 1959, longer than ever before.

The bigger the gap, the more mouth-watering bond interest is likely to seem to those, such as retired persons, to whom a dollar in hand is worth two dollars in arguable potential. And the gap grew pretty steadily through the 1960s. In 1960 the average bond interest was up to 4½ per cent, while dividends on stock had sunk to 3.4 per cent. In 1965 the mean yield on stocks was still going down—to just over 3 per cent—with bonds paying close to 5 per cent. (Stock prices, at the same time, were rising sharply—which was one reason that the dividend yield looked less impressive.) And by 1970, when the average stock yield was again 3.4 per cent, bond interest had soared to a staggering 7.84 per cent. With long-term interest rates at their highest levels since the Civil War, investors who bought at the right times were able to get top-quality bonds paying interest in the 8 and even 9 per cent range. Since this approximated the historic average return on common stocks, including both dividends and capital appreciation, it was hardly surprising that many investors decided to switch from the undeniable uncertainty of the stock market to the apparent certainty of bonds.

The certainty of bonds applies primarily to the number of dollars they pay as interest. If you buy a new $1,000 bond yielding 7 per cent, you can count on $70 interest every year—assuming the company stays solvent. But what you can't count on is being able to sell your bond to someone else whenever you choose to and get your $1,000 back. The only time you are assured of that price is on the maturity date printed on the bond. When that date, which is often many years away, arrives, the issuing corporation must pay back the original $1,000. Meanwhile, however, the price of the bond for which you paid $1,000 will fluctuate in the bond market from day to day, depending chiefly on what happens to other interest rates (as well as on any change in the corporation's credit status). If interest rates on similar, newly issued bonds rise to 8 per cent—thus paying $80 annually for each $1,000 investment—your old 7 per cent bond will seem less attractive, and its price will fall. If you have to sell it now, the new buyer will surely offer less than the $1,000 you paid, and you will have to take a loss. If, on the other hand, interest rates on comparable new bonds decline to, say, 6 per cent (in which case $1,000 bonds would yield only $60 a year), your old 7 per cent bond would be more desirable and you could sell it now in the bond market for more than the $1,000 you paid. All that affects only the selling price (and collateral value, in case you need a loan) of the bond for which you paid $1,000. Whether that selling price rose or fell, your particular bond would still pay its owner precisely 7 per cent, based on the original face value, or $70 a year in interest.

So the positive reason for turning to bonds is simple enough: If selected properly (and we will get to that shortly), they can be depended on for a set, and generous, level of income— better than is available in ordinary savings accounts and more assured than trying for capital gains on stocks. The negative aspect of bond investment lies in this very rigidity of return, and can best be understood if we consider why bond interest got so high—and why, after backing off for months, many interest rates rocketed to new records in 1973. The answer, as with so many matters affecting your money, can be found in that old devil, inflation. Bond interest rose as prices rose because smart investors were unwilling to sign away their cash for extended periods without receiving a return high enough to give them some protection against inflation. What we might call "real" bond interest —the part left over after allowing for inflation—actually never got much over 3 per cent. In fact, if you look at the interest paid during the last decade on AAA-rated corporate bonds, those con-

sidered the most safe and secure, and subtract from that interest
the rate at which prices rose in each of those years, what you will
have left is a fairly consistent 3 to 4 per cent. In terms of buying
power, that's all the bond interest really amounted to—and meanwhile, of course, the capital invested in the bond was eroding
drastically in buying power. That's why, for those other than the
very elderly, bonds are probably not the complete investment
answer: They run the constant danger of being outrun by inflation.

Over any extended period, this can be quite a drawback.
A University of Chicago study showed that over the forty-year
span between 1926 and 1965, the return on bonds was less
than half the return on stocks, when you figured in both dividends and capital appreciation. Studying a period half as long,
from 1949 to 1968, investment adviser John Winthrop Wright
concluded that the real value of $100 in common stocks had
increased on average to $250.67, while $100 invested in corporate bonds had declined in real value to $42.10. The old text-
book notion that bonds are automatically "safer" than stocks
thus begins to look considerably more dubious. It also becomes
obvious that the tantalizingly high interest paid in recent years
includes a substantial allowance for a continuing rise in prices
—this has been described as the "inflation premium"—and that
the actual return in terms of what you will have to pay your
butcher has increased very little if at all.

Another risk in buying bonds can be grasped if you understand the intense interrelationship between bond prices and
interest rates. When the average yield increases—in other words,
when bonds pay higher interest—that's not good news for everyone. As we have seen, if you already owned a bond paying, say,
5 per cent, and newly issued bonds were available paying, say,
8 per cent, the market value of your bond would have declined considerably from its original price. This is the basic
equation: When interest rates go up, bond prices go down. And
vice versa: When interest rates start to decline, the old bonds
begin to look a little more attractive—and their prices rise.
(There is even a risk on the upside—which will be discussed
more fully later in this chapter—because if interest rates fall low
enough, the company often has the right to pay off its old bonds

and issue new ones at the cheaper interest levels.) What, then, is all this stuff about bonds being "safe"?

Well, there are two things you ought to know in that department. First is the essential difference between stocks and bonds. A stockholder quite literally owns a share of the company; his financial fortunes go up and down with the company's, and his profits may vary from nil to immense. A bondholder, on the other hand, is not a co-proprietor but a lender; the company's relationship to him is akin to your relationship with the bank that holds the mortgage on your house. A bond is an obligation of a company, a debt it has incurred, and the interest usually must be paid in good times or bad; even if the company goes out of business, it has to pay its debt to its bondholders before its stockholders get a cent. Dividends on stock can be lowered or canceled, but interest on bonds is as much a legal debt as the wages due to employees. This degree of security is balanced by the knowledge that, even if the company's profits quadruple next year, the bond interest will not increase. The benefits will go to the stockholders. In the same company, bonds are a security "senior" to stocks—that is, they have a prior claim—but it is simplistic to conclude from that that "bonds are safer than stocks." Stocks in a well-managed company are more secure than bonds in a company that goes bankrupt.

The second factor relating to the safety of bonds is more reassuring. When it comes to buying stocks, "whether" is likely to be less important than "which"—and that's why we have devoted so much attention to the process of stock selection. With bonds it's almost the reverse; once you have decided "whether" to buy, "which" becomes a much less complicated proposition. The reason is that the basic question you have to ask about the company is a simple one—Will it be able to pay the interest twice a year and redeem the face amount of the bond when it comes due?—and you have some highly skilled assistance in answering that question and picking the right bond.

Every bond contains the risk that its price may fall because interest rates rise, but the other risks can be controlled—the risk that the price may fall because of financial troubles within the issuing corporation, the risk that the corporation may not be able to pay the semiannual interest and the risk that the corporation may not be able to pay the face amount of the bond when it comes due. These subsidiary risks can be instantly ruled out in the case of U.S. Treasury obligations, since Uncle Sam has unique means of paying his bills not available to corporate treasurers without access to a printing press. But if you are going for the higher interest available from corporate bonds, you will want to know—and your broker can tell you—the rating that particular bond issue has received from the professional bond-rating agencies: Standard & Poor's, Moody's and Fitch. It can be useful to compare the ratings, and to be aware that they can change from time to time. Standard & Poor's, for example, rates bonds AAA, AA, A, BBB, BB, B, CCC, CC, C, DDD, DD and D; Moody's, in descending order, tabs each issue Aaa, Aa, A, Baa, Ba, B, Caa, Ca or C.

Other than being an unpleasant echo of your schooldays, what should such ratings mean to you? Well, rather than filling pages with the exact definitions given by the agencies (e.g., AAA bonds "possess the ultimate degree of protection," BB bonds have "minor investment characteristics," etc.), let's recognize that this is a relative and subjective matter, and heed the assessment given by the New York Stock Exchange: "Obligations which merit one of the top four ratings are considered to be of investment grade by the rating agencies. To merit the very top rating, the speculative element is considered to be almost non-existent. By the fifth rating the speculative element has become quite significant, and by the seventh rating the speculative element predominates." Beyond this, you should be aware that the higher the rating, the lower the interest generally will be—companies have to pay more to investors who take on greater risks—and so you should discuss with your broker how much additional risk you may be willing to undertake in return for a fractionally higher percentage of interest.

The point of all this is that if you want to buy a bond, the rest is easy. Go to your broker (or if you don't have one, to your commercial banker), tell him how much you want to invest and with what degree of safety (for example, you might decide to stick to corporations whose financial records have earned them an A rating or above). He has instant access to lists of bonds meeting those requirements, and if he tells you differently he's talking through his Hallowe'en hat. Some brokers don't want small bond customers and try to scare them away—or into other investments. This is stupid and short-sighted, but should not discourage you; other big houses will welcome you.

Bonds are usually sold in denominations of $1,000. The commission is generally $5.00 a bond, though often there is a $25 minimum. You will note that this is a lot cheaper than the commissions on stocks, which may suggest to cynical observers why some brokers are reluctant to peddle them. Heaven forfend.

You may even be able to save that small commission if the broker has available a new issue for which his firm is part of the underwriting or selling group. Similarly, he may be able to get you a fractionally better price on some outstanding issue in which his firm "makes a market"—that is, stands ready to buy or sell on any given day. Much is said by discouraging brokers about the difficulty in reselling small amounts of corporate bonds, but rarely will the price received vary much more than about $20 per bond from that received by big institutional sellers. There's no reason in the world why the small investor who wants to buy $1,000 or $5,000 or $10,000 worth of corporate bonds should not be able to do so, and to find a pleasant and cooperative broker to handle the transaction. These days there is also the alternative of corporate bond funds, where with as little as $1,000 you can invest in a professionally managed portfolio of many different corporate bonds. This can both diminish the risk in any one individual issue and also provide the bonus attraction of a monthly interest check.

Bonds, as noted, pay interest twice a year—as opposed to stocks, which generally issue their dividends quarterly (those that pay dividends). Years ago some leading corporations paid dividends monthly (*la plus ça change*, and all that jazz), but they apparently found that the appeal to impoverished investors did not atone for the additional bookkeeping expense. There is a significant difference, however, between the payment of dividends on stock and that of interest on bonds. If you buy a stock, whether or not you get the next quarterly dividend depends on the date of purchase; after a certain date, the stock is sold "ex-dividend"—that is, without the next quarterly payment. With a bond, though, this is never true. The bond accrues interest on a daily basis, even though the corporation pays only semiannually. This means that the seller of a bond gets reimbursed for whatever interest the bond has accrued up to the date he sells, and the buyer thus nets only what remains of the next semiannual payment. Corporate bond interest, like dividends on stock (after an initial $100 exclusion), is taxed at regular income rates.

Most bonds are traded "over the counter"—that is, from broker to broker, rather than at a formal exchange—but if you are interested in bonds, it will be worth your while to take a look at the daily newspaper listings of New York Stock Exchange Bond Trading. Don't be intimidated by the long columns of confusing gray type; here's all you need to know to make sense of these listings: Observe the notations at the top of the column and then find a typical bond. You will then see something like:

83   79   Trust-Me Isle Pay 4⅝s83   67   81¾   81½   81¾   +⅝

Panic not. The key to understanding that melange lies in knowing that bond prices are quoted with the final zero removed. (Hence a typical $1,000 bond that is now quoted at, say, 104½ has not suddenly lost nearly 90 per cent of its value. On the contrary, it's showing a profit at $1,045.) In the line above we see, reading from left to right in the approved Anglo-Saxon fashion, that the highest price this year was $830 per bond (83 plus a zero), the low was $790, the bonds were issued by a company called Trust-Me Isle Pay, they yield 4⅝ per cent on each original $1,000 and that $1,000 is scheduled to be repaid in 1983. The 67 tells you that $67,000 worth of those bonds—that is, 67 units—were traded that day. The highest price during the day was $817.50 (81¾ times 10), the low was $815 and the closing price was $817.50—which happened to be $6.25 (⅝ times 10) higher than the closing price the previous day. Congratulations; you now know how to read the bond page.

In the spring of 1973 an abbreviated form of bond listings came into wide use; it would show only the following:

TrusMIP 4⅝   83   5.66   81¾   +⅝

The volume of trading has been dropped, as have been the yearly and daily highs and lows. These revised bond tables show, in order, the issuing corporation's name in shortened form, the annual interest rate (4⅝ per cent, or $46.25 per $1,000 bond), the maturity date (1983), the current yield (5.66 per cent), the closing price for the day (81¾, or $817.50 per bond)

and the net change from the preceding day the issue traded
(+⅝, or up $6.25 per bond). The current yield, a new addi-
tion to the tables that is given for most straightforward, nonconvertible bonds, is figured on the basis of the bond's closing
price for the day. In other words, if you paid $817.50, the annual
interest of $46.25 would bring you a return on your $817.50 investment of about 5.66 per cent—and that is the "current
yield."

The example given above would not be an untypical one for
a bond issued at a time when interest rates were lower than
those prevailing on the date in question. Since each $1,000 bond
pays only $46.25 interest each year (4⅝ per cent), it can no
longer compete in price with newly issued bonds that pay higher
interest. Thus the selling price, in this fictitious example, of
$817.50. This means that, if you bought the bond when it was
issued, you would now have a substantial paper loss. If you held
the bond until it was redeemed in 1983, however, you would get
your original $1,000 back. If the company's financial position
were sound, the price of the bond would rise steadily as the redemption date came nearer.

This same factor provides a buying opportunity for new purchasers. If you were to buy the bond for $817.50, the $46.25 each
year would be fully taxable as interest, but the difference between the $817.50 you paid and the $1,000 you would receive
in 1983 would be a capital gain, and taxable at the lower rates
applying to such profits. Even much smaller moves offer chances
to make money by trading bonds, but the cautions applied to
trading in stocks should perhaps be redoubled here.

The typical small investor should buy bonds with the intention of holding them until they are redeemed by the issuing
corporation, at which time he will be paid back exactly what
the bonds sold for originally. Meanwhile, he will enjoy a high
—if fixed—income from this investment. (This doesn't mean
that he has to buy bonds coming due soon. He can opt for the
higher interest available in longer-term bonds, and it's perfectly
legal for him to allow his heirs to do the actual collecting.) Trying to trade bonds, particularly in unwieldy small amounts,
means trying to outsmart both the Federal Reserve Board (on
the likely course of interest rates) and every professional bond
trader on Wall Street—a fairly formidable set of opponents. As

the sage B. Carter Randall, senior vice president of the Equitable Trust Company, once put it, "If I had one message for the average investor in bonds, the small investor in bonds, I would say, 'Don't think of bonds in terms of market price, think of them in terms of renting money at a going rate of return.'"

The security and regularity of top-quality bond income is, of course, its central attraction to older investors, especially those in retirement whose other sources of income are not large enough to put them in a high tax bracket. The speculative-bond area is better left to the professionals, or to those with good information who can afford to assume greater risks. Corporate-bond income will have much less appeal to, say, a young businessman with high current income; his emphasis should continue to be on long-term capital gains. But even those to whom corporate bonds are perfectly suited, those who choose conservatively and rejoice in the semiannual income, can have problems. We have already seen that the market price of the bond can topple if interest rates soar, and this can be unnerving to an aged investor even if he has no immediate need to sell—and knows that in the long run he or his children will get his money back. But he can also have problems if interest rates drop and his bond is "called." So let's see how that works.

Corporation treasurers not being entirely stupid, they have tried to hedge their bets when they issued bonds. Hence most corporate bonds carry a provision allowing them to be retired, or "called," prior to their official maturity date. If interest rates drop, the corporations pay off their old bonds and issue new ones at lower interest rates. Dandy for the corporation, but hard luck for the bondholder who enjoyed that high interest rate. About fifteen years ago, the nation's bondholders struck back successfully and got corporations to start issuing securities that were guaranteed against being called for a specified period of time. This "call protection" generally runs at least five years. In return for this concession, bondholders were willing to accept a moderately lower yield, thus reducing the corporation's outlay. Almost all bonds issued since the beginning of 1969 have carried this protection. What it means, though, is that the threat of redemption is not canceled but deferred. A typical utility bond issued at the time of peak interest rates, and paying over 9 per cent interest, would be callable after five years at, say, 108—$1,080 per $1,000 bond—and if interest rates were substantially lower at the end of the five years, the company would be delighted to pay the extra $80 per bond in order to cut its interest costs. Most corporate bonds are now callable after ten years. Never buy any kind of bond without finding out from your broker when and at what price it can be redeemed by the company. Redemption may be splendid in church, but it can play havoc with the budget of a bondholder.

Many experts advise the typical bond investor to look for high-quality industrial issues with ten-year call protection when they are available at yields relatively close to those of similar utility bonds. If your need is less for income than for capital gains, your search may lead you to well-rated "discount bonds," those issued at times of lower interest rates and therefore selling now at a "discount" from their face value; if you are going to retire in six years and can find a good discount bond coming due in seven, you will benefit by having less of the reward in interest when your taxes are high and more as a capital gain at a time when your over-all tax bracket is presumably lower. But whatever path the prospective bond buyer follows, he ought to be aware of one other potential pitfall—that known as "sinking funds." This sounds like something that every investor ought to worry about all the time, but actually it's not quite as sickening as it sounds.

Many bond issues have "sinking fund" provisions that require the corporation to retire a designated amount of the bonds, chosen by lot, at fixed intervals. If interest rates have fallen, and the bonds are selling at a premium over their original price, it is obviously to the company's advantage to call bonds through a sinking fund. But the opposite is true when the bonds are selling at a discount. As Nils P. Peterson, vice president of Thorndike, Doran, Paine and Lewis, Inc., put it to me, "If you buy a bond at 80 [that is, $800] that has a sinking-fund requirement, the company is going to have to come in and bid aggressively to buy those bonds—and you may be able to sell them to the company at 85 [$850] or more." In those circumstances, the sinking feeling would be in the pit of the treasurer's stomach, not yours. But in recent years investors have tended to look less at this potential benefit from sinking fund provisions and more at the potential threat to bonds paying liberal interest, and so those provisions are now often deferred in a manner comparable to call protection. It's one more question to investigate before investing, and your broker can give you the answer.

Now that you have a basic understanding of how the corporate bond market operates, you are ready to consider such twists and turns as municipal bonds, convertible bonds, preferred stocks and utility stocks—all of which are alternate vehicles for investors to whom income is an important ingredient in the portfolio mix—and we will get to them in the next chapter. Meanwhile, though, there are some points worth remembering:

(1) The typical bond investor should realize that he is sacrificing the potential bonanza of participating in a company's growth as a stockholder in return for high and relatively assured immediate income. If his bonds are chosen conservatively, he has little chance of being wiped out, but he's not going to get rich, either—and if inflation and interest rates keep rising, the market value of his bonds will fall and the buying power of the interest will be less than he expected.

(2) If his company doesn't follow Penn Central into bankruptcy, and if he or his heirs hold the bonds until they are due to be redeemed, the temporary fall in market value will vanish and the bonds will be repaid 100 cents on the dollar. Thus, for the cautious small investor, high-quality bonds can truly be what William B. Altschuler, manager of the Channing Income Fund, described to me as "an alternative to savings" for the Little Man—and at higher than bank rates—provided you don't need the savings until the bonds are due.

(3) The bond buyer should recognize that he is undertaking two kinds of risk. The first is credit risk, and this the small investor can and should minimize by buying only high-rated issues. The second is market risk, and this is affected by everything that influences the course of the nation's interest rates. For as interest rates expand, the capital invested in bonds shrinks—temporarily in terms of market value, and permanently in terms of its buying power in an inflationary economy. And even "temporarily" can run into more than a generation when you're talking about long-term bonds.

(4) The degree to which corporate bonds will be the ideal choice for the typical investor will be in direct proportion to the extent that he needs the highest possible immediate income from his investments. There will be fluke periods, such as 1969–70,

when bonds will look glittering for nearly everyone—but over the years they simply have not provided the same inflation protection as quality common stocks.

(5) Even if you decide that the bond market is not for you, you ought to be aware of what it is and how it is doing—if only because it is often an indicator of what is going to happen to the stock market. Historically, a weak bond market eventually has affected the stock averages. One reason is that, when bond yields rise high enough (thus depressing bond prices), they attract money that would otherwise go into stocks. In addition to this competitive factor, the bond trend reflects the supply and demand for money—which, as we have seen, is among the mightiest influences on the economy and stock prices. So the bond market, if it performs no other service to you, is frequently a useful "leading indicator" of what lies ahead for stocks. Even a teetotaler ought to check now and then on how the bonded stuff is going down.

CHAPTER XVII
Verrry Interest-ing

For those who look on their investments not as a beacon to a brighter future but as a way to help meet the light bill today, Wall Street offers a variety of opportunities outside the traditional corporate bond market. Their common characteristic is that they provide immediate, regular income, but beyond that they can have as little in common as a Hereford bull and a Kodiak bear. Only a charlatan would suggest that there is a single best way to get income out of investments, for the choice depends mightily on your personal situation and preferences. It is, however, possible to describe the major types of income investments in a way that may help you decide—and that is the aim of this chapter. May it reward you at least semiannually.

Murmur the words "municipal bonds" to the average American and he is likely to react with either greed or indignation, depending on whether he anticipates a purchase himself or decries it as a tax-free "loophole" for others. For the central attraction to most investors is not the noble opportunity to participate in the building of a better America but the juicy fact that the income is free of all federal income taxes, indeed does not even have to be reported on your return. Various proposals for ending this exemption were discussed while the 1969 tax-reform bill was being drafted, and have been renewed periodically since then, but at this writing the income from virtually all municipal bonds remains untouched by Uncle Sam—and if you tell your broker to choose the right issues, untouched by state and local taxes, too. Scant wonder, then, that municipal bonds have come to be regarded by a burgeoning hoard of investors as the modern version of free lunch.

The tax-exempt status of municipal bonds traces not to some shady provision sneaked into the revenue code by venal lobbyists but to a fundamental constitutional doctrine first enunciated by Chief Justice John Marshall in 1819, when he held in *McCulloch* v. *Maryland* that "the power to tax involves the power to destroy." The Supreme Court through the years has interpreted this to suggest a "reciprocal immunity," under which neither the federal government nor the states may destroy the other—and, therefore, neither can tax securities issued by the other. Isn't it nice to know that you can simultaneously save on your taxes and defend the Constitution?

Until recently, most investors regarded municipal bonds as a rarefied vehicle for banks, corporations and millionaire coupon-clippers. Since 1928 the average long-term yield on municipal bonds has been under 3½ per cent, and in the easy-money era right after World War II it dipped below even 1½ per cent. Tax-free or not, this was scarcely a return to set hearts a-thumping. Then two elements combined to set off a boom in municipal bonds. The first was the historic surge in interest rates during 1969–70, when the government's effort to squeeze inflation out of the economy led to the tightest money in a century. In May 1970 twenty-year municipal bonds were paying more than 7 per cent, tax-free, at a time when the stock market was emulating a bathysphere. This was the peak for bond interest rates, but even when they retreated, the return on quality municipal bonds remained in the same range as that paid on regular savings accounts—where the interest is, of course, fully taxable. The second element, which contributed to the first, was the huge and growing demand for new funds on the part of the nation's state and local governments. By 1972 the total of municipal bonds outstanding had reached $150,000,000,000, about one third owned by individuals and more than half by commercial banks—which presumably know a safe and sound investment when they see one.

There are three basic questions that any investor considering municipal bonds ought to ask himself: Are they worth my while? Are they safe? What are the mechanics of buying and selling? Let's take them in order.

Municipal bonds are undemocratic; they favor the rich. The desirability of a tax-free return increases in proportion to your

tax bracket. Since the return is tax-free, the issuing authorities
are able to get away with a lower interest rate than that prevailing on taxable bonds. A widow with a small income thus might
be better off forgetting about municipal bonds, buying higher-
yielding corporate bonds instead and paying the tax on their
interest. What's the cutoff point? Most authorities would agree
with Charles Garland, Jr., the partner in charge of the municipal-
bond department of Alex. Brown and Sons, who told me, "We've
usually thought that somewhere about the 30 per cent tax
bracket is the spot where a customer would find tax-free bonds
to his advantage." But you can check this out for yourself. Apply
your current tax rate for additional income to the prevailing interest paid on corporate bonds; if what is left over after paying
taxes is still higher than the return available on municipals, then
they are not for you. Don't forget to use a tax-bracket figure that
takes account of state and local income taxes, too; for example,
a New Yorker with $35,000 of taxable joint income is actually
already in a 50 per cent bracket—which means his return from
any taxable investment is sliced in half. For him, 6 per cent tax-
free is like 12 per cent from a bank or a corporate bond. For a
New Yorker making about half as much, $18,000, a 6 per cent
municipal bond would be as good as 9.37 per cent taxable—while
the lucky $100,000-a-year man would have to pull in 17.14 per
cent from a taxable investment to retain as much as a 6 per cent
municipal would pay him tax-free. Others benefit proportion-
ately, but municipals are still, on a relative basis, a case of "them
that has, gits."

Are they safe? They can be, but let's define our terms. No bond
is free of the risk that interest rates will rise further, and the
prices of all bonds will consequently fall. So municipal bonds
really are not a substitute for your savings account, which should
continue to hold the cash you want to be able to lay your hands
on swiftly. If you have a relatively short-term target for when
you will need the funds, then you should be sure to buy short-
term bonds, even though this will necessarily shave the interest
you will receive. There's no way of guaranteeing that a twenty-
year bond will be salable ten years from now at 100 cents on the
dollar.

That's the market risk, which is unavoidable; but the credit
risk, the chance of the issuer defaulting on payment, can be al-

most eliminated. The record is reassuring: Even during the Depression, less than 2 per cent of municipal-bond payments were overdue and less than one half of 1 per cent were permanently unpaid. Nowadays, with ratings on municipal bonds widely available on the same basis as those for corporate bonds, the conservative investor can sleep soundly on the nights in between the times he clips his coupons. (And he probably will have to clip them and turn them in to his bank to get the semiannual interest. Municipal bonds generally come in "bearer" form, meaning whoever has the coupon gets the interest—unlike corporate bonds, which these days usually come in "registered" form, meaning the bond is in your name and the company sends you an interest check every six months.) There are several kinds of municipal bonds, as all state and local obligations are called, but only two broad categories: general obligations and revenue bonds. The first are the blue chips.

"General obligation" municipal bonds are considered second only to a United States government bond in safety. Such bonds are backed by the "full faith and credit" of the issuing community, which means it is required to exercise an unlimited taxing power to get the interest it must pay to holders of such securities. By law, such bondholders are right up there with the schoolteachers and the policemen in their claims on the community; in fact, in Chicago during the Depression municipal employees got scrip, bondholders got cash.

The other broad category, which has various gradations, is that of "revenue bonds"—a typical example of which would be a bond issued to build a toll bridge, and backed not by the taxpayers of the community but the prospective revenues from the bridge. Obviously, there is greater risk in any revenue bond, since its future depends on necessarily inexact projections of future use. Experts consider net earnings 1¾ times greater than the annual interest payments to be respectable coverage for a revenue bond, and some do enjoy additional security features. In general, though, this is not the place for the investor seeking a safe return. One exception: Sometimes a revenue bond is "guaranteed" by another political entity, which puts its unqualified taxing power behind the bond. The guaranteeing state or local government is, in effect, assuming a general obligation to back the bond.

Clearly, there is quite a difference between a bond backed by the full faith and credit of a solvent state and one that depends on how many motorists decide to ride the new ferry. That's why the bond ratings are so important, and that's why the experienced municipal-bond house of Lebenthal and Company, which caters to small investors, says, "In recommending bonds for savings—as opposed to the more speculative portion of your funds—we favor the one bond that has earned for all municipals their reputation for safety: the general obligation."

Finally, then, what are the mechanics of buying and selling municipal bonds? Easy and getting easier, as more and more brokers compete for this business. A good municipal-bond broker should be able to offer you on any given day a selection of bonds with the precise degree of safety, return and tax advantage best suited to your personal situation. And don't let anyone tell you that this is no area for the small investor (assuming he's in the right tax bracket); if anything, believe it or not, he has an advantage—because the big financial institutions bid up the prices on large blocks. A $5,000 investor may earn about a tenth of 1 per cent more than a $100,000 investor. The bonds also come in $1,000 odd lots. You normally would not pay any commission as such; when you buy from a dealer in municipal bonds, the house makes its profit from the spread between the price at which it would sell the bond and the price at which it would buy it back. This spread averages a bit more than $20 per $1,000 bond, which is less than onerous.

If you are beginning to think that municipal bonds may be for you, here is some additional advice:

(1) If the current yield is high enough to suit your needs, don't try to be too crafty in timing your purchases. Go ahead and buy the bonds, and start getting the income.

(2) Hedge your bet by staggering the maturities of the bonds you buy. If your capital comes back at regular intervals, and you then reinvest it, you will be able to average out on interest-rate fluctuations.

(3) If you buy a "discount" municipal bond—that is, one selling for less than its face value—the quoted "yield to maturity" will include both the interest and the capital gain you will make when your bond is redeemed for the full $1,000. Bear in mind

that the latter part of the yield, the capital gain, is taxable—even though the interest is not.

(4) If you buy a bond at a "premium"—that is, at more than its face value—you cannot deduct the difference as a capital loss when you turn the bond in for $1,000. The Internal Revenue Service figures you were well repaid by the interest you received.

(5) Realize that if you stick to high-quality general-obligation municipal bonds, you run only three main risks. The tax law could be changed (check your broker or tax adviser for the current status). Your capital could be temporarily eroded because of a rise in interest rates. Or you could find that you contracted for a long-term return at a level that is no longer sufficient to keep you ahead of inflation. This last is the greatest risk in all fixed-income investments, and it's the overriding reason why no bond, even tax-free, is going to replace common stocks as the fundamental Wall Street investment.

The concept of Wall Street as a supermarket providing a wide variety of spices and sustenance to buyers with an equally wide variety of tastes and needs is inevitably unsatisfying to the kind of person who yearns to be told that there is one best food for everyone. To alleviate this craving to hear confidentially and authoritatively that there is, indeed, one sure-fire place to shop, the word was passed in many quarters in the 1960s to look in the section labeled "convertible bonds." Convertible bonds were supposed to combine the safety of corporate bonds with the profit potential of common stocks, all in the same glittering, easily accessible package. And what buyers wanted, corporations were quick to provide: convertible-bond financing increased from $2,400,000,000 in the first half of the decade to $14,700,000,000 in the second; while total bond issues listed on the New York Stock Exchange were up 25 per cent in this period, the increase in convertible-bond issues was 130 per cent. Then in 1970, when this generation underwent its version of the Great Crash, convertible bonds suddenly looked less like the most desirable product in the market than like a particularly tainted can of vichyssoise. Since those unsettling days, convertible bonds have achieved a position on the Wall Street shelves somewhere between those previous extremes. To decide whether convertible bonds should now have a place in your own investment diet, you ought to know something about their actual ingredients, their somewhat-smudged advertising campaign and some ways in which you currently may be able to distinguish the good turtle soup from the mock.

A convertible bond is a security that pays interest like other bonds but has the additional feature that it can be "converted" into—that is, exchanged for—a set number of shares of the corporation's common stock. (Strictly speaking, this type of security almost always should be referred to as a "debenture" rather than a "bond"—the difference being that the former is backed only by the company's "full faith and credit," which is to say its word, good or otherwise, and not by any enforceable mortgage on the company's assets. Rarely is specific collateral pledged behind these convertible issues. Hardly anybody in Wall Street speaks this strictly, however, so if you don't want to confuse your broker, you might as well join the crowd and call them "convertible bonds.") Here's how a typical convertible bond might work: With its stock selling at $16 a share, a company issues a convertible bond paying 5 per cent interest and convertible into 50 shares of common stock. Divide 50 into the price of the bond, $1,000, and even under the Old Math you will get a result—$20, if memory serves—that would make conversion attractive only to simpletons and philanthropists. Why pay $20 for a stock you could buy on the open market for $16? But if the stock should rise, the bond's conversion privilege would look increasingly attractive, and its price would rise, too. Meanwhile, it would keep on paying that 5 per cent interest.

Like any good hybrid, the convertible bond combines appealing characteristics of each of its progenitors. Like a bond, it pays interest and has some inherent stability—in each case, less than that of a straight bond of the same company, but still usually more income and safety than would be offered by a dividend-paying common stock of equivalent quality. Even if the company's stock price falls so drastically that the conversion feature appears worthless, the convertible bond still has some residual investment value based on its income-producing feature. So there is theoretically a floor under its descent that is nonexistent in the common-stock area. At the same time, the ceiling on potential capital gains that normally is associated with bond-buying does not hover over the convertible issues. If the company's stock roars ahead in price, that will not help the holders of straight bonds in the company—they will get only their promised interest, plus the par value of the bonds when they are redeemed—but it can cause a spectacular elevation in the price of convertible bonds. It doesn't take a financial genius to see that if the price of a company's stock doubles from $16 to $32, that would make the right to buy 50 shares of the company worth a lot more than the original $1,000—even without the interest-paying feature. To put it in show-business terms, convertible bonds have been effectively billed as topless, but not bottomless, wonders.

So what went wrong? Well, the top became uninteresting, while the bottom went tantalizingly lower than expected. Many investors in the mid-sixties rushed to buy, on exceptionally thin margin, convertible bonds in such fleetingly popular areas as the airlines and the conglomerates. When the prices declined, and the margin calls came, the convertible bonds were hit worse than the stocks—whose margin requirements had been greater. This vulnerability to sharp declines was accentuated in 1970 by the dreaded combination of a falling stock market, thus negating the value of the bonds' conversion feature, and ascending interest rates, thus lessening the prices of all bonds, convertible or not. In addition, the Cambodia panic was accompanied by melodramatic chatter about a "liquidity squeeze" that would precipitate a Depression, and those who panicked at this overheated counsel helped send convertible-security prices even lower.

This, of course, set the stage for a predictable rebound when the smoke cleared and the republic was found to be still standing —though the convertible bonds usually did not rise quite so rapidly as their common stocks. The entire experience should be taken as educational by anyone who is trying to put convertible bonds, or any other security, in perspective; there is no single panacea on Wall Street, and each prescription carries its inexorable quota of potential risks and rewards. Having said this, though, let's see how you can learn to limit your risks and maximize your rewards in the case of convertible bonds.

First, you ought to look to the credit standing of the issuing corporation. Why does the corporation want to issue convertible bonds? (These are the two most customary reasons: (1) It won't have to pay as much interest; convertible bonds pay a lower rate than straight bonds of similar quality. (2) It wants to raise capital without issuing more stock, which would immediately reduce the earnings-per-share—and thus the price—of the existing stock. Besides, bond interest is a deductible expense, while dividends on stock must be paid after taxes.) Are the corporation's motives legitimate or is the issue a cheap come-on? If the company's credit standing is not solid, even a small decline in its earning power could erode not just the value of the conversion privilege but the straight-bond value as well. So check the rating as you would for any other kind of bond. In this decade, for the first time, industrial corporations have sold AA-rated convertible bonds, so there is no question of quality not being available. Make sure you're getting it.

Second, look for convertible bonds with relatively modest "conversion premiums." The conversion premium is the percentage difference between the conversion value and the market value of the bond. Let's take our example of a $1,000 bond convertible into 50 shares of a stock now selling at $16 a share. The difference between the market value of $1,000 and the conversion value of $800 (50 times $16) is $200, or 25 per cent of the conversion value. The conversion premium is thus 25 per cent—that's the extra you are paying for getting what the common-stock buyer is not, namely a higher yield and relative safety. If the stock were well regarded, this would be considered a reasonable premium—and would give the convertible bonds special appeal, as compared to the stock, for conservative investors and trust funds. The potential for appreciation would be present, while the market risk would be diminished. The smaller the conversion premium, the more closely the price of the convertible bond will follow the price of the common stock. (If the bond's selling price is the same as its value if exchanged for stock, it is said to be selling on "conversion parity.") Conversely, if there is a large premium over the bond's conversion value, the bond's price movement is likely to be less volatile, more in line with that of bonds as a whole, and the prospects for substantial appreciation have to be viewed as long-term at best.

Third, realize that the alleged downside protection of a convertible bond depends entirely on its "investment value." This is an estimate of what the bond would be worth if it were not convertible and it had to stand or fall on its annual interest payment. In other words, what is it worth as a straight bond? Analysts for investment advisory services come up with this investment value figure by calculating the price at which the convertible bond would have to sell to provide a percentage yield comparable to those offered by straight bonds of similar quality and maturity dates. If the investment value of our $1,000 convertible bond were, say, $750 (at which point its $50 annual interest would represent a 6.67 per cent return), that would be the theoretical floor under any decline in the bond's price—a floor that, of course, does not exist under any decline in the price of the company's common stock. Two cautions, though: (1) If the bond's selling price is much higher than its investment value, that figure will provide little comfort to an investor who is losing money. (2) The investment value carries no guarantee, and could prove an insubstantial floor if the company's credit standing deteriorates—or interest rates rise.

The key features of intelligent investing in a convertible bond can be summarized even more simply. Realize that as a bond it will pay less interest and be somewhat less secure than a straightforward, nonconvertible bond of the same or a similar company. Realize that as a source of large potential profits it is only as good as the underlying stock—which should be investigated just as thoroughly as if you were buying it. Realize, in short, that you are not buying a mansion at the price of a bungalow, but a carefully constructed halfway house—a means of reducing the risk of investment in a company while at the same time reducing your potential profit if the company grows as you expect.

Now that you know that convertible bonds can be a useful investment tool, but are neither a guaranteed bonanza nor a guaranteed protection against loss, let me briefly mention one of the swingier methods of employing them. Sophisticated investors often take advantage of the lower margin requirements for buying convertible bonds, as opposed to the cash that would have to be presented to buy an equivalent amount of common stock. This fascination with speculation in convertible bonds leads to such refinements as the "convertible hedge," which typically works like this: The investor simultaneously sells short the company's common stock and buys whatever amount of convertible bonds can be exchanged for an equal amount of stock. The crafty chap is hoping that the stock will decline. If it does, he figures that the convertible bonds will descend less rapidly because of the interest they pay and their prior claim on the company's earnings. His profit on the short sale will thus exceed his loss on the bonds. On the other hand, if he guessed wrong, and the stock rises, he is protected to the extent that the convertible bonds also rise. This bit of sleight of hand works best when the bond is selling at or close to its "conversion parity," so that its moves will harmonize with those of the stock, and not too far above its investment value, so that it will not fall too far in a declining market. I would no more advise a beginner to fiddle with a technique like this than I would advise him to enter the Nepalese jungle in a swimsuit prepared to do hand-to-hand combat with a Bengal tiger.

Two final tips: (1) If you buy a convertible bond, check to see when the conversion privilege expires. If you fail to exercise this privilege before that date, all you will have left is a bond that doesn't pay much interest—and it will plummet faster than a broker explaining why it wasn't really his fault. (2) If you decide to convert, choose your time carefully. Most convertible-bond prospectuses make clear that you lose any interest accrued but not paid. So wait for the date of record for payment of that semiannual interest; collect your interest, thumb your nose at the tightwad company, and then convert. That way, you can have your interest and eat your common stock, too.

"Preferred stock" is a classy name for an income-producing security that you probably ought not to buy. Now, I realize that that sort of arbitrary statement may bring your hackles to attention, so let me assure you at the outset that this conclusion has nothing to do with your being so insufferably common that the preferred stuff is too good for you. Quite the contrary. The wise individual investor is an uncommon bird indeed, and he is likely to reject most preferred stock as offering neither the profit potential of common-stock investment nor the income potential of bonds. For him this is one of the least promising sections of the Wall Street supermarket.

If the attraction of preferred stock for you is as dubious as I have suggested, you may wonder, why do such securities continue to exist? Well, one quick answer is that their attraction for another class of investors is considerably greater—that class being the nation's corporations. Because of a quirk in the tax law, they pay tax on only 15 per cent of the dividends they receive on all industrial preferred stocks (the advantage is slightly less on some utility preferreds). No such tax advantage exists for individual investors in preferred stocks. But such large corporate investors as insurance companies are heavy investors in preferred stocks. They bid the prices of such stocks to levels where the return is significantly below what the individual investor can get on corporate bonds. The corporations are still better off, because of the special tax break they get on their income from preferred stocks, but the individual investor is settling for less than he could get from bonds—and with no compensating tax advantage. Those lacking a suicide complex are generally well-advised to shop elsewhere.

Preferred stock falls into the second of the two broad categories of investment securities—the first being borrowings by the company, such as bonds, debentures and notes, and the second being the sale of an ownership interest in the company, such as preferred and common stock. (As we have seen, a convertible bond offers an investor the option of transferring from the first category to the second.) If the company goes bankrupt, it first must pay off all its debt, which is represented by the first category of securities, before it distributes any assets to the holders of the second category. The claims of the preferred stockholders would then come ahead of the common stockholders, which is where the designation "preferred" originates. Similarly, each year the company continues in business, its first obligation is to pay off, in order of seniority, its bondholders and other creditors—then to take care of the preferred stockholders, and only finally, to see what is left for common-stock dividends and reinvestment in the business.

The adjective "preferred" can be misleading, however, because the dividend on preferred stocks is usually at a fixed rate, in good times or bad, and thus the security's price will not move up (or down) like that of the common stock, as the corporation's fortunes change. The company will generally have to pay that set dividend on the preferred stock before it can give out anything to the common stockholders, but the unvarying nature of the typical preferred-stock dividend means that this kind of security has far more in common with a bond than with a common

stock. The price of the average preferred stock responds more
to changes in interest rates than to changes in the company's
earnings. And, as noted, the dividend on preferred stocks tends
to be lower than the interest available on an equivalent investment in corporate bonds. (An exception to much of the above
is what is called a "participating preferred," which can pay its
holders a "bonus" dividend after the common shares receive a
specified amount, but this is a rapidly vanishing animal.) An additional potential drawback to preferred stocks is that their
dividend rate, while fixed, may be subject to change at the dis-
cretion of the company's directors—who have no such power to
decrease or omit the interest payable on their bonds. Such
whittling away is unlikely to happen with a solid corporation,
but I thought you might prefer to know.

The drawbacks to most preferred stocks are seldom advertised.
The New York Stock Exchange's monthly magazine, *The Exchange,* published in its April 1972 issue a comparison of the
yields on the common and preferred stock of twenty-five prominent industrial corporations—and found, not surprisingly, that
twenty-one of them had higher yields on the preferred.
"Dividend Often Higher on Preferred Stock," headlined an accompanying press release, though a far more useful comparison
would have been with the yields on long-term bonds of these
corporations. Quality preferred stocks tend to move in harmony
with investment-grade, long-term bonds, with both responding
directly to changes in interest rates.

Having emphasized that preferred stocks are essentially fixed-
return securities similar to bonds, and frequently yielding less,
let me point out some other differences between the two types
of investment:

(1) Bonds normally have a final maturity date at which time
the company promises to pay back the original price of the
bonds. Preferreds carry no such promise. Their stated "par value"
is useful only because the dividend is given as a percentage of
par value. A 4 per cent preferred stock with a par value of $100
will pay $4.00 a year in dividends, even though its actual selling
price, in a period of higher interest rates, will be considerably
below $100. Preferred stocks remain outstanding indefinitely,
unless called for redemption—a step the company is unlikely to
take as long as interest rates remain higher than they were when

the stock was issued. (The redemption price would, in any case, represent a tidy capital gain for the preferred stockholder, so there is really not much point in hunting for "noncallable" preferreds—which do exist for those who can't abide the idea of the company holding the ultimate whip hand.)

(2) Bond interest is a legal debt of the corporation. Preferred-stock dividends are not, though most preferred stocks these days are "cumulative"—meaning that any omitted dividends build up in arrears and must be paid before the common stockholders can get a penny. (Some speculative bonds pay only "contingent interest"—that is, interest that is paid only in years that it is earned—but most bonds have their interest as a legal right, and the company must pay up each year or go into default.)

(3) Bonds are less accessible to the very small investor. Their face amount is usually $1,000, and it is sometimes difficult to get precisely what you want in smaller than $5,000 lots. An investor with a few hundred dollars, on the other hand, can easily purchase preferred stocks.

(4) Preferred stocks, like common stocks, generally pay their dividends four times a year—twice as often as bonds pay interest. Some nonbudgeters profess to find this a sensational advantage.

(5) While both are considered "senior securities," in that their claims come ahead of those of common stockholders, the claims of bondholders have absolute seniority over any payment to preferred stockholders if the company goes bust.

Finally, just as there is a hybrid called "convertible bonds," so there is a jazzed-up entry called "convertible preferreds" ("cv pf" in the language of the stock tables). These, as you might guess, are preferred stocks that pay a fixed dividend but carry the additional option of being convertible into a set number of shares of the company's common stock. As with convertible bonds, their price bears a much closer relationship to that of the company's common stock than is the case with similar nonconvertible securities. As with other preferreds, convertible preferreds do not have maturity dates as do bonds—and do represent an equity interest in the corporation, which means their claims come behind those of all debt securities, including convertible bonds. Their value will depend much more on the company's earnings prospects than will that of an ordinary preferred, but even here there is an advantage to corporate buyers that you the poor individual investor do not possess: A corporation will do much better with a 4 per cent return on a convertible preferred than it will with a 5 per cent return on a convertible bond because of that tax quirk mentioned at the start of this section. You, on the other hand, are paying the same, full-rate taxes on both returns—so you may find that corporate buyers have bid up the prices of most corporate preferreds to levels that are fine for them but uneconomical for you.

The tax laws have influenced both ends of the preferred-stock equation. The supply is dwindling, in large measure because corporations can deduct their bond interest as a business expense but must pay dividends on preferred or other stock from their after-tax income—so bonds become a more desirable method of raising new capital. The demand, on the other hand, is pushed up because corporate investors get a break on preferred-stock dividends that they do not get on bond interest. All that tends to put the individual investor in the middle, more often than not—and, not to put too fine a theological point on it, you may well prefer to convert to some other brand of prayer book.

There is one class of common stocks that properly belongs in any discussion of investing for income, and that is the utilities—the "public service" companies that illuminate the lamps, power the factories and carry the telephone calls from one frequently dissatisfied customer to another clear across the republic. As an investor, you have the soul-restoring opportunity of placing these often-irritating "public service" companies at your profitable private service. But if you happen to be an old baseball fan, don't be misled by the term "utility." A baseball utility fielder is a versatile chap who can be inserted in any number of positions; a public utility, on the other hand, is far from an all-purpose investment. It is usually best anchored to the base labeled "income," though while serving there it may well provide better protection against inflation than the typical corporate bond. This can be a comforting thought if you happen to own some utility shares the next time your lights go out or the operator tells you all her circuits are engaged.

Utility stocks have had their problems in recent years, and in fact have been notable laggards when it comes to capital growth. For one thing, they were particularly hard hit by high interest rates, since they must depend so heavily on borrowing. Year after year, public utilities are the largest group of corporate-bond issuers—because the services they provide require a constant infusion of new capital to keep up with the growing needs of a growing population. (For this reason, their proportion of outstanding bonds to stock—the so-called debt-equity ratio—is notably high; the debt is, in many instances, 50 per cent of the company's total capitalization. A similar proportion in a field whose steady growth was less assured—in a steel company, for example—would be considered dangerously high.) Not only do soaring interest rates increase the costs utilities must pay; they also increase the attractiveness of corporate bonds as an investment competitive to utility stocks, since the bond yields rise along with interest rates. Recent record interest rates have made even Treasury bonds and insured bank deposits formidable competitors for funds that might otherwise have gone into utility stocks —and bid up their prices.

For another thing, utilities have been a natural target for those who see the nation's environment as threatened by the continued growth of industry. Ecologists in many cases have blocked or delayed new projects for years, while costs mounted and service suffered. As with the automobile companies, pressure to control pollution has forced on the utilities heavy expenditures that do not result in productive efficiencies or higher profits. Life is not fair, and neither is the improving of life: The understandable social concern for cleaner air and water has had uneven economic effects, and the utilities have been among the walking wounded in the war on pollution.

A third consideration is the special position of most utilities as chartered monopolies operating under government regulation. Plainly, in the present political climate, few public service commissions are about to grant to utilities the kind of large rate increases that might enable utility stockholders to double their money in the next thirty days. It's worth remembering, though, that this effective ceiling on profit growth also tends to operate as a floor (utilities seldom post losses) and thus to increase the relative safety of the investment. The wounded are still walking.

Much of the above might strike you as good arguments for not buying utilities, and indeed they are scarcely the happy hunting ground of the typical investor looking for capital gains. But they have two other strong advantages for investors contemplating or enjoying retirement, or otherwise preoccupied with the amount of money their securities can return to them each year. First, they have one quality that is strikingly missing from corporate bonds—the possibility of long-term growth, however moderate. A bond generally will increase in price only if interest rates fall, and even then its growth is normally limited by the possibility that the issuing company will call it in for redemption—and by the certainty that, when it finally matures, it won't be worth one penny more than its original price. Utilities, like other common stocks, have no such limits on their potential price. In recent years, when utility dividends often were only 2 per cent or even 1 per cent below the rate of interest on bonds of similar investment quality, many shrewd investors were convinced that this small difference would be more than overcome by the future price appreciation of the utility stocks. Those who wanted all their jam today tended to stick with bonds, whose interest definitely represented a slightly higher yield. But those who gave a greater priority to the total larder over a period of years, including dividends and capital gains, often turned wisely to this kind of common-stock investment—even in retirement years, when generous income was essential.

The second advantage of utility stocks for investors who need income but want some protection against inflation is that the better-quality utilities have a record of increasing dividends steadily over the years, as the cost of living has ascended. With a bond, obviously, there is no such protection—since the company will continue to pay the same interest for the life of the bond. The New York Stock Exchange made a list in 1972 of 22 common stocks that it said had shown "the more significant increases" in dividends over the previous ten years; all had posted dividend increases every year and were then yielding 5 per cent or more. Twenty of the 22 stocks were utilities (American Electric Power, Atlantic City Electric, Baltimore Gas and Electric, Central and South West, Central Telephone, Cleveland Electric, Columbus and South Ohio, Kansas Power and Light, Long Island Lighting, Louisville Gas and Electric, Northern Illinois Gas, Oklahoma Gas and Electric, Portland Gas and Electric, Rochester Gas and Electric, South Carolina Electric and Gas, South Jersey Industries, Southern Company, South Indiana Gas and Electric,

Toledo Edison and United Utilities). The other two, in case you're interested, were Acme Markets and Mobil Oil. Clearly, though, the domination of the list by the much-maligned utilities confirmed that, as the exchange put it, "the utility industry, whose growth is closely linked to population expansion, has historically been a stable source of dividends for the conservative investor"—and, furthermore, a source of dividends whose steady and dependable increases have provided some insurance against the ravages of inflation.

The chances that your utility stocks are going to become the Xeroxes of tomorrow are roughly akin to those of your being tapped tomorrow to become chairman of the New York Stock Exchange. While electric utilities have shown steady growth of earnings, they normally earn, at the most, 12 or 13 per cent on their equity—and if their profits ever did start to rise impressively, their customers would set up a howl that could be heard by every politician and regulatory body from Alaska to Alabama. But if you are looking for a secure investment that provides liberal income plus at least minimal protection against inflation, the power and light company might turn out, after all, to be exactly what turns you on.

Finally, gang, before we stop talking about income and let you get back to making some, there is one other area of investment with which you ought to be conversant—and that is the real estate investment trust, or R.E.I.T. It's the newest twist of all for those to whom current income is of overriding concern, but its roots go deep into the American spirit and soil.

One traditional alternative to investing in the stock market has been investing in real estate; it is, after all, part of the American dream of affluence to be able to hum along happily when the band starts playing "This Land Is My Land." Until recently, however, the chorus was dominated by relatively large investors, since their wealth enabled them to command more expertise and wider diversification than were available to the rest of us. Now, the scales are closer to balance because of the emergence of the real estate investment trusts, which permit the small investor to get into the property game by what amounts to a mutual fund for real estate. And while traditional investments in real estate can be horrendously illiquid (as you may have found out the last time you tried to sell your home), shares in real estate investment trusts have that Wall Street advantage of being readily salable on any business day at a known, specific price. If you proceed carefully and know what you are seeking (two aims we are about to assist), you may find that R.E.I.T.'s offer a useful way for you to stake out a personal claim—not, perhaps, on the entire Great American Land Boom, but at least on a corner of the supermarket parking lot.

The end of the time when real estate investment was essentially a game for the fat cats began in 1960, when Congress decided to grant tax exemption to real estate trusts that paid out at least 90 per cent of their income. This gave the R.E.I.T.'s a status similar to that of mutual funds for stocks—and brought a lot of little kittens into the game. While they had to pay taxes on the dividends the company passed along, untouched until that point by Uncle Sam, these dividends tended to be strikingly high —especially after other, more conventional sources of real estate financing began to dry up in the 1969–70 recession. The trusts provided a means for small investors to get a piece of the action, and the real estate investment trusts became star performers in the stock market.

There are two main kinds of R.E.I.T. (Wall Streeters pronounce it as one word, which they rhyme with "neat"), and both outran the Dow Jones Industrial Average. The "equity" trusts— which invest in income-producing properties—were especially impressive when money was Scrooge tight in 1968 and 1969. But an even more spectacular performance was turned in by the "mortgage" trusts—which concentrate on financing other people's properties (and which are themselves usually subdivided according to the lengths of their mortgages as "short-term," "intermediate-term" and "long-term"). There is much overlapping, and there are assorted hybrid varieties; some trusts, on the other hand, are so specialized that they finance only a specific type of property (one was formed for the single purpose of building a sports arena). Their growth over-all has been spectacular: While R.E.I.T.'s had been around in one form or another since the 1850s, they got their real impetus from the change in law in 1960, and managed to raise about $265,000,000 in capital funds from 1961 to 1967. In 1968 their growth began to accelerate: $131,000,000 raised that year alone—and in 1969 it exploded:

more than $1,100,000,000. That kind of money brought in many of the nation's largest banks and insurance companies, and in 1970 offerings soared to nearly $1,600,000,000—a heady pace that 1971 only barely failed to match.

Just as the evaporation of traditional real estate money during the tight-money era gave the R.E.I.T.'s one solid boost, so did another unexpected assist come from the White House in 1971 when President Nixon embarked on his New Economic Policy. Though most increases in corporate dividends were controlled, there was no limit on the payout from real estate investment trusts—which were still required by law to give their stockholders at least nine of every ten dollars they earned. (Since whatever is retained is taxable, many trusts make a 100 per cent distribution.) This made the R.E.I.T.'s singularly attractive as producers of increasing current income.

Some of their glamour was stripped away in November of 1971, however, when an official of the largest R.E.I.T. in the country, Continental Mortgage Investors, disclosed that his trust was facing its first decline in earnings, suggested that the whole field was getting overcrowded and warned that trouble might lie ahead. The trusts' prices promptly nose-dived, though many recovered smartly in the ensuing months. Nervousness continued, however, about the ability of the R.E.I.T.'s to thrive in a climate of lower interest rates. More than a year after the initial sell-off, it was not uncommon to find these trusts selling at prices that offered investors yields of 10 per cent or more. And when interest rates again escalated sharply in 1973, it was no panacea for the R.E.I.T.'s, which found their own money costs rising and real-estate construction less desirable. Some of the more speculative R.E.I.T.'s tumbled to prices that offered dividend yields as high as 15 per cent.

Since Wall Street rarely gives anything away, an unusually high yield is often a useful warning signal. But while some shakeout seems inevitable, the group is by no means an unbroken patch of thorns to the investor able to pick his way carefully among the more than 120 real estate investment trusts traded on the major exchanges or over-the-counter.

First, do what you would expect to do in a business that has mushroomed so quickly: Look for the track records. About thirty R.E.I.T.'s now have been active at least since 1969 in the area where the largest amount of assets is concentrated—the short-term mortgage trusts that provide construction and land-development money on twelve- to eighteen-month loans. These have been hectic, roller-coaster years for the real estate industry. See how their earnings, their dividends and their share prices have behaved over this period. (This caution is valuable no matter what kind of trust you are considering. Many R.E.I.T.'s, particularly in the equity-trust area, have had erratic earnings records. This makes them much less stable than other high-yielding investments.)

Second, see what this record can tell you about the two main qualities that analysts look for when they are gauging R.E.I.T.'s: the ability of the trust to develop good loans or investments, and the ability to raise money. (R.E.I.T.'s typically draw an original stake from the public, then borrow money to use in their investments—though some accentuate the borrowing more than others.)

Third, be aware that the pure equity trusts, and others that take some ownership interest in properties, should be judged by real estate standards—such as depreciation, "cash flow" (which covers both taxable income and reserves held for such purposes as depreciation), portfolio appreciation and leverage—rather than by such conventional Wall Street indicators as earnings per share and price-earnings ratios. Above all, take note that these trusts have a hidden bookkeeping gimmick to augment their distributed earnings. Like investment real estate companies —and indeed like all landlords—they can claim depreciation on real estate improvements that are actually appreciating in market value. This nontaxable addition to their cash flow provides expanded funds that can be retained for future operations. You should check to see to what extent you can eat your cake (in the high-dividend payout) and still have some additional cash cooking away in the trust's kitchen.

Fourth, try to determine whether the trust is being run as a sound business or just an accidental tax gimmick. How much time does the trust appear to be spending on long-range planning, for example, and what are its ultimate objectives? The best-run trusts offer an array of services that no other single institution can match. And they make an effort, whether interest rates are low or high, to maintain a constant spread between their cost of money (what they pay to borrow it) and their lending rates to others. Many R.E.I.T.'s now seek to downgrade even further the impact of the money market on their growth by making their loans at a level fixed in relationship to the so-called prime rate, thus assuring that the spread will not vary even if interest rates do. This puts the emphasis where it ought to be, on their capacity to make their assets expand by being good real estate men.

The long-range future of R.E.I.T.'s must depend on that of the real estate industry. (They are, after all, supplying capital to the industry that is the nation's largest private user of capital.) The trusts have had more than their share of problems—charges of potential conflicts of interest (as with banks that also operate R.E.I.T.'s), lack of uniform and complete reporting standards and the automatic pressures of not being allowed to retain much of what they earn—and thus having constantly to return to the market for more equity. But many experienced Wall Streeters would agree with what James P. Furniss, managing trustee of Great American Mortgage Investors, told me about his own method of evaluating a R.E.I.T.: "If it's a business that's trying to provide services over and above just being a lender or an investor, then I think they can make money whether money is easy or tight, whether their source of money is expensive or inexpensive." Your own ultimate agreement with him would probably depend on two things: your ability to avoid the fly-by-night trusts and your appraisal of the outlook for real estate. But one thing is certain, at this writing: Viewed strictly as a vehicle for current income (and some even pay monthly dividends to reinforce this image), no other form of bonds or stocks can equal the payout available from R.E.I.T.'s. If that's where your interest lies, you ought at least to take an up-to-date look at the field. The foundations might be there, for land's sake.

As a postscript to this discussion of plain and fancy bonds, preferred stocks, utilities and real estate investment trusts, don't forget that even those whose primary concern is with increasing their current income ought not to ignore the desirability of having at least part of their holdings in quality growth stocks. These securities may carry more obvious risks, and are likely themselves to yield little or nothing in the way of dividends, but they have the invaluable asset of promising long-range protection against inflation. And given the nature of the world, and its politicians, some such protection remains essential even for those entering or imbedded in their retirement years. A regular program of selling off a small percentage of such stocks would provide income, while the remainder hopefully would continue growing over the years. The income-oriented individual will want to be extra-cautious in assuring himself that the company in question is growing in more than market price alone, but he probably cannot afford to take refuge solely in fixed-income (or high-yielding, slow-growing) investments—not unless his faith in the value of politicians' promises about the future stability of the dollar is a good deal deeper than mine.

CHAPTER XVIII
Are You Exercising Your Options?

Mention the words "options market" to the average American, even the average investor, and his eyes will rapidly acquire a glaze suitable for fruit cakes. Suggest that this might be a place where he would want to put some of his money, and he will look at you as if he expected your next proposal to be that he bet against your ability to make the jack of clubs emerge from the deck and spit prune juice. Most small investors have never bought an option, and many regard them with outright suspicion as a sort of legalized version of casino gambling. The affront to conventional morality is furthered by some of the lingo involved; licentious talk about "strips," "straps," "spreads" and "straddles" may well strike those pure in heart, or otherwise uninitiated, as more suited to a burlesque show than a boardroom. (For those whose tastes run in that direction, there is also a gimmick known as "naked writing.") But options, properly used, can be a tool of the most conservative investors, as well as the most daring; they are among the most exciting, albeit least understood, areas of investing, and in this chapter we are going fearlessly to strip them of mystery and spread them out for you to see.

Disillusioning though it may be to the pruriently inclined, perhaps it would be best to begin by defining those apparently lascivious terms—a process that, I regret to report, will be approximately as erotic as a junior high school play. The basic options involved are "puts and calls," which should be more properly referred to as "calls and puts"—since the former predominate over the latter by a ratio of more than three to one. "Call" means "buy," and "put" means "sell"; remember that, and you're halfway home. A call is a contract that gives the purchaser the right to buy 100 shares of a given stock at a fixed price within a specified period of time. For example, you might pay, say, $600 for a call that entitled you to buy 100 shares of Fastryesin Kantmis at its current price of $40 a share any time within the next six months and ten days. If Fastryesin Kantmis then dutifully soared to $80 a share during the life of your option, you would have a whopping profit of $4,000 ($40 per share times 100 shares), minus only the $600 you paid for the option and about $145 for commissions and related charges. If, on the other hand, instead of doubling, the stock went down from $40 to $20 a share, your total loss would be limited to the price of the option —$600.

Let's contrast this with the situation of the more conventional investor, who upon taking a liking to Fastryesin Kantmis proceeded to buy 100 shares of the stock, either on margin or by putting up the entire $4,000 in cash. If the stock then went to $80 a share, he would have the $4,000 gain, minus commissions, but he would have had to lay out much more capital to get it. (Had the cash customer instead bought six calls for $3,600, his profit would have been immensely greater.) If, on that omnipresent other hand, the stock had descended to $20 a share, the buyer of 100 shares for $4,000 would be out $2,000—well in excess of what it would have cost him to buy a call on 100 shares at $40. In short, the buyer of a call has no limit on his potential profit if he guesses right, but has an absolute limit on his potential loss if he guesses wrong. Under no circumstances can he lose more than that one-time initial payment for the call.

Calls, then, can be an exceptionally attractive vehicle for the investor who is convinced that his market judgment is greater than his resources. With a small amount of capital, he can participate impressively in upward stock movements. Even when he misses, he knows precisely the outside limits of his risk. What, then, (to retain our racy motif) is the hooker? It will be obvious to anyone with much experience in investing: The buyer of a call must not only pick the right stock for an upward move, but must pick the right time frame in which that move will take place. Back to our example: If Fastryesin Kantmis fails to move much over the next six months, and winds up just about where it started, the fellow who bought the stock is still all even, and can afford to be patient. The fellow who bought the option has lost his $600. A call in this respect resembles the storied "one-hoss shay": It's a great little buggy during its life span, but it's not worth a darn once it expires. Even the fellow who bought the stock at $40 and saw it fall to $20 may have the hope of a come-back; the buyer of a call must permanently kiss this investment good-bye.

A put, as you may by now have surmised, is the exact opposite of a call, and is designed for those who think that a particular stock is heading downhill. The purchaser of a put on Fastryesin Kantmis at $40 a share has bought himself the right to sell 100 shares of that stock at that price at any time during the life of the contract. He doesn't have to actually own the stock when he buys the put. Puts traditionally have been cheaper than calls, given the essentially optimistic convictions of most American investors, though the difference lately has tended to dwindle. Let's say that this purchaser got a six-month-ten-day put for $500, and then that the stock of that overpriced, deteriorating Fastryesin Kantmis duly tumbled from $40 to $20 a share. The holder of the put has a profit of $2,000 ($20 a share times 100 shares), minus the $500 he paid for the put and his commission charges. Contrast this with the situation of his fellow bear, the short seller: To get that same $2,000 gain on a fall from $40 a share to $20, he would have had to put up either $4,000 cash or the required percentage of that for margin. And there's an ad-ditional—and significant—advantage for the buyer of a put. Under the tax law at this writing (and you will, of course, always be wise to check up-to-the-minute regulations with your own tax adviser before you act), the buyer of a put who holds it for more than six months and then sells it can claim his profit as a long-term capital gain. A short seller, on the other hand, always must report his gains as short-term—and pay the higher rate that ap-plies to such transactions. A put then currently offers what short selling does not: a chance to make a long-term capital gain in a declining market.

In a moment we're going to get to the techniques and strategies of the options market, but first let's ring down the curtain on the rest of the burlesque show. In keeping with a society that caters to all tastes, those terms refer to offbeat combinations of puts and calls: A "straddle," the most common variant, combines a put and a call. A "spread," which would normally be cheaper, would typically have a call priced above the market (giving you the right to buy Fastryesin Kantmis at, say, $44 a share) and a put priced below the market (giving you the right to sell it at, say, $36 a share). A "strip" is two puts and a call on the same stock at the same price. A "strap" combines two calls and a put. Even a bordello in pre-Castro Havana could hardly offer more choices than that for the visiting bourgeoisie.

We have had one caution light already in this discussion—you have to be right not only about the stock but about the timing, or you lose your total investment—and now it's time for another. What we are really talking about here is "leverage," and no investor should even dream about employing it without realizing that it can be a double-edged blade. As in physics, where a small amount of energy can lift a mighty load, so investment "leverage" is designed to make a small amount of money do the work of much more. Such leverage is involved when the investor borrows money from his brokerage firm through a margin account, thereby buying more stock than he could otherwise afford, and it is involved even more dramatically in the purchase of options, which require even less initial capital. (Do not confuse this with "high leverage" in the corporate-accounting sense—in which it refers to a company with a large amount of debt, such as bonds, compared to a small amount of equity, such as common stocks. In such a company a relatively puny increase in earnings, once the interest on the bonds is taken care of, can result in a dramatic increase in earnings-per-share for the stocks.) The investor who controls more shares than he has actually paid for, whether through a margin loan or by buying an option, stands to get a bigger profit than he would otherwise have had. But if the price of the stock goes against him, he may in turn lose more than he would have if he had made his purchase entirely in cash. Leverage is not for the faint-hearted, or the uncertain, and it is certainly not for beginners.

The option buyer has traditionally been a figure of folly to many Wall Streeters; the volume of securities under option has never amounted to more than 2 per cent of the total New York Stock Exchange trading in any year, and theories of technical analysis have grown up based on betting against the prevailing sentiment among option buyers. (When the ratio of puts to calls begins to rise, for example, these analysts apply reverse English and take this as a bullish indication. Among those who are convinced that the typical option buyer is "a rank speculator and usually wrong" is Dr. Martin E. Zweig, whose own "Zweig Forecast" closely follows the activity of what he terms "the witless options speculators.") Despite such merciless criticism, however, I am inclined to think that the average investor ought to know more about the available options—not as a substitute for more conventional investing, but as a possible supplement involving a limited portion of his funds.

There are, to begin with, two distinct types to whom puts and calls might reasonably appeal. The first, and most obvious, is the speculator whose eye is bigger than his capital; he can gain control of a large amount of stock for several months for much less money than it would take actually to buy or sell that many shares. His profit can be tremendous, and his loss can be no greater than the price of his options. The second type of potential option buyer is quite different; he's the conservative investor who just wants to buy an insurance policy. Suppose, for example, you have purchased 100 shares of a stock at $50 a share and seen its price go up to $100. You're delighted—but you're a little scared. What you could do would be to buy a put, giving you the right to sell all your stock at $100 a share any time within, say, the next six months. If the stock goes down, you are protected. And if it turns out that you were just too jittery—and the stock keeps going up—you are out only the price of the put, and you still own your stock. As these very different situations suggest, the options market is something every serious investor ought, at least, to know about—and more than two dozen Wall Street houses now have options departments to make this possible.

The risk involved in buying options has been the chief excuse for not disseminating information about them more widely, but I suspect there is also a good deal to what Robert J. Nurock, of Merrill Lynch, once remarked to me on "Wall Street Week": "Most brokers are really not that familiar with the sophisticated uses of puts and calls, and consequently if a broker does not have sufficient confidence to discuss something intelligently with his client, he shies away from it." So if you are interested in buying a call, you may well have to make the first move. Here's how to do it: Tell your account executive that you would like an "indication" of the likely price of a call on, say, Fastryesin Kantmis, and tell him how long you would like the call to run. (Options are written for periods ranging from three weeks to thirteen months, though the most common periods are ninety-five days and six months and ten days, known as "six-and-ten"; the latter can set up a possible long-term capital gain.) The price will depend on the time period you have requested and on the volatility and recent price history of the stock; a typical six-and-ten call on a reasonably volatile $40 stock would cost about $600, or 15 per cent of what it would cost you to buy the 100 shares outright. But there is no guarantee of the price—nor is there likely to be, as when buying a stock, an immediate execution. After your broker has wired your request to his firm's options department, an option clerk there will call several option dealers to get a range of tentative price offers on the option you want to buy. The report will then come back to you and you can make your decision. Options can be bought only in a margin account, which in practice means simply that same-day payment is required; you must pay full cash for the option, and you need not do any borrowing from your broker just because you now have a margin account.

If you buy a call and the stock goes down, you're out of luck—and money. But if the stock begins to rise, you have a number of alternatives. You can, if you wish, wait more than six months (but less than ten days more, or your option will have expired!) and then sell the profitable call—the option itself—to your broker. He will credit your account with the difference between the current market price of 100 shares of Fastryesin Kantmis and the lower price established in your call—minus two commissions. (If you want to take your profit as a long-term gain, it's important to do it this way. If, on the other hand, you exercised your call —buying 100 shares of the stock at $40 and then immediately selling them at the current, higher market price—your gain, though exactly the same, would be taxed at short-term rates. The Internal Revenue Service figures that your holding period for the stock would be less than a day, while your holding period for the option contract itself would have been more than six months; so don't fight City Hall: Sell the option, not the stock.) This is a nice way to take a low-taxed profit, and you don't have to put up any additional cash, even temporarily.

There are, however, other possibilities en route. Suppose, for example, that you bought your six-and-ten call on Fastryesin

Kantmis at $40 a share, and the price promptly soared within the next two months to $56 a share. You could just sit back and wait, seeing your $600 option mount ever higher in value. But you might reason that neither the stock market, nor an individual stock, ever goes straight in any one direction—and you might worry that your paper profit could evaporate. Now you have two additional alternatives: You can exercise your option, assuring yourself of a short-term profit. Or you could—get ready now —sell short 100 shares of Fastryesin Kantmis at $56 a share. You will have to put up enough cash to meet the current margin requirements for this short sale, but unlike most short sellers you can remain serene in the knowledge that your transaction is entirely without risk. If the stock goes up instead of down, you can always close out the short sale by exercising your option to buy 100 shares of Fastryesin Kantmis at $40 a share—and you will still have the profit that the call showed at the moment you sold short. If, on the other hand, the stock falls to, say, $46 a share, you can buy 100 shares of Fastryesin Kantmis in the open market, close out your short sale at a substantial profit—and still have the call. Fast-moving speculators sometimes trade several times against the same call, making a succession of profits, each of which is insured against risk by ownership of the call. Obviously, this can work only when the stock you have optioned moves up quickly and then follows an erratic course, but it is a cherished device of some market sophisticates.

There is a final option available to the holder of a profitable call: He can buy and hold the stock. Such a decision would be based on the conviction that Fastryesin Kantmis had become an excellent long-term holding. The holder would exercise his option to buy 100 shares of the stock at $40 a share. He would have a built-in profit based on the then-current selling price of the stock. (There is an additional twist for margin customers, since they would have to put up only enough cash to cover the $4,000 transaction, but would immediately get credited with a loan value based on the current higher price of the stock. If this applies to you, ask your broker what the net cost of the transaction would be under then-prevailing regulations: how much cash you would have to put up, and how much you could then immediately withdraw.)

While most options are negotiated at the current market price

of the stock—$40 in the examples we have been considering—
there is another kind of option of which you ought to be aware:
the so-called special offerings. Professional option dealers make
a practice of buying options for which they have no instant customer; they hold these options in their inventories, and then sell
them at a price that may be above or below what they paid
—depending on what happens to the stock in the meantime.
These are the options you see advertised in the newspapers,
and a typical listing might say something like this:

CLOSE	Per 100 Shares (Plus Tax)
40 Fastryesin Kantmis. . . .39⅜ Mar. 14	$625.00

Such an offering is said to be "in the money" because its "striking
price"—the price at which you have the right to buy the stock—is
below the current market price. It will naturally cost you a little
more than a regular offering at the current market price, and
still more than an offering that is "out of the money"—that is,
at a price above that currently available in the open market. (In
the example above, you are told, first, that the last closing price
of Fastryesin Kantmis was $40 a share. Then you are offered a
call that entitles you to buy 100 shares of the stock at $39.375 a
share any time before next March 14. The call will cost you
$625.00. If we assume for the sake of argument that March 14 is
still more than six months off, and thus offers long-term-gain possibilities, this would be an attractive special offering. If the cost
of a six-and-ten at the market price of $40 were $600, and you
could get an option price of $39.375 for $625, you would in effect
be buying a call "⅜ below the market"—paying $25 more for a
price advantage that, on 100 shares, would amount to $62.50.)
The premium on a special offering will commonly, though not
invariably, be increased $50 for every point it is in the money and
reduced $50 for every point it is out of the money.

Those who deride the options market can find ammunition in
the overwhelming preponderance of calls over puts, in good
markets and bad; this says something, perhaps, about the slanting
of brokerage-house advice toward the buy side—or just about the
eternal optimism of the typical investor. (Even in the bear market
of 1969, 75 per cent of all options written were calls.) It is also
frequently asserted with confidence that no more than half (if

that many) of all options written are ever exercised. There are, in fact, absolutely no reliable statistics on this subject, but available evidence suggests that these estimates are not wildly incorrect; they do, however, miss the point on at least two counts: Many options are written, as we have seen, as insurance policies; since they do provide this insurance, it is short-sighted to regard their premiums as wasted. They are no more wasted than are the premiums on fire insurance in a year your house didn't burn. And in the more speculative area it is more than possible to do extremely well with a program of buying options, even though only half (or even less) of them actually prove profitable; this is where the leverage feature can really pay off.

In recognition of their potential attractions, options have become one of the fastest-growing segments of the securities industry. In 1973 the Chicago Board of Trade opened a supplementary options market of its own, dealing only in calls on specified stocks at specified prices with specified expiration dates. These options are traded openly each market day, thereby offering the additional feature of allowing profitable calls to be sold before their expiration date at a price higher than they would bring simply by being exercised. (In our examples above, a six-and-ten call on a stock that had risen ten points would bring no more if it were sold one month after its purchase than if it were sold just before expiration—though it plainly would have more potential value with five months still to run. This prospect of further gains is reflected in the Chicago market by a higher bid price for in-the-money options that still have considerable time to run. In the broader conventional market, this advantage is enjoyed by options dealers but not by individual purchasers.) Other signs of increasing interest in the more traditional options market include the setting up of ever more options departments in major brokerage firms and the entry into the market of large institutional investors both as buyers and sellers of options. (You, too, might find the selling side of the options market more to your liking; we will get to that shortly.)

The buying of options for speculation obviously requires every bit as much research as does the outright purchase of stocks— more, in fact, since in addition to finding a stock that has fundamental reasons for growing, you have to have enough technical feel for the market to believe that the growth is going to take place quickly. Most investors probably will continue to decide that, except perhaps in some special situations, it is basically not for them. If you, though, are considering proceeding further in this area, here are some tips you may find useful:

(1) Buy six-month-ten-day options. They will generally cost about 50 per cent more than ninety-five-day options, but they give you three big advantages: You have more time to be right, you have more time for trading against an option that is proving successful and you can take your profit on the option as a long-term gain. (One-year options are sometimes available at not much more than the price of a six-and-ten; they can be even nicer.)

(2) Favor volatile stocks—the kind whose price tends to make big moves in either direction. Options on the more stable blue-chip stocks can be bought more cheaply—for good reason; their price fluctuations usually are less extreme. The option buyer should at least feel he has a chance of doubling his money. Since he's not going to come up a winner every time, he must have the capacity to make an awful lot of hay when the sun does shine—and this usually means he ought to stay with the stocks that involve more inherent risk. Remember that he has limited his loss to the price of his option; he would be foolish if he then went on to limit his profit by buying the stick-in-the-muds.

(3) Spread your risk by buying options on more than one stock —and by staggering your purchases. The purchase of a single option is a gamble; the purchase of several can be a rational program.

(4) A good time to buy calls on quality growth stocks is when "everybody" is saying that the stock market is never going to get healthy again. Not only are these stocks often ridiculously depressed at these points, but I have found that the options themselves can sometimes be obtained at bargain percentages.

(5) Consider the possibility of buying a straddle, which as you will recall combines a put and a call—and which normally will cost 1.7 times the price of a call. LeRoy Gross, the dynamic boss of Reynolds Securities' options department, told me the straddle was his "favorite weapon," adding, "We're of the opinion that nobody really knows the future price of a Natomas or an Itek or a Bausch and Lomb—these volatile stocks, nobody knows the direction for sure. So we recommend that our customers buy

straddle options on these stocks. . . . If you had a straddle on Hot Stock X, let's say, and it went up sharply, the call part of your straddle would make you money. If the stock goes down sharply, the put part would make a guy money. So what we say is, nobody knows the future but you have a chance to make money on the future no matter which direction the market may take."

(6) Something your broker may not tell you: If you have a six-month-ten-day option that looks like a sure loser, don't just let it expire. Before six months are up, sell it to your brokerage firm for $1.00. That makes it, under current law, a short-term loss for you—which is generally better than a long-term loss. The firm is happy to perform such a generous service for a marvelous customer like you. (Help it out with a little reminder.)

(7) The "striking price"—the price at which you are entitled to buy the stock, on a call, or sell it, on a put—is determined when the trade is completed, which may be some time after you place your order. If you are worried that the stock's price may change so much in the interim that you will lose interest, tell your broker that you agree to the offered price for the option "at the market, top limit 42" (or whatever), and you won't be committed at a price you don't like.

(8) Where special offerings are available, judge them depending on your confidence in the purchase you are about to make. If your confidence verges on the unbounded, it's better to pay a little more for an option that is already in the money—even though you thereby increase your loss in the event you guessed wrong. If you are less certain, you should favor options that are out of the money; it will take you longer to show a profit, if you are right, but since an out of the money option is cheaper, you will lose less if you are wrong. (If you have no confidence whatever in what you are about to do, stay out of the options market.)

Option buying, to recapitulate, is not for market neophytes—nor is it a replacement for the kind of long-range investment program that this book has been urging. But after you have had some experience, and tested your judgment "on paper" a few times against the actual market results, you may be tempted to set aside a portion of your funds for what you will frankly recognize as speculation. I would no more deny you that pleasure than I would suggest that you spend the rest of your life in a monastery.

Just realize exactly what you are doing, be prepared to take a loss
—and if you are astute (and lucky) enough to boot home a winner, you may be inclined to agree with LeRoy Gross. "It's a great
thing," he told me, "for the small fellow who wants to control a
hundred shares or two, get the feel of the stock market and not
risk very much money."

The uses of options as a conservative hedge against market
risks are limited only by each individual investor's inventiveness
and temperament. Such uses can be as simple as buying a call
on a stock when you sell it—to guard against the possibility that
you took your profit too soon. Or they can be as intricate as buying a short-term put to protect a long-term call—thus guaranteeing that the paper profit in a successful call will not disappear in
its closing days. But their strongest appeal to most investors who
buy them is probably as speculative vehicles that can deliver
major profits on minor cash. Those whose investment attitudes
are characteristically conservative, while they should be aware of
the hedging possibilities available in the purchase of options, may
find themselves drawn far more persuasively to the other side of
the deal—the sale, or "writing," of options. Those who thus, in
effect, take the house side of the bet will find themselves in the
company of wealthy individuals, who write most put and call
options, and the increasing number of large institutions that have
decided to sell options on their own portfolios. This is not basically an opportunity for the very small investor—it is usually suggested for holders of $50,000 or more in stocks—but an occasional
program could be started with $10,000 in stocks, or even less.
The advantages are twofold: (1) Most observers are convinced
that over an extended period of time, and taking all transactions
into consideration, the odds would favor the sellers of options
over the buyers. (2) While the seller of options is limiting his
profit potential on any single deal, he improves his over-all
chances of obtaining a return on his portfolio that exceeds that
available in dividends on stock or interest on bonds. On a long-
term basis an intelligent program of selling options is thought
by most experts to bring a minimum return in the range of 15
per cent a year. Many estimates go higher, and none of course
is guaranteed, but there is obviously something worth looking

into here for the substantial investor who is more interested in imitating the bank than breaking it.

Here's how you become a seller—or, to use the insiders' term, a "writer"—of options: Make sure your brokerage firm is established and experienced in this field. If it is, tell your account executive that you want his options department to know of your interest in hearing option bids. Now, let's assume that somebody else has just announced his willingness to buy our old friend, a six-month-ten-day call on Fastryesin Kantmis at $40. This firm order usually is handled by one of the approximately twenty-five companies whose primary business is dealing in puts and calls. The put and call dealer will now pass the word, both to individuals on his own list and to brokerage firms such as yours, that he is willing to pay, say, $550 for such a call. (You may remember that the price to the buyer in our example was $600; the middle men take their profit on the difference, with perhaps $12.50 going to each of the brokerage firms involved.) If you decide to become the writer of this $550 call, you may already own 100 shares of Fastryesin Kantmis or you may decide to buy the stock at the same time you sell the call. When the deal is complete, the buyer has paid $600, you have received $550 and the brokers and the dealer have divided the rest. (Your firm is not going to declare an extra dividend because of the $12.50 it just made, but it figures it is priming the pump for commissions on your purchase and sale of the stock covered by the option.)

Before we go any farther let's pause and point with pride at something you have just learned about the options business— something that is misunderstood even by many experienced investors who ought to know better: The seller of a call does not necessarily differ in his judgment from the buyer of a call. They both, in fact, expect the stock to go up. (Otherwise, of course, it would be insane to buy the stock when you were selling the call.) The difference is this: The buyer is hoping for a fantastic gain, and on a six-and-ten call he will be inclined, for tax purposes, to delay in exercising his option until more than six months has expired. The seller is content with an assured return on his investment, and he hopes the buyer will exercise his option as early as possible—so that the seller can quickly reinvest his capital. The buyer is reaching for the moon; the seller is playing the percentages.

The seller of any kind of option, if he is smart, will be bullish about the stock he is optioning. If he is writing calls, he will want to have the buyers exercise their options to purchase this stock from him as early and as often as possible; if the stock instead declines in value, even though his loss is reduced by the amount of the premium on the option he has sold, he is not really making money—and he is not turning over his capital as rapidly as a successful option-writing program demands. Now let's take the fellow who is writing not calls but puts. What he is doing is promising to buy stock at the current market price any time he is requested to do so within the life of the option he has sold. Obviously, he does not want to have to do so: for if he does he will have to pay, say, $4,000 for stock that may be worth only $3,000 or less at the moment of purchase. The option writer does best when everyone to whom he sells a call is a winner and everyone to whom he sells a put is a loser. In either case his interests are best served when the stock goes up—and that's why the Wall Street adage proclaims: "Call me ever. Put me never."

By now, if you are the devious sort, a contrary thought may be germinating: Why can't the seller of a call simply bet against the foolish optimist who is buying it? Why shouldn't he, in the example we have given, just pocket the $550 premium for selling the option—and then hope that the stock goes down and not up, thus rendering the option worthless? In that case he would not have either to own the stock or buy it; he could make easy money gambling against the (often wrong) bulls, and he could use his capital elsewhere. Well, the answer is that it has often been done —and sometimes even successfully—but it is a brutal and unnecessary risk that ought to be avoided. This, indeed, is what is known as "naked writing." Don't try it unless you're a Hemingway.

Here's why: Your refusal to own or buy the underlying stock was based on your assumption that the stock was going to go down, not up. Suppose you're wrong (believe it or not, it could happen). The stock on which you sold a call at $40 a share is now called for—when the stock is selling in the open market at, say, $70 a share. You will get roughly $4,000 (in addition to the premium that you received long ago). But you have to first go out into the open market and make a $7,000 purchase. Do that a few times and it will begin to dawn on you why naked writing is considered a less than topnotch method for making money.

The option writer should think of himself less as a speculator —that's the job of the guy who buys the options—than as a seller of insurance. In return for offering protection to the buyer of the option, on certain terms and for a certain period, he receives a reasonable premium. Just as an insurance company should, the wise option writer conducts his own affairs prudently and conservatively: If he sells a call, he makes sure he owns the stock that may be called. If he sells a put, he makes sure—even if his broker doesn't require it—that he has enough money in his account to buy the stock he has agreed to buy, at the price he has agreed to pay, if the stock should indeed be "put" to him. He tries to stick, in either case, to stocks that he regards as having little downside risk. That way, even in a declining market with his portfolio losing 10 to 15 per cent of its value, he is cushioned by the premiums he is receiving—and will be well placed to start taking profits when the market recovers.

There are two basic categories of option writers: "occasional" and "programmed." The occasional writer may simply be a fellow with a relatively stable portfolio of blue-chip stocks, whose dividend income he now and then cares to supplement by selling an option. He doesn't get too excited about what happens next. If the stock goes up and is called, he figures he can find a similar investment-grade stock into which to put his proceeds plus his premium. If the stock goes down and the option is not exercised, he is not disconcerted since he probably intended to hang on to the stock for the long haul anyhow.

Another occasional option writer might be a fellow who wanted to buy 100 shares of our Fastryesin Kantmis but thought the current $40 price a bit too high. By selling a call for $550 he reduces his effective purchase price to $34.50 (his purchase price, minus the premium he received, divided by 100). If the stock takes a temporary drop, as he feared, the option will not be exercised. If it doesn't, he has limited—but not eliminated—his profit. And there are many other possible occasional option writers, such as an investor who already has a nice profit in a stock and is about to leave on an extended vacation; if his stock goes up enough in his absence to make the call worthwhile, he has taken a good profit—if not he has the consolation of the additional income he got by selling the option.

In contrast to this sometime dabbler in option writing is the investor who consciously embarks on a "program" under which he tries to get the law of averages working in his favor to produce an annual net return of 15 per cent or higher on the stocks —the more the better—that he commits to the program. He will be, as they say, not "portfolio-oriented" but "premium-oriented" and "percentage-minded." Option writing becomes the central feature of his entire investment program, or at least a substantial portion of it. Reasoning that he is not about to triple his money by "beating the market," he decides instead to seek a more assured return that is, at the same time, well above what he could expect from fixed-income securities. A well-organized program will have him writing options fifty-two weeks a year, in good markets and bad, and thus gaining the same advantages of "dollar cost averaging" that are available in other forms of investment—such as the regular purchase of an equal dollar amount of a selected growth stock. If the option writer were so vain as to believe that he could foresee every turn of the market, he would try to make larger profits elsewhere; instead he is content with a return that can approximate 30 per cent or more during rising markets and at least curb his losses when prices are falling. The option writer prefers cash in hand to a bonanza in the bush.

Most option writers are advised to employ stocks with good earnings records and average volatility. There is less risk sometimes in the low-volatility blue chips, but the premiums are much lower. (A six-and-ten call on 100 shares of stock could run anywhere from 7 to 20 per cent of the cost of the underlying stock; calls on those old-line, sluggish blue chips would be cheapest.) On the other hand, top premiums would be paid for high-volatility, over-the-counter stocks, but the risks are commensurately greater, too. The medium range, which would include established growth stocks, is usually considered the best area of operation.

Come close now while I whisper in your ear one final advantage of option writing: taxes. At this writing, the cash you receive as a premium on a put or call that is not exercised is considered ordinary income. But if the option is exercised you have interesting capital-gains possibilities. If the option was a call on stock that you owned, you add the premium to the sale price in figuring your gain. If the option was a put, you reduce your purchase price by the amount of the premium in figuring your tax cost. So what's so interesting about that? Mainly this: Suppose you have owned a stock for four months and have a handsome profit—which you hesitate to take, for the gain would be taxed at the higher short-term rate. So you sell a sixty-five-day call on the stock. If the stock goes down, your loss is cut by the premium you received on the call. But let's assume the stock goes up, and the call is exercised at the expiration date. Your capital gain is the difference between what you paid for the stock and the total of what you received for it and what you received when you sold the option. But all of that gain is long-term, even though the call was for just over two months—since the stock to which it was attached was held for more than six months. Uncle Sam has thus taken the position that options are a helpful, and stabilizing, influence on the market, and it would be downright unpatriotic for you not to be aware of the opportunities this presents.

Option writing, then, can have appeal for investors varying from those who want an occasional supplement to their dividends to those who seek help with a specific temporary problem to those who have decided this is the way they want to spend the rest of their investment days—a decision that is best made by those who already have amassed substantial portfolios. (For knowledgeable retired people who hold growth stocks that pay slender dividends, selling options can be an alternative to selling off a portion of the stocks each year for income.)

The mechanics are as simple as signing the form to start a margin account. (Again, as in buying options, you don't actually have to incur any debt. But options are not considered by regulatory bodies as securities, and hence cannot be held in a cash securities account. And since your firm has guaranteed the option it wrote on your behalf, it requires the power to make any necessary sales or purchases to meet your obligations. It gets this power in a margin account, whereas in a normal cash account the firm has to await the customer's go-ahead.) Once you're in business, it really is the insurance business—which is why the writer of a six-and-ten option should be delighted if it is exercised after sixty days: He has been paid for six months' worth of insurance and provided it for only two. But the basic disadvantage in option writing is the other side of its conservative advantages: In contrast to the buyer of the option, you are limiting your possible gain (to the size of the premium) but not limiting

your possible loss (including the profit you could have made in a
stock that was called or the amount above the market you will
have to pay if a put you sold was exercised). The option writer
who controls his greed—who owns the stocks on which he sells
calls and who retains the cash to honor his puts—can rationally
seek a long-term return above the average for the market. But it
will seldom give him much conversation at the country club. And
sooner or later it is certain to test his character when he sees that
the stock on which he sold a call at $40 a share promptly tripled
—thus reducing his profit from the $8,000 he would have had
if he had just held the stock to the $600 or so he received for the
call. Even Atlas might not shrug that one off. But the wise, and
successful, writer of options will realize that he has consciously
surrendered the possibility of heart-thumping excitement in favor
of the less stimulating but more certain rewards of playing the
percentages.

Those who are fascinated by the potentialities of leverage in
creating large profits from small investments would count me
swinishly inadequate if I left the subject without alluding to the
fabulous possibilities in "warrants." Heaven forfend; allusion will
follow forthwith.

Your attitude toward warrants may well depend on your age.
What they are is certificates entitling you to buy a certain stock
at a certain price. They are traded just like stocks, on and off the
major exchanges. In the 1920s, when stocks were moving ever
higher, warrants zoomed along at an even more frantic pace;
they were beloved of carefree investors and a jazzy symbol of
the era. Then came the 1929 Crash, and nothing crashed harder
than warrants. They became such pariahs that they were banned
from the august New York Stock Exchange until 1970. The Big
Board, as it likes to be called, did not unbend until warrants were
issued by the American Telephone and Telegraph Company—
bluest of the blue chips and an unimpeachable symbol of corporate respectability. Led by the matronly Ma Bell, a dozen warrants became listed in the next two years.

Warrants should not be confused with "rights," which are options granted to shareholders of a company to buy new shares at
a discount from the current market value. Such rights used to
have considerable attraction, but their appeal has dwindled in

recent years. Their life, in any event, is typically short—from a couple of weeks to a few months—whereas warrants characteristically run for years, and sometimes even perpetually. (Warrants have been described as "call options issued by companies on their own stock," since both calls and warrants give their owners the right to purchase a stock at a given price—even if the stock, meanwhile, has gone way up on the open market. But there is an important time difference here, too: Whereas calls typically expire after a period of months, most warrants have a life of at least three to five years. Also, they can be freely bought and sold in the open market. A disadvantage, as compared with calls, is that you can buy warrants only if a company has decided to issue them.) The A.T.&T. case is illustrative: Each of the 31,000,000 warrants issued in 1970 entitled the holder to buy one share of A.T.&T. stock by turning in the warrant and paying $52 cash any time before May 15, 1975. (In other words, if the stock itself went to $100 a share during that period, the warrant would have to be worth at least $48—since the exact same stock could be had for the warrant plus $52.) As with all warrants, these paid no dividends and had no voting rights. All they had was a chance —a chance to see the price of the warrants advance more rapidly than the price of the related common stock. Plainly, as long as the price of the common stock remained below $52, the warrants had no intrinsic value, since the privilege they carried was available to anyone who wanted it in the open market. If the stock sold above $52, then the warrants would have some intrinsic value—plus whatever the market added for speculation.

When the stock was below $52, though, the warrants still sold for something—the something depending on how much investors were willing to pay for the assumption that the warrants would eventually have some intrinsic value before they expired. (In practice, in the first two and a half years after issuance, the warrants varied in price from $5.875 to about $13, while the approximate range of the common stock was $40.75 to $53.875.) In each day's trading, even for this ultraconservative company, the price of the warrant would have to be determined on the highly speculative basis of what was likely to happen to the price of the common stock before the warrants expired.

Once the common stock to which a warrant is related begins to move, the normal expectation is that the warrant will rise even faster, on a percentage basis—and that is where the leverage factor becomes attractive. But when a stock descends, that leverage can work rapidly in reverse; warrants can, and have, become totally worthless. This capacity for acceleration, whether going or coming, is what makes warrants so inherently speculative. Ratings services, which you can buy or examine at your broker's office, issue weekly analyses and computer tabulations that purport to give you insight into the upside and downside possibilities of the warrant as compared to the common stock. They also provide such basic information as the exercise price per share and the expiration date. (It's never necessary to exercise a warrant; you can always sell it for what it's worth in the open market.)

Despite the bargain prices at which they sometimes seem to be offered, most smart investors will not buy warrants unless they believe in the prospects of the underlying common stock. (An occasional exception might occur when the market was extraordinarily depressed, and the warrants appeared to offer opportunities for quick and heady profits.) Generally, the best warrants have been those whose related common stock had the brightest future. The New York Stock Exchange, when it reopened the door a crack in 1970, added these additional precautions: (1) maturity of about three to ten years; (2) ownership distribution comparable to common stock; (3) warrant exercise price not substantially above price of common stock at time of issue; (4) amount of warrants not to exceed 20 per cent of common stock outstanding unless approved by stockholders, with a maximum of 50 per cent.

While the Big Board was keeping the hordes away from the gate, however, warrants did not retire from the scene elsewhere. About 300 are currently sold on the American Stock Exchange, regional exchanges or the over-the-counter market. Some are issued in connection with other kinds of securities, and sometimes there is an option to buy the common stock either with cash or with other securities issued by the company. Some sophisticated investors use warrants in complicated hedging maneuvers in which they buy the common stock at the same time they sell short the warrants—or vice versa. But the sleekest glamour has attached to warrants that demonstrated the leverage feature that can be enjoyed when the (higher priced) related common stock makes dazzling moves of its own. (Two examples: Between 1962 and 1966, United Air Lines common stock rose 624 per cent; the warrants rose 2,700 per cent. Between 1956 and 1959, General Tire and Rubber common stock rose 428 per cent; the warrants rose 4,566 per cent.) A warrant whose common stock is zooming can be a supersonic creature, and once the stock approaches the price at which the warrant can be exercised, the warrant usually ascends more rapidly than the stock. The big "if," of course, lies in the performance and prospects of the common stock.

Leverage for an investor—whether he obtains it by trading on margin, buying options or dealing in warrants—magnifies the performance of the dollars he has to invest. It tends to exaggerate both his strengths and his weaknesses. The appeal of such leverage is obvious to any investor who seeks to translate the meager supply of dollars with which life has left him into a modern stock-market fortune. Yet most investors should treat leverage with care. If they have guessed wrong, about the merits of their securities or even about such an ephemeral consideration as timing, their punishment will be commensurately greater than that received by the investor who sought no more than 100 cents worth of market power per dollar. Those who insist on treating Wall Street as a casino, in which they are determined to indulge their fantasies of being the highest roller around, should remember to keep careful track both of their risks and their resources. Be aware of the odds each time you take the dice, and always save a quarter for the hatcheck girl.

CHAPTER XIX

Should You Go Against the Grain?

Pardon me for getting personal, but do you yearn for a little more action in your life? Have you lived too long in the same place and/or with the same person? Is your chief philosophical speculation a mild curiosity as to whether you are watching too much television? Do your surroundings seem drab, your regimen insufferable—and even your investments stultifyingly prosaic? Have you thought of remedying this situation by taking a fling at the exciting commodities market?

Don't. Go to Paradise Island instead. It's nice there this time of year, and when you walk into its plush, high-ceilinged casino, your heart may be syncopating but you are unlikely to con yourself into thinking that you are there as a prudent investor.

The commodities market has a hypnotic appeal for many Americans that goes beyond its sheer speculative velocity. I suspect it may have something to do with the increasingly homogenized, suburbanized nature of our culture. You take a city fellow, whether born and bred there or just unwillingly employed there, and you start to talk to him about wheat and cattle and soybeans and pork bellies, and his eyes take on a misty, faraway glow as if he were getting ready to sing the opening solo from *Oklahoma!* Mention copper or silver, and his mind transmogrifies him into the rugged boss of a nineteenth-century mining camp, courageously amassing the overnight fortune that will make him the toast of San Francisco. All this can be remarkably heady stuff for a guy who usually hangs out at the water cooler and works in the fourth partition to your left.

So the embryo investor is likely to ask himself at some point along the way a variant of this fundamental question: What interest should the typical inexperienced investor take in the pulse-thumping profit possibilities of the commodities market? My answer will not, I trust, be regarded as excessive beating around the bush. It is: none whatsoever.

Now, before all my (former?) friends in the commodities business fall about me with imprecations, let me summarize my objections: Past government surveys have indicated that fully three out of four commodities traders lose money; a former official of the Securities and Exchange Commission told me that he was convinced the current percentage of losers is even higher. History suggests that nine out of ten individual commodities transactions are unprofitable; commodities brokers admit as much when they advertise that you can be wrong 70 or 80 per cent of the time and still make money—by the classic market technique of cutting your losses and letting your profits run. The commodities business is full of professionals who for one reason or another are likely to be far better equipped to call the turn than is the casual amateur trying to pick up a few bucks the easy way. Finally, even the industry's most eloquent salesmen are unlikely to convince you that this is a smart place for the newcomer to Wall Street to be putting his money. Owen H. Nichols, speaking as chairman of the Chicago Board of Trade, told me that, while he advocated entry into the commodities market for those with what he called "speculative risk capital," he was frank to acknowledge that this was "not investment capital." And if you're still inclined to believe that you might be the one in four who makes money in commodities, be aware that at least one major brokerage house will not even take on a commodities trader unless he has a minimum $50,000 in liquid assets (car and home don't count) plus $2,000 in plainly labeled "risk capital." Those with scared money, or little money, should certainly look elsewhere, and many in the more affluent brackets may well decide to do the same.

Why, then, do so many lambs head right for the slaughter? Because the commodities market offers more of the thrills of the casino than any of the other conventional forms of investment and speculation. Profits and losses come quickly—not in months or years, as with stock investment, but in weeks or days. A little capital goes a long way—margin (the amount of money you have to put up on each trade) is 5 or 10 per cent of the total sum, a small fraction of that required on stock purchases. And a full-cash payer in the commodities market, eschewing the lures of margin trading, is as hard to find as the Abominable Snowman in Nepal. Furthermore, there are fewer limits on the free-swinging trader; for example, the speculator who wants to sell a stock short can do so only after an "uptick" (a trade at a higher price than the last previous trade), while his brother in the commodities market—who is under no such regulatory inhibitions—can sell, sell, sell all the way down. The committed commodities trader is the Action Jackson of speculation.

Is the commodities market really just another casino, then? No, it's not that simple. Commodities markets have been performing an honorable role in history since the late seventeenth century, when the powerful Japanese shoguns sought to protect themselves against variations in the price of rice. They began trading rice "futures." (Commodities "futures" carry that science-fiction designation because the purchaser of a contract has bought the right to take future delivery of the commodity in question in the month for which he bought it and at the price he paid.) In the case of any of the more than 40 commodities now traded on the thirteen American commodities exchanges, there are good, conservative reasons for participation on the part of the producers (such as corn farmers in the corn market), distributors (such as grain elevator operators in the wheat market) and users (such as chocolate manufacturers in the cocoa market). They are more interested in knowing what their costs and rewards are going to be than in gambling on the uncertainty of the market-place; hence, they seek to hedge against the risk of owning the raw or semiprocessed product by going to the commodities market and finding somebody else there who is willing—nay, eager—to assume that risk. That somebody is the commodities speculator, who guarantees them an agreed price in return for a chance at a big profit if the market price goes his way in the weeks that follow.

A producer of grain belongs in the commodities market; when he sells a future on his product, he has guaranteed himself the price he will receive when the product is ready for delivery. Major corporations belong in the commodities market; as a normal, day-to-day function of alert management, Hershey will trade cocoa, Eastman Kodak will trade silver and Swift will trade pork bellies (the unsavory name for uncured bacon). Many stockbrokers have lately come to believe that they belong in the commodities market; while their customers race in and out of fast-moving trades, they generate gorgeous commissions. And the commodities exchanges recently have been booming along to a succession of annual records, including more than $88,000,000,-000 on the Chicago Board of Trade alone in 1971, more than half the $147,000,000,000 trading volume on the New York Stock Exchange. (The comparison is, however, slightly misleading because of the extremely low percentage of commodities trading that actually has to be put up in cash.) The 124-year-old Chicago Board of Trade roared to still another record in 1972, passing its 1971 mark by October. Do *you*, then, belong in the commodities market? Probably not.

Oddly enough, the one risk that neophytes frequently fear is the one they are least likely to encounter: If you buy a commodities future, you really are not apt to see a caravan of trucks pulling up in front of your suburban split-level someday and indifferently dumping 5,000 bushels of wheat all over your petunias. What you are actually buying is a federally certified warehouse receipt, attesting that the grain is waiting for you in an elevator in Chicago. The typical speculator no more wants to take delivery on that wheat than he intends to make delivery on a wheat contract that he sells. If he buys he expects to sell the contract to someone else—hopefully at a higher price—before it expires. If he sells he is betting that the price will decline—but in either case he will complete his transaction and disappear before the expiration date. He is playing with money, not flour.

The possibility of stupendous profits is unarguably there. A commodity speculator who buys on 10 per cent margin and sees the price go up 30 per cent has just made 300 per cent on his money. If he was on 5 per cent margin, his profit was 600 per cent. Why, it's better than Aqueduct, isn't it? Well, maybe. But remember that nine out of ten trades are flat-out losers, that the rapid-fire action can be blindingly fast in reverse—and margin calls are frequent. And that three out of four players go home mad.

Those who have made money trading commodities generally ascribe their success to a strong temperament, adequate resources, a well-developed game plan—and a lot of hard work. If you are tempted, heed the words of Dickson G. Carr, nineteenth-century president of the New York Cotton Exchange: "The uninitiated believe that chance is so large a part of speculation that it is subject to no rules, is governed by no laws. This is serious error." If you are thinking of dabbling in commodities, don't; a trader in any commodity should approach the subject with the discipline of a scholar. When anything from the weather to a congressman's hangover can affect the price of your contract within the next hour, you had better be sure that your understanding of the fundamentals involved is a good deal more than cursory—otherwise you know who will soon be cursing, and it won't be that glib broker who talked you into the deal in the first place.

The leading firms that deal in commodities have free booklets available outlining the principles of commodities speculation. They will tell you not to fight the trend, not to aim at small profits (you'll never counterbalance your losses that way), to add to successful positions in ever-smaller amounts (thus avoiding complete disaster if a reaction sets in), not to add at all to unprofitable positions, not to be afraid to go short (a survey by the Commodity Exchange Authority found that "short positions of speculators tended to show profits more frequently" than long ones), to use stop orders when permitted to protect against trend reversals and never to risk more than a quarter to a half of your trading capital on any single position. Always the emphasis is on what Bernard Baruch said in his autobiography *My Own Story:* "No speculator can be right all the time. In fact, if a speculator is correct half the time he is hitting a good average. Even being right three or four times out of ten should yield a person a fortune if he has the sense to cut his losses quickly on the ventures where he has been wrong." DuPont Glore Forgan tells us that "the most successful speculators . . . take a solemn oath on exactly how much they're prepared to lose before each trade. They try to minimize losses quickly and ride profitable trends all the way." And Merrill Lynch, while emphasizing that "the key is to let profits run, but cut losses quickly," assures us that "professionals stick to their trading plan."

My own feeling is that the best advice in the world will be of scant value if you do not happen to possess the rare combination of qualities that make up a successful commodities speculator. The gambler's cool eye in assessing the technical market situation ought to be balanced by the reporter's keen ear for worldwide news developments and the scholar's complex brain for organizing and analyzing this information. Even then, the odds are formidable. The price of soybean futures on the Chicago Board of Trade can be affected by events ranging from an apparently insignificant change in the domestic economic situation to a report on the production of sunflower seed in eastern Europe. Other factors affecting supply and demand, and thus the futures price, might include the outlook for exports, for government price supports, for inventories, for the coming harvest, for domestic consumption and for the markets in competitive products—such as sorghums, wheat and corn—which are also usable for animal feed. The popular notion that all it takes is a dash of technical analysis and the ability to interpret the pattern on the charts is dangerously superficial—and demonstrably untrue, as the preponderance of losing traders suggests. The fellow who is willing and able to follow the fundamental situation, yet who is aware that in the time compression demanded by commodities trading he cannot ignore technical market factors either, may have the ability and the seriousness to vie with the professionals. But despite the increasing attention this fast-acting, fast-growing market is receiving, it is certainly no place for the dilettante, the neophyte, the shoestring hopeful or the cautious long-term investor of any financial dimensions. For most people, in fact, the conventional securities markets—stocks and bonds—are likely to prove more profitable, if sadly a little less stimulating to the adrenaline.

Before abandoning this subject of possible financial nourishment through the selective consumption of commodities, let me stress that my objection for the ordinary investor should not be construed as a social, moral or political critique of the commodities markets themselves. Such a statement might seem gratuitous, but I make it because those nineteenth-century-style trading "pits"—with traders screaming their bids and flashing cabalistic hand signals—have long been ideological targets of those who regarded them as settings for unconscionable gambling on other men's lives and fortunes. (William Jennings Bryan, in his 1896 "Cross of Gold" speech, roared with indignation against "the man who goes on the Board of Trade and bets on the price of grain.") In truth, as we have seen, the commodities speculator serves to take some of the risk out of other men's business transactions. The market tends to keep the price of raw materials steady, thus allowing those directly involved, from the original producer to the ultimate manufacturer, to make plans with greater confidence. The entire economy consequently benefits. (Even if it wanted to, the United States Government could not dictate the price of such world commodities as silver, copper, cocoa and coffee. So some kind of market is not only desirable but necessary.) What's more, the speculation fulfills an economic need, and thus should not theoretically be equated with gambling —which involves the creation of a needless risk, such as whether a coin will land on its head or its tail. (As Jack Savage, a successful commodities speculator, put it in an interview with *Barron's*, "When a man plants corn, and that corn grows, there's a risk involved from the time he plants it till the time it's harvested. That risk is there. It's not self-created.") But just as some things that may be splendid for you personally may be detrimental to the economy as a whole (such as high personal savings), so some things that may be swell for the gross national product may be cataclysmic for your family purse. So don't carry placards demanding the abolition of frozen-pork-belly futures, but unless you are prepared to be entirely serious and not a little lucky, don't rush to empty your piggy bank and buy them. The chances are that Wall Street offers you more secure avenues to eating high on the hog.

CHAPTER XX

Should Your Feeling Be Mutual?

Contrary to the tradition of the Pilgrims and the frontiersmen, and to the aspirations of manufacturers of electrical drills, not every American is by nature a do-it-yourselfer. In some areas, such as housekeeping and the assembly of children's Christmas toys, self-sufficiency has been rendered compulsory. In others, such as professional football and blue movies, spectatorial thrills are still available for those who prefer them. Mutual funds belong in the latter category.

The relationship between investment advice and the art of hyperbole has always been excessively close, but nowhere more cozy than in the realm of mutual funds—where an examination of the sales efforts of the last decade discloses a proportion of words spoken to sense conveyed that borders on the stratospheric. The notion that all you had to do to make your fortune was to turn over your savings to some hotshot band of "go-go" professionals was one of the most disastrous myths of the 1960s, leaving behind a taste so sour that many victims vowed never again to dine at the Wall Street table. What happened in part was that the cult of "performance" ("My fund gained 2 per cent more than your fund last year.") drove many money managers to the far boundaries of reasonable risk-taking, with the inevitable result that when the market turned downward in 1969 and 1970 the "go-go" funds simply went-went.

But even in the case of funds whose managements did not succumb entirely to the prevailing hysteria, widespread disillusionment set in among investors who had been sold the fiction that mutual funds were a one-way street to prosperity. Sales, which had peaked at $6,800,000,000 in 1968, remained sluggish even when the stock market improved in 1971 and 1972. Even more chilling was a situation that had been unknown in the entire half-century history of the mutual-fund industry, through boom and crash, affluence and depression: In May of 1971, for the first time, sales of new shares to the public were less than the amount of shares that were cashed in by existing shareholders. This previously unencountered terror of "net redemptions"—the excess of cash-ins over sales—recurred more often than not over the next couple of years, and after a while the rationales of mutual-fund executives and industry spokesmen began to take on a pitifully hollow ring. Something obviously had gone wrong at the gold mine.

None of this is to suggest that mutual-fund managers represent an endangered species, in need of a new ecological crusade. Close to 10,000,000 shareholder accounts were reported in 1971 by the industry association, the Investment Company Institute. These accounts represented nearly 5,000,000 families. The institute also reported that a national survey it sponsored had revealed that seven out of ten Americans say they "don't know" about funds at all—thus presumably comprising a vast untapped market for future industry growth. What is more, mutual-fund assets continued to grow (rising stock prices helping more than net redemptions hurt) to a record $60,000,000,000 at the end of 1972. If the industry was a corpse, it was an exceptionally vigorous one.

The answer for the sage investor is not automatically to avoid mutual funds—or, as some suggest, automatically to buy them—but to analyze their strengths and weaknesses as they apply to his own capacities and desires. Some people, as noted at the start of this chapter, simply have no interest in playing this particular game. They are bored by the financial page. They would like to be spared the bother of seeking out good stocks and staying abreast of developments affecting the economy and the market. They would prefer to delegate this responsibility—to let somebody else worry. Mutual funds may be for them.

Others may be interested in following the market, and even enjoy it, but find that they have no flair for it—that their performance is woeful, in good markets and in bad. Sometimes that performance can be improved—which is a key aim of this book. But in the end, mutual funds may be for them—for at least part of their funds.

I don't think the amount of money you have should be your primary consideration; the intelligent small investor can, as we have seen, do very well indeed, while at the other extreme the ability to amass or inherit impressive wealth has scant correlation with skill at investing it. In fact, according to a study by the research department of the New York Stock Exchange, the typical mutual-fund shareholder is better educated and makes more money than the average investor who owns only stock. So the answer depends less on your net worth than on the time and knowledge you are willing to devote to your investments, on your temperament and inclinations where your money is concerned. For unless you have sensational connections supplying you with brilliant information, you are going to have to work at the job of making money in Wall Street. Mutual funds provide a method for reducing this burden (if you see it as such), though certainly not for eliminating it.

The problem, you see, is not just "whether" but "which." There are well over 500 mutual funds extant in the United States, with assets ranging from a few million dollars to more than a billion. They sometimes seem to have nearly as many different objectives, though these usually emphasize either immediate income or long-term growth—or a combination of the two. The open pursuit of short-term gains has become less fashionable. The traditional method for selecting a fund was not to "buy" it at all, but to be "sold" it either by a fund salesman or by your friendly neighborhood broker, whose knowledge and consideration of your individual needs likely were subordinate to his desire for a hefty commission. To get the sale he may well have stirred dreams of sables in the closet, Picassos in the living room and villas in the Bahamas. ("Over-salesman" would have been a more accurate description of his job.) There are better ways to pick a mutual fund, and we will get to them shortly. First, though, let's consider the nature of the beast and its alleged attributes in the investment jungle.

Mutual funds are more formally known as "open-end investment companies." They are "open-end" because their managers contract to sell shares without limit and to redeem these shares on any market day for the full value of the assets they represent. The fund takes your money and pools it with its other assets; these are then used to purchase a much more widely diversified portfolio of securities than an individual investor normally could afford—shares in as many as a hundred or more different companies. If the fund's managers pick well, the fund's assets increase and so does the value of the individual shares. A well-diversified fund may, of course, have reduced not just its risks but its chances for spectacular gains—and this, perhaps, is why the ownership of mutual-fund shares has been compared in its potential for excitement with watching grass grow.

When I asked Robert L. Augenblick, president of the Investment Company Institute, to summarize what he thought an investor could get from a mutual fund that he could not do for himself, this was the reply: "First, there is professional management of the investment portfolio. The investment portfolio is managed by people who are expert in the business. Secondly, because of the greater number of stocks in the portfolio, you get diversity of investment risk—which the ordinary person, particularly the modest investor, can't achieve; he doesn't have the money to spread his interests over so many stocks. But thirdly, there are also many, many services that come with the acquisition of mutual-fund shares, such as automatic reinvestment of dividends and capital gains, withdrawal plans, the convenience of having an interest in many stocks in one certificate, and so forth."

The convenience features are undeniable, though their attractions were tarnished when back-room operations became chaotic and inefficient in the late sixties. The diversification is an obvious advantage for those who prefer investment safety to the opportunity for greater gains—or losses—that come from concentration. But it is the alleged first quality of mutual funds—"expert" professional management—that is most subject to question and that requires the most discernment on the part of the prospective investor.

All mutual funds, whether or not you pay a sales charge to buy them, collect an annual management fee. Normally, this is a fraction of 1 per cent—scarcely onerous, particularly if the fund is doing well, but capable of bringing in impressive sums in the case of a large operation. In return, the shareholder is supposed to be getting the kind of professional investment judgment, based on quality research and seasoned expertise, to which his own paltry assets would not otherwise entitle him. But does he? Does the average investor in mutual funds really do better than the average investor who does it himself? The answer to this central question is by no means as unambiguous as you might suspect.

Abraham L. Pomerantz, the peppery lawyer who once figured he had taken $80,000,000 from mutual-fund managers in lawsuits on behalf of their shareholders, told me flatly that he regarded the popular assumption of "professional management," including a better advisory organization and superior performance, as "a myth—a mirage." Pomerantz cited studies reported by the Wharton School of the University of Pennsylvania and the Twentieth Century Fund as demonstrating that year in, year out, the typical mutual fund does not do better than mere random choice. "To vulgarize it a bit," he said, "if a shareholder were to stick a pin in the financial page and pick a stock that way, he will on average do as well as this very, very expensive professional management."

Those who might regard Pomerantz as a biased witness are invited to a closer analysis of the very statistics that the mutual-fund industry itself delights in parading. In 1972, after the Securities and Exchange Commission eased its tight regulation of mutual-fund advertising, the industry embarked on a $1,500,000 campaign to improve its image with the public—nearly four times as much as it had spent in the previous year. About $1,000,000 of this went for television commercials emphasizing the dramatic growth of an average mutual-fund investment in the twenty-two years beginning in 1950—from $10,000 to $94,000, assuming the shareholder had reinvested all the dividends and capital gains he received from the fund. (Newspaper advertisements refined the final figure to $94,008.) This was contrasted approvingly with the fate of $10,000 placed in a 5 per cent savings account (compounded annually, it would have increased only to $29,256 by the end of 1971), though of course the latter was risk-free—and stock-market investment has been known occasionally to carry some risk.

Close observers would note, too, that the most impressive growth on the mutual-fund side was way back in the 1950s, when the original investment nearly quadrupled. Since then the growth of the average mutual fund has been much less dramatic, doubling rather than quadrupling from 1960 to 1970—and even that is assuming that you got in at the earliest (and lowest) point in the decade. The highest point in the chart, in fact, was 1968—so investors who went into the average mutual fund around that time were less than euphoric in the years that followed. But there is a more fundamental point about this campaign, and it was raised on "Wall Street Week" to George Putnam, chairman of the Investment Company Institute, by Frank Cappiello, who observed that the twenty-two-year mutual-fund performance worked out to about 10.7 per cent annually, on a compound-interest basis, and asked, "But that's compared to what? I mean, that's what you don't say. I mean, if I'd invested in, say, the Dow Jones Industrial Average, what would it have been?" Putnam replied that he could not answer that question but that "there was a study made that showed over a long period of time, common stocks appreciated about the rate of 9 per cent—a little bit more than that." This left the impression that in the twenty-two years in question, from the start of 1950 to the end of 1971, mutual funds probably exceeded the performance of the market as a whole. But this impression was incorrect, as several astute viewers soon pointed out.

Cappiello had asked the right question, and the right answer was that $10,000 invested in the reputedly stodgy 30 stocks of the Dow Jones Industrial Average would have increased by 1972 to $110,074, assuming that dividends were reinvested annually at the end of the year. (The funds calculated on a similar assumption.) Not only was this more than $16,000 greater than the sum the average mutual fund would have provided, but it represented a compound-interest rate in excess of 11.5 per cent. What is perhaps an even more random choice is provided by the New York Stock Exchange composite index, which keeps track of the prices of all common stocks traded there. A $10,000 investment on January 1, 1950, in the N.Y.S.E. index would have been worth a brawny $129,347 by 1972 on the same statistical basis. This result, a 12.3 per cent compounded return producing over $35,000 more than the average mutual fund, casts even greater suspicion on the condescending attitude of fund managers toward the efforts of individual investors. Anyone whose investment results surpassed the pure dartboard approach (picking stocks at random and settling for the market average) would have walloped the typical mutual fund.

How can this be? How can the despised ordinary investor, getting ordinary results—no better or worse than the statistical averages—be making more money than the fellow who has entrusted his savings to the "smart money" of Wall Street? Superficial analysts argue that this somehow cannot be true, that few individual investors really come up to the "average" results, that they "know" that the typical individual is unequipped to match wits with the superintellects of the Age of Performance. Balderdash. First, many of the high-priced money managers are considerably less brilliant than the literature praising them (or their salaries) might lead you to believe. They run in an intellectual pack, like the most pedestrian of journalists, and their capacity for independent thought is akin to that of the lemming. They talk to the same people, read the same publications and buy the same stocks. When the selling starts, they tend to panic like the rankest neophyte; several times a year there are occasions when a popular favorite gets dumped, suffers a ludicrous one-day percentage drop, and then eventually creeps up to a more sensible level. The small investor is seldom to blame. "Contrary to common belief," wrote John Winthrop Wright of Wright Investors' Service, "the average American investor generally has a stabilizing, not a speculative, influence on the stock market, and exercises superior, not inferior, investment judgment. He buys mostly good quality, profitable and well-established companies; he is usually a buyer rather than a seller and only occasionally a trader; he buys more when prices are low and declining; he is reluctant to pay very high price-earnings multiples and consequently avoids most 'growth and glamour' issues. Unfortunately, these desirable investment qualities are not widely shared by Wall Street market makers and investment managers."

Other shrewd observers agree wholeheartedly with this seemingly heretical appraisal of the Little Man's investment capabilities. Lawrence H. Weiss, president of the cut-rate, cash-and-carry firm called Odd Lots Securities, told me his 3,000 clients were able to match the performance of mutual funds by doing their own research and making their own decisions with "acumen" and "guts." Reginald B. Oliver, director of research for Pershing and Company, went even further. Pershing acts as the New York agent (executing orders and performing services) for fifty-two regional stock-exchange members, with offices in 281 cities across the country. In this capacity the firm handles between 3 and 4 per cent of the volume traded on the New York

Stock Exchange, and it claims to be in even closer touch with the individual investor than the industry giant, Merrill Lynch, which handles 10 per cent of the volume. In any event, Oliver has concluded that, despite the propaganda from mutual-fund salesmen and other interested parties, the much-maligned little guy is actually "the smartest investor of them all." Oliver cited to me an index of his customers' activity suggesting that they had been net buyers of stocks at market bottoms, or just before, had hedged a bit as the market rose and had been net sellers as it moved toward its tops. In contrast, he maintained, "certainly in the last five years the average fund has not kept up with the market." (In 1972 five out of six mutual funds failed to match the progress of the Dow Jones Industrial Average.)

Temperament and judgment aside, the individual investor has a lot going for him. Even Charles D. Ellis, who argues in his otherwise sensible book *Institutional Investing* that "the individual investor is obsolete," conceded to me under questioning on "Wall Street Week" that the individual does have some unarguable advantages.

I had quoted major and successful money managers as acknowledging that the individual investor may actually have an edge in some cases; since he is investing much less money, he can go in and out of a stock pretty easily, whereas when they want to unload a big position they may drive down the price just by doing that. Ellis, who is a vice president of Donaldson, Lufkin and Jenrette, replied that the individual investor does have two advantages:

"One, he has small positions, so that his transaction costs are relatively small. He simply pays the commission. [One mutual-fund management organization, you will recall, has calculated that active managers of a large institutional portfolio require a 31 per cent average change in stock prices for them to get out and get back in without losing money.]

"The second advantage is that because he is small he can also deal with very small companies. He can deal with virtually any company. Large institutional investors dealing with a billion dollars simply can't deal with very large numbers of small companies. And statistically, small companies do better than large companies."

I would add at least one other tremendous advantage for the

wise individual investor: If he holds authentic growth stocks, stocks whose earnings and prospects (not just their prices) continue to rise, he can relax and not be concerned with how his "performance" this particular year compares with that of the fellow down the street—content that over the years he will come out well ahead. For, believe me, he will.

There is one final reason for skepticism about another frequent claim of the mutual-fund brigade: that it is uneconomical, both in terms of the time he must expend and the commissions he has to pay, for the average guy to buy small amounts of stock himself instead of turning over his funds to professional management. For the fellow who decides to do it himself, obtaining and sifting the best advice available from his broker and other sources, is in a position to learn from his mistakes. As the head man of Merrill Lynch, Donald T. Regan, put it, "This is the only way to learn. And the learning curve of individuals, we find, is greater; if they put their money in the hands of someone else, then they forget it forever." The individual investor is not only having his own fun, he may actually be learning something along the way.

But even though the typical mutual fund may do worse even than the market averages, you may decide that its performance is greater than your own is likely to be, given your lack of aptitude for matters financial or your lack of time that you are willing to devote to them. Fair enough. For you, then, the question may indeed become not "whether" but "which." Read on.

(1) Buy a "no-load" fund. This suggestion alone will narrow your choice impressively; nine out of ten funds carry a "load"— though this proportion is decreasing as the "no-load" bandwagon inexorably begins to roll. What is a "load"? It is a sales charge that you pay for the privilege of handing over your money to the mutual fund. Typically, on small investments, it runs about 8½ per cent. This means that when you think you are investing $10,000 you are really putting to work only $9,150; the rest goes to the broker or salesman and to others involved in the retailing operation. There is no evidence whatsoever that this payment is worth it to you. On balance, there is no conspicuous difference in the performance records of the average load fund and the average no-load fund; the only difference is that with the latter you are instantly 8½ per cent better off. The counterargument is that you have to approach the no-load funds yourself, while

with the load funds you have a benign counselor who will guide you to the perfect investment. Don't you believe it. First, the salesman may sell only the funds managed by a single management company; the brokerage firm may have a tie-in with one or more operations. In either case your choice has been narrowed for reasons unrelated to your needs. Second, it is ludicrous to suppose that you are incapable of deciding whether you want a fund that emphasizes capital growth or a fund that emphasizes current income, and thus ought to sacrifice an immediate 8½ per cent off the top for the privilege of being guided. (A list of names and addresses of no-load funds will be found in Appendix C.) Don't for a moment believe that you are accepting second-best in return for not having to pay a sales charge; in 1971 three no-load funds ranked 1-2-3 in growth among all the 526 funds rated by the Arthur Lipper Corporation, and another four no-load funds were in the top fifteen. Led by the dramatic success of the T. Rowe Price group of Baltimore, whose three funds account for more than a quarter of the no-load industry's assets, the field is expanding as an increasing number of top brokerage firms establish their own no-load funds and as more and more load funds change their status to keep up with the public's growing awareness that an $.08 stamp is cheaper than an 8½ per cent load.

(If you follow mutual-fund prices in the newspaper, you can readily recognize the no-load funds: They are the ones whose "bid" and "asked" prices are identical. The "asked" price is what you will have to pay to buy a share of any mutual fund. The "bid" is what you will get if you redeem a share. The difference, if any, is the "load," or sales charge. Do not confuse this with the management fee, normally a fraction of 1 per cent annually, which all mutual funds charge subsequent to your purchase; it is sometimes said that these average a hair higher for no-load funds, but this is a minuscule consideration. To buy a no-load fund you write—or phone—the management company, take five minutes to fill out the forms they send you and mail the forms back with your check. You have just saved yourself 8½ per cent of your investment. As severe a critic as Abe Pomerantz said, "I adhere to my judgment that the mutual fund as an institution has fallen down on its promise. I wouldn't say that about the no-load fund, because the no-load fund, while charging no admission fee, has—so it has been said by eminent statisticians—as good a performance rate as the load fund, which charges almost 10 per cent.")

(2) Follow the advice of Al Smith, who campaigned for the presidency on the slogan "Let us look at the record." The long view is particularly appropriate here, since the last few years have been testing times for investors of all descriptions. A record of the fund's performance both in roaring bull markets and in nose-diving bear markets will tell you something about the managers to whom you are thinking of entrusting your shekels. Wiesenberger's Investment Companies, a thick manual widely available in libraries, summarizes much valuable information. *Forbes* magazine annually reviews the mutual-fund industry and gives each fund a report-card grade, from A+ to F, for its comparative performances "in UP markets" and "in DOWN markets." Painful for many highly paid egos; instructive for you. There is, naturally, no guarantee that any fund (or any stock) will do well in the future just because it has done well in the past, but if a fund has reasonably and consistently met your objectives over several years, it is obviously a better bet than one your friends or your broker assure you "simply can't miss" because it is headed by a brilliant seven-year-old Tibetan lama with direct access to the stars.

(3) Reassess yourself and your own investment objectives. This makes it more certain that you will be choosing a fund whose own stated objectives match what yours truly ought to be. If you decide you are investing for long-term growth, then don't get discouraged six weeks later and sell out at a loss. Mutual funds make poor trading vehicles at the best of times; the most successful generally are those that invest for the long haul in companies whose profits are growing faster than the rate of inflation and the economy as a whole. (If that sounds familiar, it is because it is a splendid philosophy for the individual investor, too.) If you buy a bond fund, or other income-oriented fund, then don't get mad if your capital doesn't grow. The dream of a risk-free investment, growing spectacularly and paying lusty dividends all along the way, exists only in opium dens, not in Wall Street.

(4) Consider a balanced investment program—partly in funds, partly handled yourself. Even advocates of funds-for-all acknowledge that the average guy will be happier if he keeps a

couple of thousand dollars around to follow his own speculative impulses. My point is more serious. You may, as noted, actually learn something from your personal investing—when you make money, and when you don't. And you may even find, wonder of wonders, that you are doing better on your own than in the fund. Such a discovery is not only joyful for the bank account, it elates the ego to an extent comparable to election to the United States Senate. (Warning: An old Wall Street maxim counsels "Don't confuse wisdom with a bull market.")

Finally, remember that there are possibilities other than conventional mutual funds for those who seek investment safety in crowds. If your assets are substantial, bank trust departments and investment-management companies will be eager to give you advice for a fee. Lately, more and more of the latter have been wooing smaller accounts, starting with as little as $5,000. The annual fee is typically 2 to 2½ per cent of the value of the account, with a minimum of $200 or so. That's just for the advice, which is unlikely to be exclusive; commissions are extra.

Another possibility is the "closed-end investment companies," which are traded like common stocks—often on the major exchanges. These differ from "open-end" mutual funds in that there is a limited number of shares and nobody guarantees you that you will get what their assets are worth on the day you sell; you get what the market will pay. Typically, these closed-end companies sell at a discount from the total value of their holdings, so to some people they seem like terrific bargains as compared with regular mutual funds. This can be an illusion. There is no guarantee that a closed-end company that is selling today at a 15 per cent discount will not be selling at a 20 per cent discount when you want to sell it. (Some such companies sell at a premium—for more than their stock holdings are worth. In either case the premium or discount is a sort of price-earnings ratio, giving the market's assessment of the likely future performance of the investment company's managers. The bigger the discount, the gloomier the assessment. But the actual correlation between discounts and market performances historically is inexact, reflecting passing factors of supply and demand.) *The Wall Street Journal* each Monday lists the discounts and premiums on closed-end investment companies. Some are seasoned with records of achievement over more than four decades. Since the discounted companies offer a route for acquiring a diversified stock portfolio at a "negative load"—that is, at less than the stocks alone would cost—such closed-end companies can provide cut-rate opportunities. Over the years discounts frequently change, sometimes to premiums—and vice versa. And the cost of purchasing closed-end companies is only the usual small stock-exchange commission. Just remember that the discount won't necessarily change when you—or the investment company's management—think it should.

And if you are a good old-fashioned American joiner, don't forget about the institution known as the Investment Club, which is cunningly designed to combine individual greed with group therapy. Such clubs are not a bad way to learn, especially if there is at least one investor in the gang who knows what he is doing, and if you really believe that it is possible to intermix friendship with finance and make a profit by majority vote. A typical club meets once a month, usually in the home of one of its twelve to fifteen members. Two or three of those present report on a study they have made of some likely corporation; the others discuss whether or not to invest in it, and if you are lucky it winds up with a profitable decision and a nice cup of coffee. For reasons about which I hesitate even to speculate, all-women's clubs seem to do better at this than all-men's clubs. (The clubs in general are more successful than cynics suggest; Thomas E. O'Hara, chairman of the National Association of Investment Clubs, told me that over the thirty-two years the association had existed its average club had earned at a compounded annual rate of 14.7 per cent.) It has been said of investment clubs that they are valuable to the economy because they don't panic during crashes; they panic during booms, because that's when the treasurer disappears. If you want to learn how to organize an Investment Club that will make money in the market and not lose it in Rio de Janeiro, write for information to the National Association of Investment Clubs, 1515 East Eleven Mile Road, Royal Oak, Michigan 48067. A cheerful method that can either make or lose you your shirt and your friends.

In the end we cannot leave the subject of group investment without returning to the question with which we started: Are mutual funds for you? They may well be the total answer for many investors and the partial answer for many others, but in no case should an investor assume that the decision to buy a mutual fund instead of investing for himself is the only one he has to make. Picking the right fund is as challenging a task as picking the right stock. There is no assurance that one who would fail at the latter would succeed at the former, especially if he is unwilling to do the homework suggested in this chapter. (One possible hedge, advocated by T. Rowe Price himself: Buy into two or three funds, each managed by a different firm. Another, which is valuable whether you decide to buy funds or stocks or both: Don't throw in your entire nest egg at once; dollar-average your initial investment over a period of months, so that you don't get trapped by your enthusiasm at the market high.)

For those to whom the stock listings have no magic, for those who feel their time would be more profitably spent elsewhere, for those who would rather delegate than do, watch than perform, the funds have obvious attractions. For those who want at least to test their own investment potentialities, to learn before they abdicate, individual investing will have greater charms—and possibly even greater profits. How about you? As the little-cigar commercial used to put it, "You know who you are." Or, to paraphrase the venerable gag about marriage: Mutual funds are a wonderful institution—but not every man is ready for an institution.

CHAPTER XXI

The Fault, Dear Brutus . . .

If there is a universal neurosis of our times, surely it is paranoia. The political and social movements of the era have enshrined it, telling virtually any identifiable group that it was a special object of discrimination—and had every right to feel grievously put-upon. Sometimes this reassurance was justified, but it scarcely mattered: rarely if ever was it rejected. People crave being told that their failures to become rich and famous, attractive and popular, or whatever they desire, can be ascribed not to their personal shortcomings but to the malfeasances of society. When they review their lives and their disappointments, the dominant emotion is usually "once more, with feeling—of persecution." And since Wall Street, as we have seen, can invoke the major impulses of mankind—including lust, power, status and greed—it is hardly surprising that its literature overflows with accusations that malign forces rig the marketplace against the honest innocents whom we all see ourselves to be. The perfect rationale for failure has always been that life was fixed; if we lose money in Wall Street, the fault clearly cannot be ours alone. It must be that the brokers are avaricious, or that the specialists on the market floor are dishonest or that the plutocrats who run the exchanges have made it impossible for the poor little guy to make a profit. To believe otherwise would entail a more rigorous examination of ourselves—a process that, while it is immediately promising and eventually rewarding, is at all times considerably less comfortable.

Don't misunderstand me. As host of "Wall Street Week," I have carried the banner for the small investor—and I think he often deserves better than he gets. He deserves more professional service from his broker. He deserves more competition *among* brok-

ers—not least in *price*. He deserves the option of having his
charges "unbundled"—of not having to pay for services he neither
wants, requests nor uses. He deserves more readable, more
reliable and more uniform reports from companies and their
accountants. He deserves a continuation and expansion of the recent regulatory concern that his assets are being identified, sepa-
rated and safeguarded by their custodians. He deserves better
representation on such bodies as the board of the New York Stock
Exchange, which has still not wholly abandoned its smug concept of itself as a private club. He deserves, above all, recognition of his central importance to the free marketplace of capital
—and a wooing, in fact and service, that will match the previous
wooing, through advertisements and salesmen.

But if Wall Street is not yet Valhalla for the Little Man, it is
not a den of thieves, either—however much losers yearn to be
told the contrary. It reminds me, in this sense, of my own profession of journalism, in which outsiders almost invariably over-
estimate the malice and underestimate the incompetence.

There will always be those who regard the stock market as if
it were a sort of mass version of the Godfather game—all very
polite and full of dazzling offers that you can't refuse, but in the
end about as honest as a Mafia kiss on the lips. Yet when I bluntly
asked William J. Casey, who as chairman of the Securities and
Exchange Commission did much to make Wall Street a safer
clime for the small investor, "How honest is Wall Street?" he replied without hesitation, "By and large, I believe that Wall Street
is honest. There are dishonest people in all spheres of life, but
I believe that the Wall Street community has policed itself well.
The troubles have been carelessness rather than dishonesty."
There are those who might view Casey as an interested witness;
I refer them to the testimony of Senator Harrison A. Williams,
Jr., the New Jersey Democrat who as chairman of the Senate
Securities Subcommittee found much to criticize in the way Wall
Street does business—and who confessed to me that he and Casey
"disagree fundamentally on a few things." Yet when I put it to the
senator directly—"How square a deal does the average investor
get these days on Wall Street?"—his response was not funda-
mentally different: "Well, what do you mean by 'square a deal'?
He gets an honest deal. . . . I'm not questioning any honesty."
Or turn to Manuel Cohen, who was an employee of the SEC for

twenty-seven years, starting as a junior attorney and culminating in his appointment by President Kennedy as a commission member in 1961 and his service as chairman from 1964 to 1969. When I suggested that he was the man who should know how crooked Wall Street was, Cohen said flatly, "I don't think Wall Street is more crooked than any other segment of industry—perhaps no more crooked than any other segment of society. In fact, Wall Street is probably the most regulated segment of all of our business society."

It would be a disservice to all these gentlemen to leave the impression that they were just Pollyannas enraptured by the status quo. Each of them recognized that further change was not only inevitable but desirable. Scandal has scarcely been unknown in Wall Street's past, and it would be rash to predict that it will spontaneously evaporate in the future; it will, as always, require vigilance to expose it. But what they wouldn't buy, and what is always so easy to sell to those who would rather have solace than facts, is that the wheel is basically rigged.

But to say that the market is essentially honest, if improvable, is not to say that it is therefore easy to make money in Wall Street. The short cuts are usually dead ends. It is ironic that the same fellow who will pore lengthily over elaborate performance charts before making a bet at the racetrack will commit his life's savings in the stock market on an unchecked tip from his barber. We all hunger for inside information, yet even that longed-for commodity tends to be immoderately overrated; the record of insider transactions in stocks demonstrates that top managements can be as fallible, and as prey to overenthusiasm, as the veriest tyro. It takes more than advance access to company developments to put them in accurate market perspective. Yet how we all desire, however subconsciously, to believe that the market really is crooked—and that we, oh joyous day, have just been put in touch with one of the crooks. (According to Clifford Irving, the most widely read publication at the Allenwood [Pennsylvania] Prison Farm was *The Wall Street Journal.*) No matter how often we get scalded by hot tips, we never quite accept that the cool and careful approach to the market is the surer way to success.

Yet there is a better way—or, more accurately, there are better ways. For as we have seen in this book, Wall Street provides merchandise for shoppers with vastly different financial needs and desires. Some will be looking for long-term growth—for that quality stock with a unique product or service that, in each new business cycle, ends up in earnings and in price a little higher than before. It is a course that takes initial care, continual attention and permanent patience, but it has been a consistent winner for millions. Others will define their goals differently; they may, for example, require a more immediate return on their securities or wish to test their speculative agility in the options market. The important thing is that neither these nor other aspirations have any exclusive claim to legitimacy or probability of success—but that the investor's goals must in some way be defined before he begins. The investor who has reasonable objectives, thoroughly understood both by him and by his broker, is automatically miles ahead of the fellow who has no intelligent concept of what he is or ought to be after ("Is it the right stock for *you?*") and consequently is ludicrously susceptible to blowing his entire bundle in a wild attempt to get rich quick. Get your laughs from other people's pathetic and avoidable blunders with their money; your squandering of your own life's savings, you will find, seldom provides an equivalently hearty giggle.

The stock market is irrational in the short run, rational in the long. That's why those who attempt to outtrade the traders have the odds against them—and are most inclined to suspect chicanery. The market, as we have seen, is subject to steaming, hurtling reactions, which it quickly regrets and reverses; day by day it is a zany schoolgirl in the college of life. It takes passionate likes and dislikes to passing news developments and to individual stocks and groups of stocks. Not much later it exercises the privilege, traditionally accorded to women and stock markets, of changing its mind. To try to guess the next hour's crush is as dangerous as it is unnecessary. That is why, for example, the wise individual will spread, or "dollar average," his initial investment over a period of months—to avoid the possibility that, on the day after he finally decides to give Wall Street a try, the market will make one of its periodic decisions to throw all the good news in the wastebasket and take a hysterical dive. It is also why some of the most seasoned investors continue year after year to show more interest in the earnings of their stocks than their prices. More often than not, if the company is making the progress it ought to be making, the market will eventually take care of itself.

The sensational may make better copy, but the undramatic makes more money—not just "buying and holding" but "buying and watching," not panicking the first moment the traders decide the price-earnings ratio is too high but not throwing caution to the winds the first time the stock rises eight points, either. The investor who can discipline himself to this degree of perception and maturity, who can read and learn from the kind of detailed advice that is in this book, will find not only that Wall Street is no casino but that it is an enterprise in which the odds can be made to operate in his favor. If the average long-term return on stocks is about 9 per cent, he should do that or better. He will not pick a winner every time—no one I have yet encountered has—but he will realize that he does not have to, that he can do just splendidly with a decent batting average and a willingness to learn from his errors. He will recognize, above all, that he carries within himself the possibilities of success or failure in Wall Street—that the fault for persistent losers lies not in their brokers, or in their specialists, or in their stars. Recognizing that, he will make himself a winner.

May you be that prosperous investor—and may you have an extraordinary amount of fun in the process. Good luck and good hunting.

Appendixes

APPENDIX A

Commissions on Stock Trades

Twice in eighteen months during 1972 and 1973, the New York Stock Exchange raised the cost of doing business there. A new commission rate schedule was put into effect by the exchange in March 1972 after the proposals had been reviewed by the Securities and Exchange Commission, endorsed by the members of the exchange and approved by federal price stabilizers. These rates were, in turn, increased in September 1973—by 10 per cent on transactions up to $5,000 and by 15 per cent on orders ranging from $5,001 to $300,000. (Each time you place an order for more than $300,000 you can negotiate your own commissions, you will be pleased to know.) The SEC envisioned ending all fixed commissions by April 1, 1975, at which time firms would be free to post their rates without reference to what their competitors were charging.

Meanwhile the commissions as given in this appendix now apply on all exchanges and must be paid twice—when you buy the stock and when you sell it. As explained in Chapter IV, the new basic schedule adopted in 1972 and raised in 1973 replaced a set of rates established in 1958 and subjected to a surcharge in the spring of 1970. The method of computing commissions was changed in 1972 to use a scaled percentage of the money involved in each order, as requested by the SEC. This meant that the commission percentage went down as the amount of dollars increased. Under the 1958 schedule the percentage was the same whether you bought 100 shares, 400 shares or 1,000 shares. (Really big spenders were given a reduced rate for 1,100 shares or more.)

On balance, the 1972 schedule was expected to yield about 5 per cent more than the 1958 rates—but the results proved inadequate to improve the uncertain health of the brokerage industry, and the larger increases that produced the current, updated schedule were sped through the following year. Stock commissions are, of course, a perennial subject of controversy; the following information will make you an instant expert:

CURRENT COMMISSION RATE SCHEDULE

Round Lots

Shares Per Order	$5	$10	$20	$30	Price of Stock $40	$50	$75	$100	$200	$400
100	$ 18.04	$ 27.50	$ 41.80	$ 53.90	$ 63.80	$ 71.50	$ 74.75	$ 74.75	$ 74.75	$ 74.75
200	36.08	55.00	77.00	101.20	121.90	142.60	149.50	149.50	149.50	149.50
300	54.12	73.70	108.10	139.15	170.20	201.25	224.25	224.25	224.25	224.25
400	68.20	90.20	135.70	177.10	218.50	259.90	299.00	299.00	299.00	299.00
500	81.95	106.70	163.30	215.05	266.80	301.30	370.30	373.75	373.75	373.75
600	93.50	128.80	190.90	253.00	301.30	342.70	411.70	448.50	448.50	448.50
700	105.05	146.05	218.50	287.50	335.80	372.60	453.10	523.25	523.25	523.25
800	116.60	163.30	246.10	315.10	365.70	402.50	494.50	586.50	598.00	*
900	128.15	180.55	273.70	342.70	391.00	432.40	535.90	639.40	672.75	*
1,000	139.70	197.80	301.30	370.30	416.30	462.30	577.30	692.30	747.50	*
2,000	243.80	347.30	462.30	554.30	646.30	738.30	968.30	1,198.30	*	*
2,500	292.68	404.80	531.30	646.30	761.30	876.30	1,163.80	1,451.30	*	*
5,000	519.80	646.30	876.30	1,106.30	1,336.30	1,577.80	*	*	*	*
10,000	876.30	1,106.30	1,566.30	2,026.30	*	*	*	*	*	*

* Not computed; negotiated rates.

CURRENT COMMISSION RATE SCHEDULE

Odd Lots

Shares Per Order	$5	$10	$20	$30	Price of Stock $40	$50	$75	$100	$200	$400
10	*	$ 7.04	$ 9.24	$11.44	$13.64	$15.84	$21.73	$25.30	$39.60	$61.60
20	$ 7.04	9.24	13.64	18.04	22.44	25.30	32.45	39.60	61.60	74.75
30	8.14	11.44	18.04	23.87	28.16	32.45	43.18	51.70	74.75	74.75
40	9.24	13.64	22.44	28.16	33.88	39.60	51.70	61.60	74.75	74.75
50	10.34	15.84	25.30	32.45	39.60	46.75	59.13	71.50	74.75	74.75
60	11.44	18.04	28.16	36.74	45.32	51.70	66.55	74.75	74.75	74.75
70	12.54	20.24	31.02	41.03	49.72	56.65	74.75	74.75	74.75	74.75
80	13.64	22.44	33.88	45.32	53.68	61.60	74.75	74.75	74.75	74.75
90	14.74	23.87	36.74	48.73	57.64	66.55	74.75	74.75	74.75	74.75
99	15.73	25.16	39.31	51.40	61.20	71.01	74.75	74.75	74.75	74.75

* Not computed; negotiated rates.

The Major Stock Averages

There is no more widely disseminated fact about Wall Street than the daily stock averages, and few that cause greater confusion. The un-initiated hear a broadcaster report that "the Dow Jones Industrial Average dropped 20 points" (about a 2 per cent movement) and are terrified at the thought that their own $50 stock may now be worth only $30. Or disappointed investors note that the averages keep rising, while their stocks keep falling, and suspect that there must be some hanky-panky somewhere. To them, these market "averages" are reminiscent of the Pullman-car porter who, when asked by a first-time traveler what his average tip would be, replied, "Five dollars." When the traveler dutifully handed over a five-dollar bill the follow-ing morning, the porter thanked him and said, "Congratulations. You're the first person to come up to the average since I've been work-ing here."

The confusion may abate if you understand that the major stock averages differ from one another both in their statistical methods and in their coverage. Let us begin, as most people do, with the Dow Jones Industrial Average. It is not necessarily the most reliable index of the market's strength, and it is far from the most comprehensive, but it is the most widely known and it is usually the first number that investors want to hear. (Its perennial battle to rise above 1,000 became a sort of national sport before that barrier finally was pierced for the first time in the postelection euphoria of 1972.) It is one of four stock averages prepared by Dow Jones & Company, publisher of *The Wall Street Journal, Barron's National Business and Financial Weekly* and *The National Observer.* The industrial average keeps track of the prices of 30 industrial common stocks; the others include one average comprising 20 transportation common stocks, one for 15 utility common stocks and a "composite" average including all of the 65 just mentioned. Dow Jones also compiles six bond averages and one composed of yields on a group of bonds. But it is the Dow Jones Industrial Average that draws the most rapt attention from Wall Street to Main Street.

First compiled on May 26, 1896, and first published on a daily basis a year later (it opened at 41), "the Dow," as it is usually abbreviated, obtained its average simply by adding up the prices of twelve leading companies—surely you remember such biggies as American Cotton Oil and Distilling & Cattle Feeding—and then dividing by twelve. (The only survivors from the original list are American Tobacco—now American Brands—and General Electric.) The list expanded to 20 companies in 1916 and to 30 in 1928; since then, there have been 30 different individual substitutions in the list (the most significant was when IBM was dropped in favor of American Tel & Tel), but the total has stayed the same. The list of stocks presently in use is printed each Monday in *The Wall Street Journal;* at this writing there have been no changes since 1959 and this is the current list:

Allied Chemical	Exxon	Procter & Gamb
Aluminum Co	General Electric	Sears Roebuck
Amer Brands	General Foods	Std Oil of Calif
Amer Can	General Motors	Swift & Co
Amer Tel & Tel	Goodyear	Texaco
Anaconda	Inter Harvester	Union Carbide
Bethlehem Steel	Inter Nickel	United Aircraft
Chrysler	Inter Paper	US Steel
Du Pont	Johns-Manville	Westinghouse El
Eastman Kodak	Owens-Illinois	Woolworth

These 30 companies have had widely differing results over the years but each remains an authentic titan of American industry, and together they account for about one fifth of the earnings of all United States corporations. Their "average" is no longer compiled simply by adding up their closing prices and dividing by 30. This method would give misleading results when one of the stocks splits. (If a company whose stock is selling for $50 a share orders a two-for-one stock split —giving each stockholder two new shares in exchange for each old one—and the new stock then sells for $25 a share, the average should remain unchanged. If you just divided the total by 30, the average would drop—because one of the 30 components would be down from $50 to $25.) Such changes are now accounted for by a numerical "divisor," which is applied to the raw total of the 30 stock prices and which changes itself every time there is a split or similar change—or when a new stock is substituted for an old one. This divisor, which necessarily changes frequently, is given each day on the next-to-last page of *The Wall Street Journal* under the tables providing the statistics of the averages. Its purpose is only to assure that changes unrelated to a rise or fall in a stock's price do not affect the over-all Dow Jones Industrial Average, and that today's average is absolutely comparable with yesterday's, and last year's, and that of a generation ago.

The Dow Jones Industrial Average is, however, a "price-weighted" average in that changes in the higher-priced shares have a greater impact than those in the lower-priced shares. This has long bothered some statisticians, and they have a preference for averages that are "size-weighted." "Size-weighted" averages are computed by adding up the daily market value of each component company (multiplying the price of each share by the number of shares in that issue outstanding), and then adding together all these market values to get an aggregate market value of the issues in the index. This is the method used in the Standard & Poor's indexes, which then relate the total aggregate market value to the base period of 1941–43, which is figured as 10. Under this method price changes in stocks with large public ownership count for more than changes in stocks with smaller capitalizations. But there is no need to bother about a changing divisor, since stock splits are adjusted for automatically. The market value of a company with 100,000 shares worth $50 will be precisely the same ($5,000,000) if the stock splits two-for-one and the company now has 200,000 shares worth $25.

Standard & Poor's Corporation launched its new indexes in 1957 to replace older indexes the company had prepared since 1926 and to provide broader coverage than was given by the Dow Jones Industrial Average. Standard & Poor's publishes a 425-stock industrial average, a 20-stock railroad average, a 55-stock utility average and a 500-stock composite of the three, as well as other indexes for individual industries. The "S & P 500," as the composite is often called, includes all the 30 Dow Jones industrial stocks—and they account for more than a quarter of the composite's current price. A similar percentage is represented by a second group of 30 stocks with large capitalizations: outstanding growth stocks such as IBM, Xerox, Minnesota Mining, Coca-Cola, Merck and American Home Products. This means that the remaining 440 stocks of all types have a combined weighting of only 45 per cent.

To meet objections that even a 500-stock index was insufficiently comprehensive to reflect the interests of the average investor, the New York Stock Exchange and the American Stock Exchange brought out their own averages in 1966. (Five years later the National Association of Securities Dealers utilized its Automated Quotations system to begin its own NASDAQ over-the-counter averages, including an 1,800-stock industrial index and a 2,600-stock composite.) The major exchanges differed in their statistical methods, with the New York Stock Exchange following the lead of Standard & Poor's in making its averages size-weighted and the American Stock Exchange experimenting with a totally "unweighted" index simply designed to show the average change, in dollars and cents, of all Amex shares. The New York Stock Exchange countered by regularly compiling a second figure, separate from the index change but almost invariably confused with it, which it calls "the market"—as in the phrase "The market was up 9 cents"—and which is intended, unlike the New York Stock Exchange index itself, to show the change in an average share of common stock.

Sophisticated investors found that the New York Stock Exchange approach provided a more useful market measurement, and in September 1973 the American Stock Exchange in effect followed its big brother's example—replacing its old index with what it called the Amex Market Value Index, a size-weighted average under which 100 represents the total value of the Amex list on August 31, 1973, and also beginning to give each day an entirely separate "market" report indicating the price change of an average Amex share. Lest it seem just a belated copy cat with these twin maneuvers, the junior exchange simultaneously installed a battery of other indicators, including indexes for stocks in eight industrial categories, for companies in seven geographical regions of the United States and for all foreign-issued securities traded on its premises. Its computers were thus equipped to deliver just about everything short of a partridge in a pear tree.

With the statisticians themselves going off in so many different directions, it is no wonder that ordinary investors feel baffled as to which average, if any, can be believed. Recently, the widely watched averages have tended to overstate the market's improvement; in 1972, for example, three fifths of all publicly traded stocks actually declined. According to calculations by Indicator Digest, Inc., in late February of 1973, the average New York Stock Exchange stock was only 23 per cent above its 1970 low and fully 43 per cent below its 1968 high. The typical American Stock Exchange issue had done even worse. But such indicators as the Dow, the S & P 500 and the New York Stock Exchange index all had shown much better performances because a minority of stocks did spectacularly well. The big rewards came not to those investors who threw darts at the financial page, and counted on the "averages" to rise, but to those who tied their fortunes to a few carefully selected growth stocks.

As proof that such methods consistently produced results in a period of inflation and erratic over-all economic performance, consider one final market average: the David L. Babson & Company Growth Stock Index. It lists twelve companies (American Home Products, Coca-Cola, Dow Chemical, Eastman Kodak, Honeywell, IBM, Merck, Minnesota Mining, Procter & Gamble, Provident Life & Accident, Sears Roebuck and Xerox). In the seven years ending in February 1973 the Dow had declined 5 per cent, while the S & P 500 and the New York Stock Exchange composite index each rose 17–18 per cent. In contrast, the average stock in the Babson Growth Stock Index increased in price every year and had doubled by the end. Whether the reason was merely that institutional interest had centered in the leading growth stocks, or that such stocks have inherently better characteristics in an era of inflation, the record showed that "growth" was more than a figure of speech when it came to figuring the averages.

No-Load Mutual Funds

For those who decide to buy shares in mutual funds, we discussed in Chapter XX the advantages of choosing a no-load fund. The load is a sales charge—typically 8½ per cent of a Little Man's investment —that he must pay for the privilege of investing in the fund. No-load funds carry no such sales charge. Since no salesman is getting paid, nobody is going to try to sell such funds to you, and you have to make the initial approach yourself. No-load funds vary in quality and performance, as do load funds, but more than 1,000,000 shareholders now have chosen them, and their net sales increased even in 1972— when the entire mutual-fund industry showed net redemptions (an excess of shares cashed in over new shares sold) that reached $1,700,-000,000. Many smart investors consider no-loads the wave of the future for all mutual funds, and more and more load funds are changing their status and climbing aboard.

The No-Load Mutual Fund Association, Inc., 475 Park Avenue South, New York, N.Y. 10016, listed the following no-load funds as of January 1973:

Fund	Objective	Founded	Total Net Assets 6/30/72 (in millions)
Aberdeen Fund 919 18th St., N.W. Washington, D.C. 20006	Long-range capital growth and income	1933	$ 37.88
Able Associates Fund 174 Birch Drive Manhasset Hills, N.Y. 11040	Capital appreciation	1971	2.00
The Acorn Fund, Inc. One First National Plaza Chicago, Ill. 60670	Capital appreciation	1970	22.23

Fund	Objective	Founded	Total Net Assets 6/30/72 (in millions)
Afortress Income Fund, Inc. 8 Pennell Road Lima, Pa. 19060	Income	1969	.31
Afuture Fund, Inc. 8 Pennell Road Lima, Pa. 19060	Capital appreciation	1967	65.42
Aid Investment Fund, Inc. 701 Fifth Avenue Des Moines, Iowa 50304	Long-term capital appreciation	1960	.55
Alliance Growth Fund, Inc. Box 1032, Wall St. Station New York, N.Y. 10005	Capital appreciation	1968	.39
American Enterprise Fund 50 Broad Street New York, N.Y. 10004	Long-range capital appreciation	1957	.82
American General Growth Fund, Inc. P.O. Box 1931 Houston, Texas 77001	Growth of capital	1964	5.23
American Investors Fund 88 Field Point Road Greenwich, Conn. 06830	Capital growth	1957	220.68
American Patriots Fund 2300 Russ Building San Francisco, Cal. 94104	Capital growth	1971	.14
Americare Growth Fund, Inc. 601 Sixth Avenue Des Moines, Iowa 50304	Long-term capital growth	1971	.31
Argonaut Fund, Inc. 1020 Prospect Street La Jolla, Cal. 92037	Capital appreciation	1967	1.06
Armstrong Associates, Inc. 3200 First Nat'l Bank Bldg. Dallas, Texas 75202	Long-term capital growth	1968	4.94

David L. Babson Investment Fund, Inc. 301 W. 11th Street Kansas City, Mo. 64105	Long-term growth of capital and income	1959	77.85
B.A.I. Fund, Inc. 200 Park Avenue New York, N.Y. 10017	Growth of capital	1969	.11
Bank Stock Fund, Inc. 105 E. Colorado Avenue Colorado Springs, Colo. 80902	Capital growth	1970	.28
The Barclay Growth Fund 30 Broad Street New York, N.Y. 10004	Capital growth	1968	5.14
Beacon Hill Mutual Fund 75 Federal Street Boston, Mass. 02110	Long-term growth of capital	1964	4.05
Beacon Investing Corp. 7 Whittier Place Boston, Mass. 02114	Growth of capital	1962	16.56
Berger-Kent Special Fund 899 Logan Street Denver, Colo. 80203	Capital appreciation	1969	11.13
Bondquest Debenture Fund 80 Broad Street New York, N.Y. 10004	Income	1972	.13
Bridges Investment Fund 8401 West Dodge Road Omaha, Neb. 68114	Long-term capital growth	1963	1.23
The Burnham Fund, Inc. 60 Broad Street New York, N.Y. 10004	Capital appreciation	1969	16.93
California Venture Fund 611 W. Sixth Street Los Angeles, Cal. 90017	Aggressive growth	1969	.77
The Cambridge Appreciation Fund, Inc. 11 West 42nd Street New York, N.Y. 10036	Capital appreciation	1969	.21

Fund	Objective	Founded	Total Net Assets 6/30/72 (in millions)
Capital Preservation Fund 459 Hamilton Avenue Palo Alto, Cal. 94301	Income	1972	.10
Chesapeake Fund, Inc. 527 St. Paul Place Baltimore, Md. 21203	Long-term growth	1969	.77
Columbia Growth Fund, Inc. 621 S.W. Morrison Street Portland, Ore. 97205	Capital appreciation	1967	32.42
The Columbine Fund, Inc. 1600 Broadway Denver, Colo. 80202	Capital appreciation	1970	4.66
Compustrend Fund, Inc. 424 Falls Building Memphis, Tenn. 38103	Capital growth	1969	.48
Comsec Fund, Inc. 88 East Broad Street Columbus, Ohio 43215	Capital growth	1970	.78
Concord Fund, Inc. 366 Madison Avenue New York, N.Y. 10017	Capital appreciation	1949	2.02
Consultant's Mutual Investments, Inc. 211 S. Broad Street Philadelphia, Pa. 19107	Capital gains	1962	15.85
Continental Mutual Investment Fund, Inc. 9255 Florida Boulevard Baton Rouge, La. 70815	Long-term capital appreciation	1959	1.27
Contrails Growth Fund, Inc. 2 First National Bank Place Chicago, Ill. 60670	Long-term capital	1968	2.43
Davidge Capital Fund, Inc. 1747 Pennsylvania Ave., N.W. Washington, D.C. 20006	Long-term growth	1972	.43

The Davidge Fund 1747 Pennsylvania Ave., N.W. Washington, D.C. 20006	Capital appreciation	1969	10.81
de Vegh Mutual Fund, Inc. 20 Exchange Place New York, N.Y. 10005	Long-term capital appreciation	1950	109.61
Dodge & Cox Balanced Fund 35th Floor—Crocker Plaza San Francisco, Cal. 94104	Income and long-term growth	1931	16.15
Dodge & Cox Stock Fund 35th Floor—Crocker Plaza San Francisco, Cal. 94104	Long-term growth and income	1964	10.69
Doll Fund, Inc. Thacker Lane Mendham, N.J. 07945	Capital appreciation	1967	.47
Drexel Equity Fund, Inc. 1500 Walnut Street Philadelphia, Pa. 19101	Long-term capital appreciation	1960	38.47
Drexel Hedge Fund, Inc. 1500 Walnut Street Philadelphia, Pa. 19101	Capital appreciation	1968	2.30
Drexel Investment Fund 1500 Walnut Street Philadelphia, Pa. 19101	Capital growth	1968	4.76
East/West Fund, Inc. 9100 Wilshire Blvd. Beverly Hills, Cal. 90212	Long-term capital appreciation	1970	.11
Edie Special Growth Fund 530 Fifth Avenue New York, N.Y. 10036	Long-term capital appreciation	1969	49.35
Edie Special Institutional Fund, Inc. 530 Fifth Avenue New York, N.Y. 10036	Long-term capital appreciation	1969	46.53
E & E Mutual Fund, Inc. 4400 No. High Street Columbus, Ohio 43214	Growth and income	1957	2.88
Eldorado Fund, Inc. 18158 Westover Southfield, Mich. 48075	Capital appreciation	1968	.52

Fund	Objective	Founded	Total Net Assets 6/30/72 (in millions)
Endowments, Inc. P.O. Box 7583 San Francisco, Cal. 94120	Growth of capital	1969	8.97
Energy Fund, Inc. 120 Broadway New York, N.Y. 10005	Long-term capital	1952	151.06
The Evergreen Fund, Inc. 600 Mamaroneck Avenue Harrison, N.Y. 10528	Capital appreciation	1971	30.70
F. G. Mutual Fund, Inc. 4680 Wilshire Blvd. Los Angeles, Cal. 90010	Long-term capital appreciation	1972	.20
Financial Dynamics Fund 900 Grant Street Denver, Colo. 80201	Capital appreciation	1967	53.70
Financial Industrial Fund 900 Grant Street Denver, Colo. 80201	Growth with income	1935	318.09
Financial Industrial Income Fund 900 Grant Street Denver, Colo. 80201	Income	1959	114.53
Financial Venture Fund 900 Grant Street Denver, Colo. 80201	Capital appreciation	1968	21.39
Finomic Investment Fund 600 Jefferson–Cullen Ctr. Houston, Texas 77002	Capital appreciation	1972	.11
First Multifund of America 299 Park Avenue New York, N.Y. 10017	Long-term capital growth	1965	14.96
First Spectrum Fund, Inc. 230 Park Avenue New York, N.Y. 10017	Capital appreciation	1971	.26
The 44 Wall Street Fund 150 Broadway New York, N.Y. 10038	Capital appreciation	1968	2.73

Fund for Mutual Depositors 200 Park Avenue New York, N.Y. 10017	Long-term capital growth	1969	23.84
General Securities, Inc. 133 South Seventh Street Minneapolis, Minn. 55402	Capital appreciation	1951	8.05
Samuel Greenfield Fund 25 Broad Street New York, N.Y. 10004	Capital appreciation	1966	1.53
Growth Industry Shares 135 S. La Salle Street Chicago, Ill. 60603	Capital growth	1946	50.15
Guardian Mutual Fund, Inc. 120 Broadway New York, N.Y. 10005	Capital appreciation	1950	59.27
Hartwell and Campbell Fund 345 Park Avenue New York, N.Y. 10022	Capital appreciation	1965	14.52
Hartwell and Campbell Leverage Fund 345 Park Avenue New York, N.Y. 10022	Capital appreciation	1968	17.90
The Hawick Fund, Inc. 134 Peachtree St., N.W. Atlanta, Ga. 30303	Capital growth	1968	2.30
Hedge Fund of America, Inc. 555 Fidelity Union Tower Dallas, Texas 75201	Capital appreciation	1967	22.84
The Hornblower Growth Fund 8 Hanover Street New York, N.Y. 10004	Capital growth	1969	1.81
Hyperion Fund, Inc. 126 Barker Street Mount Kisco, N.Y. 10549	Capital appreciation	1969	6.43
Interfund, Inc. 23–148th Ave., S.E. Bellevue, Wash. 98007	Long-term capital appreciation	1970	1.16
The Inverness Fund, Inc. 345 Park Avenue New York, N.Y. 10022	Capital appreciation	1968	.53

Fund	Objective	Founded	Total Net Assets 6/30/72 (in millions)
Investment Guidance Fund Investment Plaza Cleveland, Ohio 44114	Capital appreciation	1967	3.67
Investment/Indicators Fund 120 Montgomery Street San Francisco, Cal. 94104	Capital growth	1966	6.69
Ithaca Growth Fund, Inc. 100 Fairview Square Ithaca, N.Y. 14850	Capital appreciation	1969	.06
Ivy Fund, Inc. 411 Stuart Street Boston, Mass. 02116	Long-term capital growth	1961	64.28
Janus Fund, Inc. 444 Sherman Street Denver, Colo. 80203	Capital growth	1968	24.26
The Johnston Mutual Fund 460 Park Avenue New York, N.Y. 10022	Growth and income	1947	282.02
The Kaufmann Fund 111 Broadway New York, N.Y. 10006	Capital appreciation	1967	.77
La Salle Fund, Inc. One IBM Plaza Chicago, Ill. 60611	Capital appreciation	1971	1.19
League Investment Fund 15600 Providence Drive Southfield, Mich, 48075	Capital growth	1971	.90
The Lenox Fund 666 Fifth Avenue New York, N.Y. 10019	Capital growth	1967	14.06
Loomis-Sayles Capital Development Fund 225 Franklin Street Boston, Mass. 02110	Capital appreciation	1961	79.38
Loomis-Sayles Mutual Fund 225 Franklin Street Boston, Mass. 02110	Capital growth	1929	174.19

Mairs & Power Growth Fund W. 2062 First National Bank Building St. Paul, Minn. 55101	Long-term capital appreciation	1958	11.98
Market Growth Fund 80 Broad Street New York, N.Y. 10004	Capital appreciation	1964	.95
Mates Investment Fund 237 Madison Avenue New York, N.Y. 10016	Long-term capital appreciation	1967	4.92
Mathers Fund, Inc. One First Nat'l Plaza Chicago, Ill. 60670	Capital appreciation	1965	104.09
The Medici Fund, Inc. 120 Broadway New York, N.Y. 10005	Capital appreciation	1966	1.01
Montrose Investors, Inc. 1900 L St., N.W. Washington, D.C. 20036	Capital appreciation	1972	
Mutual Shares Corp. 200 East 42nd Street New York, N.Y. 10017	Capital gains	1949	8.67
Mutual Trust 301 West 11 Street Kansas City, Mo. 64105	Income	1944	9.40
Naess & Thomas Special Fund 201 North Charles Street Baltimore, Md. 20201	Capital gains	1949	8.67
The Nassau Fund One Palmer Square Princeton, N.J. 08540	Appreciation and in- come	1957	8.81
National Industries Fund 1880 Century Park East Los Angeles, Cal. 90067	Capital growth and income	1958	12.24
Nelson Fund, Inc. 345 Park Avenue New York, N.Y. 10022	Capital appreciation	1955	5.02
Neuwirth Century Fund Middletown Bank Bldg. Middletown, N.J. 07748	Long-term capital appreciation	1967	12.00

Fund	Objective	Founded	Total Net Assets 6/30/72 (in millions)
Neuwirth Fund, Inc. Middletown Bank Bldg. Middletown, N.J. 07748	Capital growth	1966	43.72
Neuwirth Income Development Corporation Middletown Bank Bldg. Middletown, N.J. 07748	Income	1970	.38
New York Hedge Fund 116 John Street New York, N.Y. 10038	Capital appreciation	1968	.70
Nicholas Strong Fund 312 East Wisconsin Avenue Milwaukee, Wis. 53202	Capital appreciation	1968	100.99
No-Load Selected Funds 3300 Whitehaven St., N.W. Washington, D.C. 20007	Capital appreciation	1971	.12
North American Growth Fund 1112 Security Life Bldg. Denver, Colo. 80202	Long-term capital growth	1971	.10
Northeast Investors Trust 50 Congress Street Boston, Mass. 02109	Income	1950	58.36
Oceanographic Fund, Inc. 15 Exchange Place Jersey City, N.J. 07302	Growth	1967	16.60
One Hundred and One Fund 1600 Broadway Denver, Colo. 80202	Income and capital growth	1966	3.60
One Hundred Fund, Inc. 1600 Broadway Denver, Colo. 80202	Capital growth	1966	47.22
O'Neil Fund 10960 Wilshire Boulevard Los Angeles, Cal. 90024	Capital growth	1965	14.82

The One William Street Fund, Inc. One William Street New York, N.Y. 10004	Capital growth	1958	301.21
Pax World Fund Inc. 224 State Street Portsmouth, N.H. 03801	Income	1970	.24
Penn Square Mutual Fund 451 Penn Square Reading, Pa. 19603	Capital appreciation	1957	150.15
Pennsylvania Mutual Fund 80 Broad Street New York, N.Y. 10004	Capital growth	1962	9.66
Pine Street Fund, Inc. 20 Exchange Place New York, N.Y. 10005	Growth and income	1949	52.98
Platt, Tschudy, Norton Fund, Inc. 600 Dain Tower Minneapolis, Minn. 55402	Capital appreciation	1970	3.03
T. Rowe Price Growth Stock Fund, Inc. One Charles Center Baltimore, Md. 21201	Growth and income	1950	1,236.16
Rowe Price New Era Fund One Charles Center Baltimore, Md. 21201	Capital appreciation	1968	146.20
Rowe Price New Horizons Fund, Inc. One Charles Center Baltimore, Md. 21201	Capital growth	1960	508.19
Pro Fund, Inc. Valley Forge Colony Bldg. Valley Forge, Pa. 19481	Capital growth	1966	47.82
Professional Portfolio Fund P.O. Box 208 Honolulu, Hawaii 96810	Capital growth	1962	1.31
The Prudential Fund of Boston, Inc. 50 Congress Street Boston, Mass. 02109	Long-term capital growth	1949	3.11

Fund	Objective	Founded	Total Net Assets 6/30/72 (in millions)
Redmond Growth Fund, Inc. 1750 Pennsylvania Ave., N.W. Washington, D.C. 20006	Capital growth	1969	9.97
The Reserve Fund, Inc. 1301 Avenue of Americas New York, N.Y. 10019	Income	1971	.10
Rochester Fund 31 E. Main Street Rochester, N.Y. 14614	Long-term growth	1967	1.49
Sagittarius Fund, Inc. 375 Park Avenue New York, N.Y. 10022	Capital appreciation	1966	.81
Scudder Development Fund 345 Park Avenue New York, N.Y. 10022	Long-term capital	1970	31.35
Scudder Special Fund 345 Park Avenue New York, N.Y. 10022	Long-term growth	1956	216.78
Scudder International Investments, Ltd. 44 King Street, W. Toronto 1, Ontario	Capital growth	1964	15.95
Scudder, Stevens & Clark Balanced Fund, Inc. 10 Post Office Square Boston, Mass. 02109	Growth and income	1928	93.05
Scudder, Stevens & Clark Common Stock Fund, Inc. 10 Post Office Square Boston, Mass. 02109	Capital appreciation	1929	167.21
Sequoia Fund, Inc. One New York Plaza New York, N.Y. 10004	Capital growth	1970	12.52
Shasta Fund, Inc. Monchanin, Del. 19710	Capital appreciation	1971	.08

Sherman, Dean Fund, Inc. 140 Broadway New York, N.Y. 10005	Capital growth	1968	6.50
Smith, Barney Income and Growth Fund, Inc. 1345 Avenue of Americas New York, N.Y. 10019	Income and capital	1967	4.55
Smith, Barney Equity Fund 1345 Avenue of Americas New York, N.Y. 10019	Capital growth	1968	89.21
Standard & Poor's/Inter- Capital Dynamics Fund 1775 Broadway New York, N.Y. 10019	Capital appreciation	1968	14.17
Standard & Poor's/Inter- Capital Special Fund 1775 Broadway New York, N.Y. 10019	Capital appreciation	1969	16.81
State Street Investment Corp. 225 Franklin Street Boston, Mass. 02110	Growth	1924	438.99
Steadman American Industry Fund, Inc. 919 18th Street, N.W. Washington, D.C. 20006	Long-term capital growth	1958	56.25
Steadman Associated Fund 919 18th Street, N.W. Washington, D.C. 20006	Income	1939	68.17
Steadman Fiduciary Invest- ment Fund, Inc. 919 18th Street, N.W. Washington, D.C. 20006	Long-term appreci- ation	1956	10.62
Stein Roe & Farnham Bal- anced Fund, Inc. 150 S. Wacker Drive Chicago, Ill. 60606	Growth and income	1949	199.79
Stein Roe & Farnham Capital Opportunities Fund 150 S. Wacker Drive Chicago, Ill. 60606	Long-term capital appreciation	1963	24.98

Fund	Objective	Founded	Total Net Assets 6/30/72 (in millions)
Stein Roe & Farnham Stock Fund, Inc. 150 S. Wacker Drive Chicago, Ill. 60606	Appreciation and income	1958	186.08
Stratton Growth Fund Benjamin Fox Pavillon Suite 412 Jenkintown, Pa. 19046	Capital growth	1972	.20
Summit Capital Fund, Inc. 555 Fidelity Union Tower Dallas, Texas 75201	Capital appreciation	1968	1.64
Technivest Fund 28 State Street Boston, Mass. 92109	Capital growth	1968	47.80
Tudor Hedge Fund 120 Broadway New York, N.Y. 10005	Capital appreciation	1968	17.25
The Twenty Five Fund 1600 Broadway Denver, Colo. 80202	Capital appreciation	1968	3.38
United Services Fund, Inc. 110 East Byrd Blvd. University City, Texas 78148	Capital appreciation	1970	1.09
Variable Stock Fund, Inc. 441 Stuart Street Boston, Mass. 02116	Long-term growth	1957	3.72
Viking Growth Fund 6006 N. Mesa Street El Paso, Texas 79912	Long-term capital growth	1956	2.90
Viking Investors Fund 6006 N. Mesa Street El Paso, Texas 79912	Appreciation and income	1961	.28
Washington Investment Network, Inc. 1700 K Street, N.W. Washington, D.C. 20006	Capital appreciation	1968	.32

Weingarten Equity Fund 331 Madison Avenue New York, N.Y. 10017	Capital appreciation	1967	10.32
Westernamerican Fund 212 College Club Bldg. 505 Madison Street Seattle, Wash. 98104	Capital appreciation	1967	1.80
The Willow Fund, Inc. One Chase Manhattan Plaza New York, N.Y. 10005	Long-term capital appreciation	1969	17.42

Total Net Assets—No-Loads $7.149 billion

APPENDIX D

Institutional Favorites and Dividend Increasers

The New York Stock Exchange periodically publishes a number of lists of stocks with particular characteristics of interest to different categories of investors. The following two, based on statistical material compiled by Standard & Poor's Corporation, may be of special appeal. You should, of course, regard them as no more than a preliminary screening of stocks that may merit further study.

First is the list of institutional favorites—the stocks most widely held by pension and mutual funds, insurance companies, foundations and similar high-caliber professional investors. Widespread institutional ownership is no guarantee of a stock's future success, but it is certainly a factor of which you ought to be aware. These were the institutional favorites as of February 15, 1973:

Stock	Number of Institutions Holding Stock
Int'l Bus. Mach.	1022
General Motors	763
Exxon Corp.	734
Amer. Tel. & Tel.	687
General Electric	627
Eastman Kodak	607
Texaco Inc.	599
Xerox Corp.	514
Ford Motor	414
Gulf Oil	403
Sears Roebuck	396
Mobil Oil	394
Gen'l Tel. & El'tr'cs	373
First Nat'l City Corp.	345
Westinghouse Elec.	338

Goodyear T. & Rub.	329
Minn. Mng. & Mfg.	323
Stand. Oil Indiana	319
duPont (E.I.) Nem.	309
Dow Chemical	303
Union Carbide Corp.	301
Atlantic Richfield	299
Texas Util.	293
Merck & Co.	292
Int'l Tel. & Tel.	286
Burroughs Corp.	281
Standard Oil (Cal.)	278
Warner Lambert	272
Int'l Nickel of Can.	267
Southern Co.	266
Caterpillar Tractor	264
So. Calif. Edison	253
Phillips Petroleum	251
Amer. Elec. Pwr.	240
RCA Corp.	240
Com'w'th Edison	236
Amer. Home Prods.	232
Chase Manhattan Cp.	227
Pfizer Inc.	225
Int'l Paper	220
Honeywell Inc.	219
Florida Pwr. & Lt.	215
Penney (JC) Co.	214
Polaroid Corp.	214
Coca Cola	213
Continental Oil	210
Procter & Gamble	205
General Foods	201
Fed. Dept. Stores	200
Avon Prods.	199
Virginia Elec. & Pwr.	198
Monsanto Co.	196
Bristol Myers	189
Houston Lt. & Pwr.	185
Central & So. West	179
Gillette	179
Morgan J.P.	177
Weyerhaeuser	174
Deere Co.	172
Sperry Rand	171

Stock	Number of Institutions Holding Stock
Pacific Gas & Elec.	170
Amer. Cyanamid	167
Kresge (SS)	167
Gulf States Util.	164
Middle South Util.	164
Illinois Power	160
Tenneco Inc.	157
Philip Morris	153
Chrysler Corp.	149
Western Bancorp	146
Amer. Airlines	145
Control Data	145
Reynolds (R.J.) Ind.	145
Johnson & Johnson	144

About half the stocks on the New York Stock Exchange have paid dividends continuously for at least twenty-five years, and the exchange has a long list of those which have not missed a quarter for four decades or more. You might be more interested, though, in the following list of those whose earning power enabled them to increase their dividends significantly each year from 1962 to 1972. In many cases that meant that the latest dividend represented a relatively low yield on the current price—because investors are likely to bid up the prices of stocks with rapidly growing earnings. But those who bought such stocks in 1962 saw their dollar dividends increase as much as tenfold or more in the ensuing decade.

Stock	Indicated Percentage Yield 2/15/73	Percentage Increase in Dividend '62–'72
Air Prod. & Chem.	0.5	139
Allied Maintenance	1.1	260
Amer. Elec. Power	6.4	86
Amer. Home Prod.	1.5	130
AMP Inc.	0.6	280
Atlantic City Elec.	6.6	55
Avon Products	1.1	479
Baltimore Gas & El.	6.8	69
Baxter Labor.	0.3	227
Block (H & R)	1.6	z999

Central & So. West	4.7	93
Central Tel & Util	4.0	160
City Investing	3.9	477
Cleve. Elec. Illum.	6.7	128
Coca Cola Co.	1.1	173
Colgate Palmolive	1.6	94
Columbia Broadc't'g	3.0	153
Columbia Gas System	5.9	65
Columbus S. Ohio El.	7.1	75
Consol. Foods	3.0	184
Dart Industries	0.7	62
Diebold	0.8	196
Disney (Walt) Prod.	0.1	155
Dr Pepper Co.	0.8	593
Dun & Bradstreet	2.2	134
Eastman Kodak	1.0	140
Eckerd (Jack) Corp.	0.5	z999
Emerson Electric	1.3	281
Emery Air Freight	0.9	384
First Virginia Bankshs	3.5	246
First Wisc. Bkshrs	4.3	84
Florida Pwr & Lt	3.0	86
Gen'l Amer. Oil Tex's	1.2	113
Genuine Parts	1.0	258
Ga.-Pacific Corp.	2.5	248
Heublein, Inc.	1.8	351
Int'l Bus Machines	1.3	592
Intl. Flavors & Frag.	0.5	688
Johnson & Johnson	0.4	306
Kansas Pwr. & Lt.	5.3	86
Long Isl. Light'g	6.2	79
Louisville Gas & El	5.5	112
Manhattan Indus.	3.9	56
Masco Corp.	0.4	580
Mayer (Oscar)	2.0	184
Minn Mng & Mfg	1.2	141
Missouri Pub. Serv.	5.1	35
Mobil Oil Corp.	4.3	125
Nevada Power	3.4	129
Northern Ill. Gas	6.8	82
Oklahoma Gas & Elec	5.0	100
Pargas, Inc.	5.4	628
Portland Gen'l Elec.	7.1	75
Procter & Gamble	1.4	107
Riviana Foods	2.8	179

Stock	Indicated Percentage Yield 2/15/73	Percentage Increase in Dividend '62–'72
Rochester Gas & El.	5.7	67
Rochester Telephone	2.3	138
Rohm & Hass	0.8	146
Rorer-Amchem, Inc.	2.4	458
Servomation Corp.	2.2	552
South Carolina E & G	6.2	74
Southern Co.	6.8	70
Southern Ind. G & E	5.1	108
Sterling Drug	1.6	108
Toledo Edison	6.5	130
United Telecommun.	4.9	96
Weis Markets	2.5	z999
Winn-Dixie Stores	3.1	107
Xerox Corp.	0.5	z999

z=exceeds 1,000 per cent

highs indicate that an intermediate bottom has been reached; five or fewer new lows suggest an intermediate top. This is based on the general theory that when everybody is tickled pink, it's time to sell, and when everybody is scared to death, it's time to buy. How's your courage index this week?

(4) An institutional block ratio. This one keeps track of the urgency of buying or selling by the big boys, who are also prone to hysteria. If close to three quarters of their purchases of 10,000 shares or more come at higher prices than the last previous trade, batten down the hatches.

(5) A low-price activity ratio. This is an indicator of speculative sentiment, the growth of which is supposed to signal the concluding stages of a rally. The ratio compares weekly volume in the *Barron's* Low-Price Stock Index to volume in the seasoned blue chips of the Dow Jones Industrial Average. A neutral indication would be about 9 per cent; 10–15 per cent suggests an intermediate top is arriving.

(6) A comparison of volume on the American Stock Exchange with volume on the New York Stock Exchange. As noted in Chapter XIII, the higher the percentage of Amex trading, the more cause there is supposed to be for worry.

(7) An odd-lot short-sales ratio. Odd lots are trades of fewer than 100 shares; short sales are sales made on borrowed stock that the seller hopes to replace by buying the stock at a lower price in the future. These odd-lot short sellers are regarded as uninformed small investors. When they get active—thinking the market is going lower—technicians often assume the opposite. If the ratio of odd-lot short sales to all odd-lot sales runs as high as 1.5 per cent or more, it's taken as a highly bullish indication.

(8) A New York Stock Exchange specialist short-sale ratio. Here we have the reverse situation. The specialists who make the market in each individual stock are regarded as the most informed players in the game. Also, they are assigned to go against the tide—which, the technicians assume, is probably heading the wrong way anyhow. So when the specialists' short selling increases, others get worried. If more than 60 per cent of all short sales are made by specialists, it's taken as a sign that an intermediate top has been reached. On the other hand, when that percentage gets below 45 per cent, it indicates an intermediate bottom—and good news ahead.

(6) An equity financing index. This one is based on the theory that a rapidly increasing supply of new issues is a bad sign for the market. If the total primary and secondary offerings registered for sale, as compiled by *The Investment Dealers' Digest*, goes over

$1,000,000,000 a month, a market top is suggested; a more favorable figure, indicating a bottom, would be below $600,000,000.

(10) A bond-market indicator. In the belief that an improving bond market usually precedes an improving stock market, and that a declining bond market is an unfavorable portent for stocks, this keeps track of the recent strength of long-term government bonds. A good sign, indicating higher stock prices ahead, would be a one- to two-month improvement taking the bond prices up at least two points.

When the difference between the number of indicators showing positive readings and the number negative is 5 or more (for example, 7 up, 1 neutral, 2 down; or, 1 up, 3 neutral, 6 down), the index is thought to be clearly indicating a coming change in the market's direction. (Remember that we are talking always of changes only in the market's three- to six-month "intermediate" term—not in the market's long-range course.) A highly positive reading on the index would suggest that the market was "oversold" and about to rally; a heavily negative balance would indicate that buying excesses had set in and that a downturn should be expected.

There are some who swear by this kind of market alchemy and there are others who swear at it. It will primarily be of use, I suspect, to dedicated traders (not to investors) and to those who want to understand what the devil those technicians are talking about. The index's predictive value, whether for the next minute or the next millennium, is certainly not guaranteed—least of all by a skeptic like me.

Index